*The
Selection of
National Party
Leaders
in Canada*

John C. Courtney

The Selection of National Party Leaders in Canada

Archon Books
1973

© J. C. Courtney, 1973

Published in Canada by the Macmillan Company of
Canada Limited and simultaneously published in the
United States of America as an Archon Book by
The Shoe String Press, Inc., Hamden, Connecticut.
Printed in Canada.

Library of Congress Cataloging in Publication Data

Courtney, John C
    The selection of national party leaders in Canada.

    Bibliography: p.
1. Liberal Party (Canada)   2. Progessive Conservative
Party (Canada)   3. Leadership. I. Title.

JL196.C68   329.9'71   72-14046

ISBN 0-208-01393-8

This book has been published with the help of a grant
from the Social Science Research Council of Canada,
using funds provided by the Canada Council.

To Helen

Contents

List of Tables

Preface

It is not an altogether uncommon experience in universities for students to plant the seed of inquiry on some particular subject in the mind of their professor. I trace the origins of this work to just such an event. In November 1966, at the time of Dalton Camp's re-election as president of the Progressive Conservative party and that party's approval of a motion to hold a leadership convention before the end of the following year, I agreed to a request from several students to deliver a series of lectures on party conventions and party leadership in Canada. When I began to prepare the lectures, however, I found surprisingly little literature on the topic other than a few articles in assorted journals, the occasional passing references in biographical works, and a handful of party *Reports*. Little else had been written on the subject. And the more I gave serious thought to the matter, the more I was puzzled. What was Canada, with a parliamentary system based on the British model, doing with a convention system for the selection of her party leaders, when "conventions" were an American, non-parliamentary contribution to politics? Why were the more traditional and informal processes of leadership selection formerly used by Canadian parties abandoned? What were the reasons for the change to leadership conventions? What had been the effects of such a change — on Canadian parties, government and politics? To attempt to answer such fundamental questions has been my purpose in writing this book.

As a good deal of the flavour of Canadian politics has been produced from a unique blend of British and American political institutions and practices, I have incorporated some of the essentials of leadership selection in both the United Kingdom and the United States. The Canadian reader should, I believe, have such information available to him so that he might assess more knowledgeably the leadership selection practices in his own country, and understand more clearly their historical antecedents as well as their relationship to developments in parties in the other two countries. The book, however, is not intended as a full-blown comparative analysis of leadership selection in Britain, Canada and the United States. It concentrates, instead, on Canadian leadership selection. Within those sections on Canada, the emphasis is placed almost entirely on the Liberal and Progressive Conservative parties. Apart from occasional comparative references to, and a short chapter on, the CCF–NDP, the study focuses on the two older parties, for they have monopolized political power federally and dominated Canadian political history. As its title suggests, the book is restricted to *leadership selection* of *national* parties in Canada. It does not examine, except in a very incidental way, the policy-making and organizational concerns of Canadian parties, nor does it consider the selection of provincial party leaders. These are vast and important topics, but they deserve nothing less than separate and complete studies.

I am greatly indebted to those who have read with such care various parts of the book during its formative stages. For the historical sections, Professors Mary Hallett, of the University of Saskatchewan, Roger Graham, of Queen's University, and Lovell C. Clark, of the University of Manitoba, made a number of helpful suggestions. Both Senator Paul C. Lafond, former general secretary of the Liberal Federation of Canada, and Mr. Richard D. Thrasher, one-time national secretary of the Progressive Conservative

Party, gave me their comments on Chapter 5. Professor Walter Young, of the University of British Columbia, carefully scrutinized the chapter on the CCF–NDP, and Senator Eugene Forsey offered his views on a number of the constitutional questions examined in the book. Professors J. A. A. Lovink, of Queen's University, and Lawrence LeDuc, of the University of Windsor, offered very constructive comments on Chapter 8 and Appendix G, the two parts of the book in which the reader will find game theoretical explanations used to account for convention voting behaviour. (As the reader will discover, such explanations are necessarily speculative. Nonetheless, it is hoped that they will raise for him as many intriguing questions about the nature of convention coalitions as they have for the author. Perhaps future data-based studies of subsequent conventions will produce the necessary evidence to support or reject those theories.) From my own political science colleagues at the University of Saskatchewan I have had great assistance. Norman Ward and David E. Smith have both read a number of sections of the book dealing specifically with Canadian leadership selection, and D. J. Heasman has offered many helpful comments on British as well as Canadian leadership selection practices. As a result of their thorough perusal of parts of the book, J. M. Porter and Duff Spafford have introduced to me invaluable arguments and lines of reasoning on more aspects of this work than I would care to enumerate. To all these people, I must acknowledge my grateful thanks for their many suggestions — some of which I have followed, others of which I have not. It need scarcely be added that the faults of the book are mine, not theirs.

I am happy to acknowledge the financial support given this study by the Canada Council and the Principal's Humanities and Social Sciences Fund of the University of Saskatchewan. The grants provided by those two bodies have made it possible for me to gather information from a variety of sources. I have been able to examine particularly relevant papers in the Public Archives of Canada and to interview, in both Canada and Britain, many politicians too numerous to name individually. They have included parliamentarians, party officials, leadership candidates, organizers, and convention delegates. To those who so willingly spent time with me discussing leadership selection, my thanks. The response to my short mail questionnaire by 1,335 (or 55 per cent) of the delegates to the 1968 Liberal convention was most encouraging, for it suggested a genuine willingness on the part of party activists to participate in studies of this sort. Professor Hugh Thorburn, of Queen's University, has kindly provided some additional information on 1967 Conservative and 1968 Liberal delegates from his work on those conventions, and Professor R. C. Brown, of the University of Toronto, has furnished the ballot totals for Arthur Meighen's selection as Conservative leader in 1920. Party officials of the Liberal, Progressive Conservative and New Democratic Party national headquarters in Ottawa could scarcely have been more cooperative in answering numerous requests for factual information. I found the exchange of opinions with Professor D. V. Smiley to be most helpful in clarifying some of my thoughts on party conventions. The Hon. and Mrs. R. A. Bell, both of whom made a number of excellent suggestions with respect to Canadian leadership conventions, have once again lived up to their reputation as perceptive students of Canadian politics.

The research assistance provided by Mrs. Robert Enright of the Department of Economics and Political Science at the University of Saskatchewan has been invaluable, and Miss Marie Franz has typed the entire manuscript in a most competent fashion. With humour and a sound grasp of Canadian history and politics, Mrs. Diane Mew has performed her editorial tasks most skilfully. Finally, my parents and my wife and children, who have seen this work through from beginning to end, deserve a special acknowledgement; without their patience and understanding, the book could not so easily have been completed.

Saskatoon, Saskatchewan   J. C. C.
Victoria Day, 1972

*The
Selection of
National Party
Leaders
in Canada*

1

Leadership Selection in Britain and the United States

To an outsider, perhaps the most striking feature of party leadership selection in Britain is the singularly dominant position of the parliamentary parties. Carefully guarded and widely accepted as the font of future leaders, the parliamentary parties in Britain enjoy a rather special immunity from their extra-parliamentary associations — an immunity no longer shared by their Canadian namesakes. To the British politicians the implications are clear. Every politician with leadership aspirations realizes that to be considered seriously for the party leadership he must convince his parliamentary colleagues of his political skills and judgment. For his part, every member of parliament knows that one of the roles he is expected to perform is that of selecting, together with his parliamentary colleagues, the leader of his party. This he regards as one of *his* responsibilities as an elected public representative. He argues, therefore, that the extra-parliamentary wing of his party has no place in the formal election of the party leader. Although there are understandable differences between the Labour and Conservative parties, the two parties share, in fact, a good deal in common on the matter of leadership selection.

1

From Lord Salisbury to Lord Home the British Conservative party chose to "elect" its leader formally only after he had been called upon by the monarch to serve as prime minister, a practice which underscored quite clearly the royal prerogative of the Crown as part of the British constitution. From 1937 to 1963 the body so constituted to elect the party leader following his acceptance of the prime ministership was composed of all Conservative MPs and peers, prospective Conservative parliamentary candidates and the 150-member executive committee of the National Union of Conservative and Unionist Associations. Prior to 1937 Conservative leaders had been elected at a joint meeting of Conservative peers and MPs only, although prospective Conservative candidates were invited to participate in the 1922 meeting which offered the leadership to Bonar Law. If a leadership vacancy occurred when the party was in opposition the Conservative MPs selected a leader for their group in the House of Commons, as did Conservative peers in the House of Lords, leaving the post of "Leader of the Party" unfilled until governmental power had been reassumed and the monarch had acted. Then, without ballot and by acclamation, the party once again formally "elected" its leader after he had been called upon by the monarch to form the government.[1]

This "subtle and complex"[2] process by which British Conservative leaders were chosen was based on the premise that at the appropriate time the person best suited to lead the party would "emerge" from within the parliamentary ranks of the party. According to one Conservative MP the principle might be explained in the following terms: "Great leaders of parties are not elected,

---

[1] Thus, technically, Austen Chamberlain was never formally elected to the leadership of the Conservative .party for he never served as prime minister. On leadership selection in the Conservative party, see R. T. McKenzie, *British Political Parties: The Distribution of Power Within the Conservative and Labour Parties,* 2nd ed. (London: Heinemann Educational Books Ltd., 1963), pp. 22-23; chapter III, "The Election of the Leader and the Appointment of the Chairman of the Party Organization," in the National Union of Conservative and Unionist Associations, *Interim and Final Reports of the Committee on Party Organization, 1948 and 1949* (London: Conservative Central Office, 1949); and "Electing the Leader," *The Times* (London), January 22, 1957, p. 9.

[2] McKenzie, p. 23.

they are evolved. . . . I think it will be a bad day [when we] . . . have solemnly to meet to elect a leader. The leader is there, and we all know it when he is there."[3] Writing at a time when such a process was still in use by the Conservative party, R. T. McKenzie stated that the party did not elect its leader

> by any procedure which would ordinarily be called demo-
> cratic. A potential Conservative Leader . . . is called into the
> councils of the party by the current Leader (into either the
> Cabinet or the Shadow Cabinet). Increasingly he is groomed
> by the old Leader and recognized by the party as the heir
> apparent. If the emerging Leader has rivals they must either
> outshine him or supersede him in the affections of the old
> Leader and of the party. And they must do so *long before
> the party meeting assembles to elect a new Leader.* There
> can be no question of forcing a contest at that late date.
> Convention requires that on that occasion all potential rivals
> should affirm their unswerving allegiance to the tribal chief.
> The tribe then speaks with one voice and the new Leader
> has "emerged."[4]

Subsequent to Harold Macmillan's selection as leader in 1957, McKenzie wrote: "The Conservative system of selecting Leaders tries to take into account both intensity of feeling aroused by the potential rivals for the Leadership, and the 'political weight' of their supporters *and* opponents. It is because Conservative elder statesmen and party managers clearly understand that, even among Conservatives, some men are 'more equal' than others that they are so reluctant to count heads in determining who should lead the party."[5]

Widespread dissatisfaction within the Conservative party with such an informal procedure for the selection of the party's leader followed Harold Macmillan's resignation in October 1963. Macmillan, hospitalized at the time, had an announcement read to the annual party conference by the man who ultimately succeeded him, Lord Home, to the effect that the "customary processes of consultation" should soon begin so that a new leader might be

---

[3] Captain Ernest Pretyman, as quoted in McKenzie, p. 52.
[4] McKenzie, p. 54. (Italics in original)
[5] McKenzie, p. 590. (Italics in original)

chosen. In the opinion of one of the leading contenders for the Conservative leadership, R. A. Butler, the timing of Macmillan's announcement could not have been worse:

> The fact that the P. M. asked for the processes of selection of his successor to be undertaken in the middle of a party conference was bound to create consternation, confusion and intrigue, and indeed it did. I cannot imagine an atmosphere less suited to such a declaration with scores of journalists, television interviewers, *et hoc genus omne.* It turned Blackpool into a sort of electoral Convention *à l'Américaine.* After that there was no peace.[6]

The timing of the announcement was not the only aspect of the proceedings to which exception was taken. The wholly informal and unstructured way in which opinions were canvassed and weighed by various party notables had the effect of producing severe strains within the party. Macmillan, according to the chief whip of the Conservative party, had sent a directive

> to the Cabinet that there was to be a system of selection which he carefully detailed, in which I as Chief Whip was to sound the whole of the party in the Commons, the Chief Whip in the Lords was to sound the active peers in the Lords, the Lord Chancellor was to sound the Cabinet, and the leaders of the National Union were to collect opinion in the country, through the agents, through chairmen, and the Young Conservatives, and candidates and so forth. And all this information was collated and put together.[7]

---

[6] Lord Butler, *The Art of the Possible* (London: Hamish Hamilton, 1971), p. 242. A description and analysis of events of the time and of the selection of Lord Home is given in Butler, chapter 11, and Anthony Howard and Richard West, "Lord Home Emerges," in Anthony King (ed.), *British Politics: People, Parties and Parliament* (Lexington, Mass.: D. C. Heath and Co., 1966), pp. 69-80. See also Iain Macleod's critical account of the changeover, "The Tory Leadership," *The Spectator,* January 17, 1964, pp. 65-67; McKenzie's analysis of Macleod's account in *The Observer,* January 19, 1964; and the book which prompted Macleod's article, Randolph S. Churchill, *The Fight for the Tory Leadership* (London: William Heinemann Ltd., 1964).

[7] BBC interview with Rt. Hon. Martin Redmayne entitled "The Commons in Action," *The Listener,* LXX (December 19, 1963), 1013.

To a number of Conservative MPs, such an informal system left far too much in doubt. One subsequently criticized the 1963 leadership changeover this way:

> Uncertainty as to who was entitled to be consulted, the absence of any formalised procedure, the fact that those who took soundings both decided who were to be sounded and what weighting was to be given to the opinions of those who had been sounded and — most important of all — the fact that those who took the soundings and made the weightings were the only people to scrutinise the results of this somewhat arbitrary poll, . . . led to a feeling that this [should] never happen again.[8]

The fact that the Conservatives were led into "the best-publicized and most brutal struggle for power in the party's history"[9] seemed, more than anything, to prove the inadequacy of the party's traditional processes for choosing their leaders.

The criticisms prompted the new leader, Sir Alec Douglas-Home, to announce early in 1965 that a different method would be followed by the party in future leadership selections. Formal votes would henceforth be taken with a maximum of three ballots; voting would be restricted to Conservative MPs. New nominations would be called for on the second ballot, thereby permitting, if necessary, the emergence of a compromise candidate in the event of a first ballot deadlock. The voting arrangements were designed in the hope of obtaining as broad a consensus as possible in support of the new leader, given the obvious strictures of a formal voting mechanism. As had been the case in the past, the name of the candidate chosen by the party in the Commons would be presented subsequently to the meeting of Conservative MPs and peers, prospective Conservative candidates and members of the executive committee of the National Union for the official election

---

[8] Memo of Humphry Berkeley, MP, to Sir Alec Douglas-Home, December 9, 1964, as published in George Hutchinson, *Edward Heath: A Personal and Political Biography* (London: Longman Group Ltd., 1970), Appendix II, pp. 218-219.
[9] Howard and West, "Lord Home Emerges," p. 69.

as leader of the party.[10] (For the text of the procedure adopted in 1965, see Appendix A.) Not all Conservative MPs were satisfied with the new procedure. According to the chairman of the 1922 Committee (composed of Conservative private MPs) the new system may well prove to be too rigid to operate successfully and may, in fact, be so highly structured that adequate informal soundings of the views of "the party in the country" may no longer be assured.[11] Although it may wish to alter some of the particulars of the voting mechanism in the future, it seems unlikely that the Conservative party could retreat from a position of entrusting, by way of some formal electoral arrangement, the selection of its leader to its MPs exclusively.

The Parliamentary Labour Party has studiously avoided acceptance of the principle that the royal prerogative should be exercised by the monarch in such a way as to select a party's leader, such a practice leading, according to the Labour party, to the involvement of the Crown in party politics. The Conservatives have been subjected to Labour criticism on this account when they have deferred to the monarch in the selection of the prime minister and their new party leader.[12] It might be argued that the Labour party can afford the luxury of such criticism, for it has never been placed in the potentially embarrassing position of having to choose a new leader when in office. Yet in fact, prior to the 1965 change in the Conservative selection technique, the Labour party's position in this regard had been clearly stated. A policy declaration on leadership selection when the party is in power was drawn up by the PLP leadership in 1957 and the procedures outlined in the statement

[10] On the application of the new selection system at the time of the resignation of Sir Alec Douglas-Home and the selection of Edward Heath (so far Heath has been the only Conservative leader to have been chosen by the new technique), see *The Times* (London), July 23, 1965, pp. 12 and 13, July 26, 1965, p. 10, July 27, 1965, p. 10 and July 28, 1965, p. 10. See also chapter 3, "Conservatives: Reforming Under Fire," in D. E. Butler and Anthony King, *The British General Election of 1966* (London: Macmillan, 1966).

[11] Interview with Sir Harry Legge-Bourke, MP, chairman of the 1922 Committee, London, July 29, 1970.

[12] See, for example, Labour's criticism of the way in which Harold Macmillan was chosen as Conservative leader, *The Times* (London), January 22, 1957, p. 8.

would, presumably, be followed in the event of a leadership vacancy created by death or resignation when the Labour party formed the government. Citing the 1922 Bonar Law precedent "as being most in accord with the spirit of the Constitution," and "the only one that accords with the *democratic* organization of the Parliamentary Labour Party," the statement made it clear that the Commons members of the party would meet at once to elect a new leader who would then be in a position to accept office as the new prime minister.[13] What attracted Labour to the Bonar Law example was that he had been elected party leader immediately *before* being called upon by the King to form a government. For the Conservatives, this was clearly regarded as an exception to their usual practice.

In its early years in parliament the Labour party elected a chairman (as distinct from a leader) who "was regarded more as a spokesman and representative than as an initiator of policies and a leader of men." [14] But by then both Conservative and Liberal parties had established a model which proved impossible for the small group of Labour supporters to ignore.

> By the time Labour representation came to Westminster, the British party system had reached a definite stage in its development. The two major parties were clearly divided, without that blurring at the edges which still characterized the party system in the 1850's and 1860's. Conservatives and Liberals were mass parties with "pseudo" democratic organizations in the country. Neither the National Liberal Federation nor the Conservative National Union had any decisive influence over the leadership of its party. The management of elections and the conduct of parliamentary policy were firmly vested in leaders who, by virtue of their personal qualities and, more often, their former office as Prime Minister or appointed successors of such, ruled over their parliamentary bloc without more than an occasional challenge in the exercise of their authority.[15]

[13] *Ibid.* (Italics added)
[14] W. L. Guttsman, "Changes in British Labour Leadership," in Dwaine Marvick (ed.), *Political Decision-Makers* (Glencoe, Ill.: Free Press of Glencoe, 1961), p. 97.
[15] *Ibid.*, p. 118.

Shortly it had become apparent that "the process of election to the [Labour] chairmanship had begun to resemble the process by which Conservative Leaders have always been chosen. Intense behind-the-scenes discussion, negotiation and bargaining resulted in the unopposed election of the Chairman" by his parliamentary colleagues.[16] Finally, in 1922, when the Labour party became the official opposition and its chairman the leader of the opposition, the electoral contest for the chairmanship became the occasion for the first selection of a "Leader" of the parliamentary party. When in opposition, the PLP has, since 1922, selected one person to serve as both its leader and chairman of the party at the commencement of each parliamentary session, calling for nominations and, if necessary, taking a secret ballot to decide the winner; whereas in office, the PLP has used annual elections to choose the chairman of the parliamentary party, the leader serving as prime minister and remaining free from pre-sessional intra-party elections. Within the PLP electoral contests have been held on six occasions. In 1922, 1935, 1955 and 1963, Ramsay MacDonald, Clement Attlee, Hugh Gaitskell and Harold Wilson were chosen, respectively, as leader; in addition, Gaitskell's leadership was challenged twice, both times unsuccessfully, by Harold Wilson in 1960 and by Anthony Greenwood in 1961.

The similarities of leadership selection procedures in the Conservative and Labour parties are more numerous and of much greater significance than the differences. Although its origins as a party were extra-parliamentary and it might have been expected, therefore, to allow extra-parliamentary participation in its leadership selection, Labour's "concepts of leadership have widely assimilated the attitudes that had been customarily held by men of the older political parties."[17] Both parties have now reached essentially the same position on the constitutional question of the discretionary power of the Crown in selecting the prime minister. By restricting the practical exercise of the royal prerogative when a leadership vacancy occurs in the governing party, the parties

[16] McKenzie, p. 339.
[17] Guttsman, "Changes in British Labour Leadership," p. 93.

have further limited the discretionary powers of the Crown by obliging the monarch to accept their choices. What is even more significant, however, is that without challenge from the extra-parliamentary party, the leading parliamentary officers of both parties have assumed the power to formulate the parties' respective positions on methods of leadership selection. In 1957, it was the members of the opposition shadow cabinet who designed and announced Labour's policy on leadership selection in the event of a leadership vacancy in office, just as it had been the Labour MPs, who, in 1922, had unilaterally assumed (without apparent opposition) the right to choose the party's first leader in the Commons quite independently of the extra-parliamentary organization. It was Sir Alec Douglas-Home himself who, as leader and following consultations with and advice from certain party notables, promulgated in 1965 the voting procedures to be followed in selecting future Conservative leaders — a fact which in itself is remarkable evidence both of the authority and power of the Conservative leader and of the subservience and the weakness of the party outside parliament on matters pertaining to parliamentary leadership.

Both the Conservative and Labour parliamentary parties have had no difficulties in preserving unto themselves the power to choose their own leaders. Underlying this fact is the notion that parties in Britain are first and foremost parliamentary entities and as such the parliamentarians should be entitled to select the person they wish to have lead them with no interference from the party outside parliament. Why should this be so? One explanation may well have been offered by Samuel Beer when, in reference to the nineteenth-century growth in the British Conservative and Liberal parties of local constituency associations and national bodies based largely upon those local associations, he stated:

> Conceivably these changes in the formal structures of the parties might have revolutionized the way in which leaders were chosen and their policies when in power or in Opposition were determined. Control over the extra-Parliamentary organization and through it, over the Parliamentary party, might have gravitated into the hands of party bureaucrats

and professional organizers, as has sometimes been the case on the continent. Or perhaps the party organization might have become in fact, as well as form, radically democratized. . . .

Yet neither of these varieties of party government materialized. . . . A striking fact about British politics, now as then, is that these highly professional operators never acquired independent political power comparable to the power of the American "boss" or the continental party "bureaucrat."[18]

It is likely also true that the existence of annual party conferences in Britain has made it easier for the parliamentary parties to retain the power to choose their leaders, for the party conferences serve as legitimate outlets through which a good deal of the political energy of party activists is dissipated. If through regular party conferences the party activists have gained the impression of having contributed to the well-being of the party, then the likelihood of their promoting the idea that they should participate directly in the selection of the party leader has been reduced accordingly.

If, as has been suggested, "because of deferential norms [in Britain], there is no support for the Jacksonian belief that all electors are capable of holding public office," [19] one may also apply the same line of reasoning to the absence of mass party conventions for the selection of party leaders in Britain. For even though the Labour and Conservative parties exhibit mass party characteristics, there is no support for the belief that all party men are capable of selecting party leaders. The implications are obvious. To be selected as leader of the party a candidate must meet the standards established by his parliamentary colleagues. He must have proven ability to lead and to administer. He must have established a commendable record as a parliamentarian and almost assuredly have served as a junior minister, then as a minister in the cabinet (see Tables 1-1 and 1-2). He must have demonstrated some skill as a debater and diligence as a party supporter and worker. In the final analysis he will be the man whose selection, over all others, will be confirmed and legitimized by an

[18] Samuel Beer, "The Conservative Party of Great Britain," *Journal of Politics,* XIV (February 1952), 44-45.
[19] Richard Rose, *Politics in England* (Boston: Little, Brown and Co., 1964), p. 41.

Table 1–1: Leaders of the Conservative Party, 1885-1970

Name	Year of Election as Leader	Age at Time of Election	Parliamentary Experience at Election	Ministerial Experience In Cabinet	Not in Cabinet[a]
Marquis of Salisbury	1885	55 yrs.	32 yrs.	4 yrs.	nil
A. J. Balfour	1902	53 yrs.	28 yrs.	9 yrs.	6 yrs.
A. Bonar Law	1911[b]	53 yrs.	11 yrs.	nil	2 yrs. 4 mo.
A. Chamberlain	1921[b]	57 yrs.	29 yrs.	8 yrs. 5 mo.	nil
A. Bonar Law	1922	64 yrs.	22 yrs.	5 yrs. 10 mo.	2 yrs. 4 mo.
S. Baldwin	1923	55 yrs.	15 yrs.	2 yrs. 1½ mo.	3 yrs. 9½ mo.
N. Chamberlain	1937	68 yrs.	19 yrs.	11 yrs. 2½ mo.	4½ mo.
W. Churchill	1940	65 yrs.	38 yrs.	18 yrs. 1½ mo.	2 yrs. 4 mo.
A. Eden	1955	57 yrs.	32 yrs.	11 yrs. 2½ mo.	4 yrs. 4 mo.
H. Macmillan	1957	62 yrs.	31 yrs.	5 yrs. 4½ mo.	5 yrs.
A. Douglas-Home	1963	60 yrs.	27 yrs.	8 yrs. 6½ mo.	3 yrs. 7 mo.
E. R. Heath	1965	49 yrs.	15 yrs.	5 yrs.	8 yrs.

a Includes junior ministers.
b Leader of the Conservative party in the House of Commons.

Sources: David Butler and Jennie Freeman, *British Political Facts, 1900-1960* (London: Macmillan & Co. Ltd., 1963).
Charles Moritz (ed.), *Current Biography, 1962* (New York: H. W. Wilson Co., 1962).
Joseph Thomas, *Universal Pronouncing Dictionary of Biography and Mythology*, 4th rev. ed. (London: J. B. Lippincott Co., 1915).
Who's Who, 1968 (London: Adam & Charles Black, 1969).
Who Was Who, 1929-1940 (London: Adam & Charles Black, 1947).

Table 1–2: Leaders of the Parliamentary Labour Party, 1922-1970

Name	Year of Election as Leader	Age at Time of Election	Parliamentary Experience at Election	Ministerial Experience In Cabinet	Ministerial Experience Not in Cabinet[a]
J. Ramsay MacDonald	1922	56 yrs.	12 yrs.	nil	nil
Arthur Henderson	1931	67 yrs.	28 yrs.	5 yrs. 2½ mo.	4 mo.
George Lansbury	1932	73 yrs.	10 yrs.	2 yrs. 2½ mo.	nil
C. R. Attlee	1935	52 yrs.	13 yrs.	nil	1 yr. 11½ mo.
Hugh Gaitskell	1955	49 yrs.	10 yrs.	1 yr.	4 yrs. 5 mo.
Harold Wilson	1963	46 yrs.	18 yrs.	3 yrs. 6 mo.	2 yrs. 2 mo.

[a] Includes junior ministers.

Sources: David Butler and Jennie Freeman, *British Political Facts, 1900-1960.*
Who's Who, 1968.
Who Was Who, 1929-1940.

intra-parliamentary party contest and vote. "We choose our leader," in the words of Lord Home, "not for what he does at a party conference but because the leader we choose is in every respect the whole man who is fit to lead the nation." [20]

Parliament's place as a centre for political activity is enhanced by the British system of choosing party leaders, for the group to which a prospective leader is obliged to appeal is defined first and foremost according to parliamentary, not extra-parliamentary, parameters.[21] And this means, clearly, that a candidate whose support comes more from the party outside parliament than from his parliamentary colleagues stands to suffer the fate of Aneurin Bevan. The selection of Gaitskell in 1955

> illustrated how narrow in effect the limits are within which the Parliamentary Party can exercise its discretion. . . . The defeat of Bevan's candidacy indicated that support of the party organization in the constituencies, which Bevan un- questionably enjoyed, was not sufficient to win the leader- ship. The factors in Gaitskell's success were his parliamentary skill, ministerial experience, and the prospect that he could

---

[20] Douglas-Home at the 1963 Blackpool Conservative Conference, as quoted in Macleod, "The Tory Leadership," p. 67.
[21] A common attitude shared by British MPs is that their leader's sense of responsibility to his parliamentary colleagues is greater, given the role that the parliamentary party plays in his selection, than it would be if he were selected by several thousand party delegates meeting in convention. On the whole, the attachment to parliament as a forum for political de- velopment appears to be a good deal stronger among British MPs than their Canadian counterparts. One Labour MP (Douglas Houghton), who stressed parliamentary skills as being more important to a leader than any other single characteristic, voiced disappointment over the design of the House of Commons chamber in Ottawa because there would be a tendency in such a chamber, he felt, to play down the importance of parliamentary skills. The Canadian chamber's large physical size, combined with the Canadian practice of allocating fixed seats to all members of the House, reduced the likelihood, he argued, of producing many first-rate parlia- mentary debaters. Citing Winston Churchill's dictum that effective parlia- mentary debate could best be achieved in a small legislative chamber with a "sense of crowd and urgency" about the great issues debated there, Houghton concluded that the political leaders produced in Canada would, on the whole, be less skilled as orators and as parliamentarians than their British counterparts. Interview with Douglas Houghton, MP and chairman of the PLP during the years of the Wilson government, London, July 21, 1970.

provide the party with effective and continuous leadership before the electorate. Important trade union support came to him as a consequence of these factors. Since none of his competitors possessed all of these qualifications, Gaitskell's election was in fact a foregone conclusion. That the party organization could not command the selection of the Leader, but that the Parliamentary Party, judging by the relatively narrow standards of parliamentary and electoral success, did, is an illustration of the extent to which the requirements of the system of government rather than the logic of the party structure, define the position of the party Leader.[22]

In the United States a nominating convention to select presidential and vice-presidential candidates was held as early as 1808. Up to that time it had been customary for congressional caucuses to nominate the presidential candidates, a practice derived at least in part from the favourable view held by many United States' politicians of the British parliamentary model, which by that time had established the principle of selection of the prime minister by legislative majority.[23] Other more practical considerations, such as the amount of time required to travel from one part of the country to another, and the absence of widespread public involvement in federal politics, combined to reinforce the position of the congressional caucus as the vehicle by which presidential and vice-presidential candidates were selected. In 1808 the leaders of the Federalist party were especially anxious to defeat the Republican presidential candidate, James Madison, but as the insurgent Democrats had already nominated a candidate of their own, the question facing the Federalists "was whether to run their own candidates, or . . . to back the insurgent already in the field." [24] To come to a decision on this point "that would be binding on the

[22] Gerhard Loewenberg, "The British Constitution and the Structure of the Labour Party," *American Political Science Review,* LII (September 1958), 782.
[23] Paul T. David, Ralph M. Goldman and Richard C. Bain, *The Politics of National Party Conventions* (Washington, D.C.: The Brookings Institution, 1960), p. 9.
[24] Samuel E. Morison, "The First National Nominating Convention, 1808," *American Historical Review*, XVII (July 1912), 744.

whole party" [25] a caucus of congressional members of the party was deliberately by-passed in favour of a convention of delegates at which some eight states were represented. A congressional caucus was relatively unattractive to the Federalists in 1808. For one thing, they had too few elected members at Washington to make a caucus practicable; for another, the party had previously discovered the caucus to be ineffective in producing party harmony. More importantly, four years earlier it had been established that "the noncongressional Federalist leaders of Massachusetts and New York . . . were more powerful in their home states than the party minority was in Congress." [26] For these reasons a secret meeting of Federalist leaders (a "convention") was held in New York City to nominate candidates for the presidency and vice-presidency. By repeating in 1812 what they had done in 1808 the Federalists left to posterity "the germinating idea of a national nominating convention."[27]

Not until 1831, however, when the first open nominating convention was held by the Antimason party, was there another national nominating convention. A secret convention, such as the Federalists had held, would scarcely have been acceptable to a party pledged to the abolition of secret societies, especially at a time when the new democratic ethos was becoming more and more widely accepted; therein lies the reason for the Antimason's decision to open their meeting and its deliberations to public scrutiny. Indeed, to a party of such recent origin with more extra-legislative than congressional support, a caucus of congressional members appeared singularly unattractive when compared to a meeting capable of drawing delegates from several states and generating much public discussion and publicity. Subsequent to the Antimasonic convention of 1831, there was a convention of National Republicans that same year. Like the Antimasons, the Republicans had few supporters in Congress and they "needed a device to give them at least a semblance of nationwide representa-

---

[25] *Ibid.*

[26] David, Goldman and Bain, p. 14.

[27] Thais M. Plaisted, "Origins of National Nominating Committees and Platforms," *Social Studies,* XXX (April 1939), 201.

tion." [28] In the following year a Democratic-Republican convention met after Congress had adjourned (timed so as "to prevent an improper interference by members of Congress" [29]) to select Andrew Jackson and Martin Van Buren as its presidential and vice-presidential nominees.

Subsequent candidates for the presidency were no longer chosen by congressional caucuses, for with the 1832 convention the new technique of extra-congressional selection had become established. A major innovation in American party politics had been effected initially, at least, because of unacceptable congressional representation, and it had been accomplished in a remarkably short period of time. Jackson himself had contributed significantly to the change by his obvious and successful reliance on an extra-congressional organization. His popular support base had left him free of indebtedness to congressional leaders and, therefore, free of the congressional caucus. Ultimately the widespread acceptance of national nominating conventions was easily fostered by two separate and by no means incompatible developments of nineteenth-century politics.

> The convention prevailed over the other nominating methods because it best satisfied the ideological demands of the Jacksonian era that government should be responsive to the people's direction. It also solved the technical difficulties of conducting politics in a democracy. In the nominating convention, idea and experience harmonized; a popular theory created an institution which passed the pragmatic test imposed by politicians. [30]

For these reasons the national party convention soon developed into a powerful and popular political institution of its own.

---

[28] David, Goldman and Bain, p. 18.
[29] As quoted in David, Goldman and Bain, p. 18.
[30] James S. Chase, "Jacksonian Democracy and the Rise of the Nominating Convention," *Mid-America*, XLV (October 1963), 231-32. Chase states: "The Convention satisfied the great political touchstone of Jacksonian democracy — popular sovereignty. Every public question was to be decided by the people acting through their chosen agents; elected officials were considered, even by themselves, mere agents reflecting the voters' desires. Any other course constituted a dangerous tendency toward aristocracy, or even monarchy" (p. 232).

The switch from congressional caucuses to national nominating conventions has occasioned a diminution of the importance of congressional politicians in the selection process, while at the same time the influence of state party notables in the selection process has increased. State delegations have become the basic electoral units at national conventions, and the power of the state party organizations, state and local machines, and state and local bosses has been magnified accordingly. Struggles by competing delegations from the same states for recognition and acceptance at the conventions have amply demonstrated both the inability and the unwillingness of the national organizations to apply standards of uniformity to delegate categories and to methods of delegate selection. Such struggles have appeared as reminders of the distinctly federal composition of national party conventions. At the same time, open and public voting by state delegations and individual delegates has fulfilled a requirement of Jacksonian democracy more suitably than secret congressional caucuses, just as national nominating conventions have embodied more truly than did congressional caucuses the principle of separation of powers in the selection of presidential and vice-presidential candidates. Philosophically, then, the national nominating convention has been well-suited to the style and understanding of politics in the United States.

Significantly the change from caucus to convention selection brought with it an enlargement of the group from which the potential leader may be chosen, as well as alterations in the criteria applied to judge potential presidents. "The congressional caucuses," according to David, Goldman and Bain, "in picking most of the nominees stayed largely within the circle of their own observation and acquaintanceship." [31] But within a decade of its adoption

> the new system had effectually broken the tendency to pick presidential nominees from a small circle of nationally known statesmen. It gave scope to the campaigning efforts of the sectional leaders, made room for factional candidacies, and provided machinery for selecting a compromise candidate

[31] David, Goldman and Bain, p. 159.

when the leading factional candidates had defeated each other. The field was open to state government officials as well as federal, to legislators as much as executives, *and to persons with no previous governmental experience,* if for some other reason they had developed that intangible quality known as "availability."[32]

V. O. Key, Jr., has commented upon the same feature of American politics:

> Had the congressional caucus by some chance survived as the means for nominating presidential candidates, the odds are that Presidents and the presidential system itself would have been radically different. The convention provides a channel for advancement to the Presidency independent of the Congress, a channel that can probably be navigated by men who could not make their way to the top through Congress and that probably is closed to others who can achieve leadership in Congress.
>
> If these estimates are correct, the convention profoundly conditions the character of the American governmental system. It does not limit access to the Presidency to those who climb the ladder within the narrow confines of the inner circles of the representative body; nor does it restrict competition to those who gain the deference of their fellows within any narrowly defined group of party notables. The convention operates flexibly with a range of freedom that enables it to elevate to leadership men it judges to be suited to the needs of the time rather than merely to promote those who have worked their way up the bureaucratic ladder of party status.[33]

A structural change, in other words, could obviously have widespread political consequences. Had the congressional caucus managed to retain its control over presidential nominations,

> the chances are that the old war-horses of the party organization in Congress would have had the edge in the race for the Presidency. A Taft would have won over an Eisenhower, a Garner over a Roosevelt, a Johnson over a Ken-

[32] *Ibid.,* p. 159. (Italics added)
[33] V. O. Key, Jr., *Politics, Parties and Pressure Groups,* 5th ed. (New York: Thomas Y. Crowell, 1964), p. 433.

nedy. Those factors conducive to advancement in hierarchies would have governed in the successive screenings on the way to the Presidency. An institution so transient as a national convention can be unconventional in its choices, a circumstance that is sometimes frightening; yet it permits the occasional choice of leaders who probably could not have made their way up a tighter party hierarchy.[34]

That an entirely new and different type of person was capable of being selected as a presidential candidate was made possible by the adoption of the national party convention. Such a fundamental alteration, brought about as it was by way of a change in leadership selection practices, was eventually repeated in Canada when, early in the twentieth century, the national political parties abandoned the traditional processes used up to that time (processes modelled on the British experience), replacing them with the party leadership convention. By so doing, Canadian parties opted for a leadership selection system which had the marked effect of opening up party leadership positions to non-federal and non-legislative politicians, just as it had in the United States.

Whereas the American national nominating conventions have developed within and, in their own way, contributed to, a system of forceful state and local parties, the British arrangements for leadership selection have reinforced the status of the already powerful parliamentary groups. The one leadership selection method seems to have been well suited to the decentralization and localization of political power, the other to its concentration. One is more in keeping with the separation of legislative and executive powers, the other with their fusion, which, after all, one would expect given the American and British systems of government. As it has turned out, the nominating convention has proved to be much truer to the American governmental model than the earlier congressional caucus selection method because it has distinguished more precisely the office of the president as an entity separate from the congressional branch of government. Moreover, there is a touch of irony in the fact that of the two political systems the one with

[34] Key, p. 398.

the mass membership political parties, the annual party conferences, and the elaborate extra-parliamentary party organizational structure, is not the one that through its membership and
its conferences formally selects its leaders. The hierarchical career
pattern is so imbedded as one of the fundamentals of British
political leadership recruitment and selection that the flexibility
granted American political parties with regard to the co-optation
of notables into the presidential candidacy is, for all intents and
purposes, an option unavailable to British parties. In Britain the
enthusiastic party activist has been kept occupied with aspects of
his party's work other than formal participation in the selection of
its leader. Not so with his American counterpart. The nominating
convention has enabled thousands of party activists to participate
in some way (even if it meant, for many of them, nothing more
than casting a vote) in the choice of a presidential candidate.
And that sort of message is not long lost on party professionals.
They, more than anyone else, want to generate sufficient intra-
party excitement to sustain an electoral machine, to enthuse the
public at large and, most important of all, to win elections.

2

Conventions in Pre-Confederation Canadian Politics

Gatherings of supporters of particular legislative groups or individuals were held on various occasions in pre-Confederation British North America. Not infrequently these assemblies were referred to as "conventions," and they were instrumental in adopting and utilizing for the first time some of the techniques and procedures later to be accepted by party conventions in twentieth-century Canada. Such rallies were held for a variety of reasons, but never to select the leader of a party. That was not to come until the early twentieth century. In pre-Confederation Canadian politics, conventions proved to be especially well-suited to both John A. Macdonald and his Conservative allies and to George Brown and the Reform party. As a result, conventions for policy and organization purposes found early acceptance in the history of both the Conservative and Liberal parties.

As early as 1818 an attempt was made to influence government policy by way of pressures exerted by an extra-governmental body constituted as a "convention." In that year, Robert Gourlay, a fiery Scot newly arrived in Upper Canada, sought redress of grievance with reference to, among other things, landholding policies in the province.[1] It was as legitimate to petition governments collectively as individually, Gourlay maintained. He therefore advanced

> a scheme of township meetings at which representatives would be chosen, who would later meet in a provincial convention to "dispatch commissioners to England with the petitions, and hold correspondence with them, as well as with the supreme government." That is, Gourlay proposed the assembling of a popular body that would assume at least some of the authority of the provincial legislature.[2]

The Attorney General of the province held that although neither the township meetings nor the convention were "unconstitutional," they were "a most dangerous type of popular movement" and he was issued instructions "to seize the first opportunity to prosecute [Gourlay]."[3] In the event, Gourlay's convention was held. It was not well attended, was decidedly cautious in its deliberations, and adopted nothing more than two moderate addresses. All this should have made obvious "that the convention was not really trying to usurp the role of the legislature,"[4] but the potential threat such an innovation presented to the Governor and the legislators led the legislature within four months of the convention to adopt a law prohibiting the assembling of unauthorized conventions of delegates. The legislative assembly

> passed a resolution that no member of [Gourlay's] convention should be allowed a seat in the house. Further resolutions pronounced the assembly the only constituted representative of the people and the recent convention of delegates illegal. On October 31 a bill in conformity with these resolutions passed both houses.[5]

---

[1] For a description and an analysis of Robert Gourlay and his place in Canadian history, see Aileen Dunham, *Political Unrest in Upper Canada: 1815-1836* (Toronto: McClelland and Stewart Ltd., 1963), pp. 51-61, and Gerald M. Craig, *Upper Canada: The Formative Years 1784-1841* (Toronto: McClelland and Stewart Ltd., 1963), pp. 93-100.
[2] Craig, p. 96.
[3] *Ibid.*, and Dunham, p. 57.
[4] Craig, p. 97.
[5] Dunham, p. 57.

The popular mood was too much for the legislature, however. There was "much feeling in the province" [6] that the banning of unauthorized conventions was an extreme measure, and within two years the act itself was repealed.

The reaction to Gourlay's proposal by the Governor and his legislature is worth examination. The American and French revolutions were relatively recent events and their considerable impact on government institutions was well known to British officials. The Attorney General of Upper Canada recognized that fact when he allowed that the word "convention" had "unfortunate overtones of the American and French Revolutions." [7] He had no doubt feared such a meeting as Gourlay proposed on that ground alone. But "conventions" were also known in English political history. That they were regarded with suspicion by the British North American authorities is understandable given the history of that word in English politics.

In the American colonies from 1689 on, a variety of gatherings had been held under the common rubric of "convention." Such meetings

> usually consisted of, or closely resembled, a colonial legis-
> lature minus the governor, or minus the governor and
> council, and not summoned by the governor, and . . . they
> were called conventions because, of all the words denoting
> a political assemblage, convention was held to be the fit and
> technical term by which to designate such bodies as these.[8]

During and immediately following the American Revolution the idea of "convention" as a body apparently able to express the will of the nation

> proved invaluable as both the former colonies and the
> nation needed a means compatible with the natural rights
> philosophy of government for writing and ratifying their
> new constitutions. Implicit in the convention was the idea
> that its delegates incarnated the sovereignty of the people; its

---

[6] Craig, p. 98.
[7] Craig, p. 96.
[8] J. Franklin Jameson, "The Early Political Uses of the Word Convention," *Proceedings of the American Antiquarian Society,* XII (1899), 184.

sessions enacted the social compact. Private associations, such as the great religious denominations, whose large and scattered memberships made primary meetings impracticable, also employed the convention after 1776 as the supreme governing body of their organizations. These conventions possessed, on a more modest scale, the same sovereign functions as the state constitutional conventions and the delegates proceeded on the assumption that their authority sprang directly from the rank and file.[9]

The precedents for the application of the term "convention" to such meetings in the American colonies were to be found in seventeenth-century English politics. They were, specifically, the 1660 assembly of parliament, which restored Charles II, and the English Revolution of 1688

> in which the leading part, in representing the nation, was taken by a body which was substantially a parliament, but which was not summoned by the king and lacked his presence and concurrence, and which therefore called itself a convention until the day when, having declared William and Mary king and queen, it declared itself a parliament.[10]

The word first seems to have appeared as a political term in England thirty years before the English Revolution, when it was used to denote a parliament defective in some way or another. For some time to follow "convention," not uncommonly, was a term that carried with it cognizance of the irregularity of the meeting itself, the implication that the gathering was not perfectly legal, or that it was not completely within the framework of the constitution. Early nineteenth-century British North American official reaction to suggestions of a convention becomes more understandable, then, given the historical association of the word with an improper, non-parliamentary, quasi-Cromwellian gathering.

However, by the mid-nineteenth century the term began to gain favourable acceptance in Canadian politics. As it happened, the

[9] James Staton Chase, "Jacksonian Democrocy and the Rise of the Nominating Convention," pp. 231-32.
[10] Jameson, 185.

newly formed British American League, most of whose members were Conservatives, was experiencing an internal struggle for control of the League's policy, and several of its supporters, including John A. Macdonald, wished to settle the matter once and for all. It looked to them as if a convention of League supporters would be the best means. Therefore, a convention was called for July 1849 in Kingston, with a second meeting to follow later that year in Toronto. According to Donald Creighton, "the first task of 1849, as Macdonald and the moderates saw it, was to defeat the desperate annexationist proposals" of the pro-American Montreal extremists.[11] To present an acceptable alternative to continental union Macdonald sought support for certain principles before the convention met, urged League organization meetings at the local level to select "the best man as a delegate," and pleaded with certain individuals to attend the convention as voting delegates. Writing to D. B. Stevenson of Prince Edward County, Macdonald stated:

> As the Conservatives are resolved to have a meeting or Convention here at the end of this month or beginning of the next, it is of great importance to have a full attendance. . . . The reason why some persons hold back from forming Constitutional Associations or *Leagues* is that the purpose or views of such combinations have not been promulgated. Now the only way to attain that, is to have this Convention, where some specific line of action, & fixed policy may be adopted. The great aim is to make it not so much a political or party as an economical movement, protection to native industry & home manufacturers, connection with Great Britain, reciprocity with the United States in agricultural products, and repeal of the municipal and tariff monstrosities of last session, no French domination, but equal rights to all. *These* are the ruling principles of the League. Pray lose no time. Form a *District* Constitutional Association in connection with the League. Have a meeting in every township & let each township send its best man as a delegate — every society with 100 members send one delegate, 300 — two, 600 — three & 1000 & over 4 delegates. Be sure and

---

[11] Donald Creighton, *John A. Macdonald: The Young Politician* (Toronto: Macmillan of Canada, 1952), p. 142.

> come yourself as one delegate, as the discussion on protec-
> tion will be very full & warm and in the absence of Cayley
> you have studied the subject most.[12]

With the adoption of a declaration favouring federal union of all
British North American colonies by the convention, and with the
rejection of an annexationist policy, the efforts of Macdonald and
others directed toward the organization of district associations and
the selection of as many sympathetc delegates as possible had paid
off. Moreover, it was shown that conventions could, if properly
organized and directed, prove to be highly effective and useful
means of accomplishing political tasks.

Within five years Macdonald, anxious to obtain the best candidates for the forthcoming election to the legislature of the Province
of Canada, decided that the bounds of the party should be enlarged "so as to embrace every person desirous of being counted as
a 'progressive Conservative'." [13] Stressing the care that must go into
the selection of the right candidates for election to public office
as well as the need to ensure the selection of Conservative supporters, Macdonald wrote:

> Take care that amid a multiplicity of candidates on our
> side, a Rad may not succeed — especially a Rad armed with
> Crown patronage, which we know would be unscrupulously
> exerted or rather distributed. The only way to cure this is
> an early choice of candidates at a Conservative Caucus Con-
> vention. I am opposed to the Yankee system of caucus as a
> general rule, but sometimes as in your case, it is the only
> way to avoid disunion.[14]

The "convention," which for this purpose Macdonald seemed to
equate with "caucus," was regarded as an acceptable mechanism
both for widening the basis for support of the party and for the
selection of candidates for election to the legislature.

However, the Conservatives were not alone in experimenting
with the newly acceptable form of political organization. Twice

---

[12] J. K. Johnson (ed.), *The Letters of Sir John A. Macdonald, 1836-1857*
(Ottawa: Public Archives of Canada, 1968), p. 155. (Italics in original)
[13] Macdonald to Captain James McGill Strachan, *ibid.,* p. 202.
[14] *Ibid.,* pp. 202-203.

during the late 1850s party conventions were held in Toronto by Reformers under the "guiding spirit" of George Brown.[15] Six delegates from each constituency in Canada West were invited to attend a one-day convention in 1857 with the intention, according to J. M. S. Careless, of constructing "a definite party union or Reform Association, based on a well-understood set of principles and policies."[16] Several policies favouring representation by population, non-sectarian national education and free trade were debated and adopted by the meeting. Indeed, a new party organization called the Reform Alliance was established, giving permanent structure to the fusion of Toronto urban and western Upper Canadian rural Reformers. All in all, the Toronto meeting was judged a great success — so successful that it could only lead to a favourable impression of party conventions by the various Reform leaders and a desire for further meetings of a similar sort.

By 1859, in order "to buoy up [the party's] enthusiasm,"[17] another convention was thought to be necessary. With nearly six hundred delegates present (four times the number of delegates at the 1857 meeting), what has been referred to as "the first great party convention in Canadian history"[18] was held. Although differing views have subsequently been expressed on the relative success or failure of the meeting in the area of policy agreement,[19] several important decisions were made relating to representation and organization of the convention which were important in themselves. Delegate status was accorded not only to the several constituency and township representatives, but also to Reform MPPs

[15] J. M. S. Careless, *Brown of the Globe*, 2 vols. (Toronto: Macmillan Company of Canada, 1959 and 1963), I, 235. A group of Upper Canada Clear Grits, dubbed "the Calebites" by the *Globe*, met twice in convention in 1850 to adopt a number of resolutions favouring, among other things, universal suffrage, election of all "public functionaries," and election of the governor. See Careless, I, 113.

[16] Careless, I, 234.

[17] Elwood H. Jones, "Ephemeral Compromise: The Great Reform Convention Revisited," *Journal of Canadian Studies*, III (February 1968), 21.

[18] George W. Brown, "The Grit Party and the Great Reform Convention of 1859," *Canadian Historical Review* (hereinafter cited as *CHR*), XVI (September 1935), 246.

[19] *Cf.* Brown, 263-65; Careless, I, 321-22; Jones, 26-27; and Frank H. Underhill, *In Search of Canadian Liberalism* (Toronto: Macmillan Company of Canada, 1961), p. 61.

and editors of newspapers supporting the Reform party. Five separate committees were established on credentials, procedure, resolutions, organization of the party, and finance.[20] All in all, according to one student of the convention, in spite of its ultimate failure to unite the Reform party behind Brown's leadership and its failure to unite the party on a common policy of federation, the convention was "impressive for its size, ambition, organization and free expression of opinion." [21]

The Reform party of Canada West assembled once more in convention prior to Confederation. Meeting in Toronto in June 1867, the six hundred delegates rejected the idea of serving in a coalition government with Macdonald's Conservatives following the official creation of the Dominion on July 1. By doing so the delegates accepted one of the ideas foremost in George Brown's mind when he called the meeting. "Incensed at the refusal of [William] McDougall and [W.P.] Howland to resign" from Macdonald's cabinet, the *Globe* publisher determined to read the two Reformers out of the party.[22] "He called a convention for late June. The Reform Party would greet Confederation with purified ranks and a new set of goals."[23] Once again the party was to be united, and once again a convention was the means whereby that would be accomplished. "Party unity would be focused not so much on a specific set of reforming resolutions as on a general agreement that Liberals would close ranks against the principle of coalition, and fight the elections for a genuinely Liberal government." [24] An important stage in the emergence of a political party had been reached and the convention was the tool whereby the party leaders felt they could best consolidate their troops.

The 1867 convention's significance stemmed not simply from its rejection of coalition government in Canada and its preference for

---

[20] *Globe*, November 10, 1859, p. 2. Brown states that of the sixty-two signatures attached to the circular calling the 1859 convention, forty-three were of newspaper representatives (Brown, 251).
[21] Jones, 27.
[22] Dale C. Thomson, *Alexander Mackenzie: Clear Grit* (Toronto: Macmillan Company of Canada, 1960), p. 95.
[23] *Ibid.*
[24] Careless, II, 245.

party politics. The convention itself was more highly organized than any previous one. It included as *ex officio* delegates "all Reform members of the House of Assembly, all Reform candidates for the House of Commons and House of Assembly, and all editors of Reform newspapers in Upper Canada" in addition to the maximum number of five delegates from each municipality.[25] A committee on credentials was set up, which meant that the delegates ("the cream of Upper Canada" — according to Brown — "Wardens, reeves, J.P.'s, coroners, merchants, manufacturers — the pick of the local politicians, business men and professionals")[26] were to present their credentials upon registration at Toronto's Music Hall. As well, arrangements and resolutions committees were established. The colourful member of the British Columbia legislature, Amor de Cosmos, travelled east for the convention to urge support for British Columbia's immediate entry into Confederation, thereby broadening the basis for delegate status beyond the immediate borders of Canada West and giving promise to Brown's dream of a truly national Reform party coming into existence sometime in the future.[27] Brown's stated intention not to run again for parliament combined with the real desire on the part of the delegates to see him lead the party in parliament after the forthcoming elections led to the adoption by acclamation of a resolution urging him not to retire from active politics and to seek, once again, a position in the legislature.[28] The resolution stated:

> That this Convention cannot separate without expressing to the Hon. George Brown the gratitude of the Reform party, *of which he has been so long the able leader,* for his services to the people of Canada, and also the earnest hope that he will reconsider his intention of retiring from parlia-

[25] *Globe,* June 14, 1867, p. 2. See also Supplement to the *Daily Globe,* June 28, 1867.
[26] As quoted in Careless, II, 247.
[27] Careless, II, 246; and P. B. Waite, *The Life and Times of Confederation: 1864 to 1867* (Toronto: University of Toronto Press, 1962), p. 319.
[28] Careless, II, 250-51, and James Young, *Public Men and Public Life in Canada* (Toronto: William Briggs, 1902), pp. 360-61.

mentary life, and accept a position in the Legislature of the country.[29]

The resolution, which in fact led Brown to change his mind and seek election to parliament that year, came close to conferring officially the leadership of the party on Brown by its adoption. With the 1867 assembly, conventions had moved one step closer to selecting a party leader.

[29] Young, p. 361. (Italics added)

3

Leadership Selection in the New Dominion

Early post-Confederation history of the selection of party leaders in the new Dominion clearly indicated the degree to which British-modelled attitudes and practices had a firm grip on Canadian politics. The statement of the preamble to the British North America Act that the constitution of Canada was to be "similar in Principle to that of the United Kingdom" applied as much to the operative side of Canadian politics as to its formal, institutional and constitutional side. This meant that the traditional processes of private, behind-the-scenes "soundings" of parliamentarians, of formal parliamentary caucus votes, of the application by the Governor General of the discretionary power of the Crown were the techniques relied upon in varying degrees by Canadian parties in naming their leaders. The techniques varied, of course, with the particular circumstances, most notably whether or not the party was in power or in opposition, but the contemporary observer of the first half-century of post-Confederation Canadian politics would rightly have gained the impression that Canadian party leaders were chosen in essentially the same ways as their British counterparts. The selections from Macdonald

31

to Meighen (1920) in the Conservative party and from Mackenzie to Laurier in the Liberal party bore witness to the extent to which the British leadership model was followed in post-Confederation Canadian history.

The parties in parliament admittedly deferred to the wishes of the Governor General when the Crown was involved in selecting a new prime minister. But in turn such deference was clearly based upon an implicit understanding that informal processes of contacting various party notables and weighing their expressed opinions would be undertaken by the Governor General. In this respect the Sovereign's representative, like the monarch herself, performed an essential governmental act, with some latitude of discretion (the degree of which related specifically to the occasion), and with profound implications both for the country and for the party. The retiring leader and other key individuals in the parliamentary party, therefore, were in positions to play a substantial part in choosing the new leader and, by and large, they did. Their influence was commensurate with their place in the party hierarchy. By the same token the parliamentary parties' less prominent members enjoyed relatively little influence in the selection of the leader although this was a feature much more characteristic of the party in power than in opposition, for in opposition the caucus vote on the party leadership was a vehicle that allowed an element of formal participation for backbench MPs. It would be impossible to equate that vote, however, with any measurable degree of influence over the outcome, given the likelihood of a "leadership-followership" connection between the relatively few, but important, party notables on the one hand, and the many, but nonetheless comparatively unimportant, backbench MPs and senators, on the other hand.

Parties in Office

The choice of Macdonald in 1867 as Canada's first prime minister was to be expected. His substantial ministerial experience, his role in the negotiations of the 1860s on Canadian confederation, as well as his leadership of the Canadian delegation in London during the winter of 1866-67 marked him for the prime ministership. Macdonald was so informed during the London meetings. "Lord Monck," Macdonald wrote to his sister, "is to return to Canada as Governor General, and has, but this is *entre nous,* charged me with the formation of the first Government as Premier."[1] Two months later Monck confirmed the appointment:

> I write this note to authorize you [Macdonald] to take the needful measures, so as to have a ministry ready to be sworn into office and to commence the performance of their several functions on the 1st July. I entrust this duty to you as the individual selected for their chairman and spokesman by unanimous vote of the delegates when they were in England, and I adopt this test for my guidance in consequence of the impossibility, under the circumstances, of ascertaining, in the ordinary constitutional manner, who possesses the confidence of a Parliament which does not yet exist.[2]

The election of 1867 gave more than enough parliamentary supporters to the government side for Macdonald to be assured of the leadership of a loosely defined but nonetheless discernible group. A national political party was in its early stages of development and its first leader was to retain his position in the party for a quarter of a century and through six more elections.

In a period of little more than five years, from June 1891 to July 1896, Canada had six different prime ministers: Macdonald, Abbott, Thompson, Bowell, Tupper, and Laurier. It was an extraordinary period in Canadian party history.[3] Macdonald's death had

---

[1] Joseph Pope, *Memoirs of the Right Honourable Sir John Alexander Macdonald,* 2 vols. (Ottawa: J. Durie and Son, 1894), I, 319.
[2] Sir Joseph Pope, *Correspondence of Sir John Macdonald* (Toronto: Oxford University Press, n.d.), pp. 45-46.
[3] The political history of the period is covered in Lovell C. Clark, "The Conservative Party in the 1890's," *Report of the Canadian Historical Association* (1961), pp. 58-74; Lovell C. Clark, "Macdonald's Conservative Successors, 1891-1896," in John S. Moir (ed.), *Character and Circumstance: Essays in Honour of Donald Grant Creighton* (Toronto: Macmillan Company of Canada, 1970), pp. 143-62; and John T. Saywell, "The Crown and the Politicians: The Canadian Succession Question: 1891-1896," *CHR,* XXXVII (December 1956), 309-37.

come at a time (June 1891), when the Conservative party's many factions were becoming increasingly quarrelsome (even though the Macdonald government had just been returned to office in the recent election) and when, incredibly, there was no readily apparent successor to the party leadership. The man who might well have succeeded Macdonald, could not. It had been recognized for some time before Macdonald's death that the Old Chieftain's faithful French-Canadian colleague, Sir Hector Langevin, would succeed him. An arrangement to that effect, which had been agreed upon some years earlier, had to be abandoned because of the scandal charges which just prior to Macdonald's death had been launched against Langevin's department (Public Works). The subsequent inquiry disclosed such a state of affairs in the department that Langevin, although acquitted of personal wrongdoing, was obliged to step down from the cabinet. In retrospect, this seems the closest the Conservative party has ever come to choosing a French Canadian as its leader.

For different reasons, neither of the next two most logical potential successors to Macdonald was available. Sir Charles Tupper, then Canadian High Commissioner to London, claimed he would not accept the leadership of the party if it were offered him (although the sincerity of the disclaimer itself has been questioned by one of Tupper's biographers[4]). Tupper was so distantly removed from the Canadian capital that nothing short of a unanimous appeal by Conservative MPs could conceivably have led to his return, and such an appeal was an impossibility given the range of opinions of Conservatives over Tupper. The other possible leader, indeed the most obvious successor to Macdonald, was Sir John Thompson. An experienced politician, Thompson was highly regarded by many of his colleagues. Yet he was unacceptable to some influential Conservatives, the Ontario Orangemen in particular, not so much because of his Roman Catholicism but because he had been a Catholic convert from Methodism. Although offered the prime ministership by the Governor General, Thompson declined to accept, "bowing instead to the 'sectarian

---

[4] J. W. Longley, *Sir Charles Tupper* (Toronto: Makers of Canada [Morang], Ltd., 1916), pp. 211-15.

climate' of the time." [5] At the same time, Thompson was in a powerful position, for the Governor General requested his recommendation for the next prime minister. Thompson recommended J. J. C. Abbott, who in turn accepted the premiership when it was offered to him by the Governor General.[6]

Abbott, if nothing else, was frank. In his speech to the Senate about acceptance of the call to form a new government he made it clear, almost apologetically so, that the reason for his selection was the lack of agreement on other possible leaders:

> But the position which I to-night have the honour to occupy, which is far beyond any hopes or aspirations I ever had, and I am free to confess beyond any merits I have (cries of no, no), has come to me very much probably in the nature of compromise. I am here very much because I am not particularly obnoxious to anybody.
>
> Hon. GENTLEMEN — No; no.
>
> Hon. Mr. ABBOTT — Something like the principle on which it is reported some men are selected as candidates for the Presidency of the United States — it is not that they are so able, it is not that they are so wonderfully clever, or such great statesmen, but it is that they are harmless, and have not made any enemies. I am inclined to think that that sentiment has had a great deal to do with the position in which I am placed.[7]

Abbott was right. He was held to be an acceptable compromise leader, although less so by his own province of Quebec than

---

[5] Clark, "The Conservative Party," p. 62.

[6] In so doing, Thompson effectively blocked D'Alton McCarthy from the party leadership. McCarthy's claim was not a strong one. He was one of the most outspoken of the Ontario Orangemen in parliament and had made the effort during the search for a new leader to press his own claim for the leadership on Thompson, no doubt pointing out at the same time that Thompson's Roman Catholicism made him unacceptable to the Protestant wing of the party. See J. Castell Hopkins, *Life and Work of the Rt. Hon. Sir John Thompson* (Toronto: United Publishing Houses, 1895), p. 190, and Steven Muller, "The Canadian Prime Ministers, 1867-1948: An Essay on Democratic Leadership" (unpublished Ph. D. dissertation, Department of Political Science, Cornell University, 1958), pp. 256-57.

[7] Canada, *Debates of the Senate* (June 17, 1891), p. 98.

Ontario, and his age (70) made it all too clear that his leadership would be short-lived. He was regarded, in other words, as a stopgap leader. His was to be a holding operation during which time the way would be prepared for Thompson to succeed him. It was agreed that Thompson would lead the party in the Commons with Abbott, the first of two prime ministers in the Senate, leading the government party in the upper house.

Abbott remained as prime minister for a year and a half. During that time Thompson emerged according to one contemporary observer as "the practical chief of the Administration [and] . . . the real leader of the Conservative party." [8] He was clearly expected to be the next prime minister and party leader, and it was felt that the religious difficulties would be minimized if he were able to bring into his cabinet some acceptable Ontario Protestant. To Abbott, there was no doubt about the leadership succession. "I am convinced," he wrote Thompson, ". . . that the feeling of the party points directly and unmistakeably [sic] to yourself." [9] On medical advice, Abbott submitted his resignation to the Governor General in November 1892, and Thompson accepted the request to form a new government. The retiring leader's role had been one of allowing the party sufficient time to sort out its affairs and to reach agreement on the leadership under a Roman Catholic. He had also paved the way for the leadership transition by acquainting the Governor General with his own views and those of the party on the succession. [10]

Unfortunately for the Conservatives, Thompson died at the age of fifty, only just over two years after he had become prime

---

[8] Hopkins, p. 239.

[9] Public Archives of Canada (hereinafter cited as PAC), *Thompson Papers,* vol. 166, 20780, letter from Abbott to Thompson of November 10, 1892.

[10] See Saywell, "The Crown and the Politicians," p. 314. At least some of the Ontario Conservative Orangemen who had previously reacted unfavourably to the suggestion that Thompson become party leader had, during the course of Abbott's premiership, changed their minds. Writing to Thompson to assure him of the support of the "boys," one Ontario MP and Orangeman, Sam Hughes, stated: "What! the pervert? the ultramontane? the roman catholic? the defender of Mercier's Jesuit Estates Act? *Yes,* all say yes." Hughes to Thompson, August 20, 1892, as quoted in Clark, "Macdonald's Conservative Successors," p. 146. "Pervert" was the expression current at the time to refer to a Roman Catholic convert.

minister. The situation in the Conservative party was a repeat of that following Macdonald's death, for no acceptable successor was readily available in Canada. But to some, at least, the choice once again "pointed unmistakably to Sir Charles Tupper, the High Commissioner to London." [11] They argued that Tupper was the one man who could restore harmony in the crumbling Conservative party. Yet their views were anything but shared by the Governor General and his wife (Lord and Lady Aberdeen) who were determined not to see Tupper as the first minister. In her diary, Lady Aberdeen made His Excellency's intentions perfectly clear: "Never if he [Aberdeen] could help it should Sir Charles be again in Canadian politics. He is another of those who are able mysteriously to provide largely for his sons & daughters."[12] Lord Aberdeen cabled the Colonial Secretary of the British government for advice, and consulted with Sir Frank Smith, a Conservative senator for nearly a quarter of a century. Both agreed that the senior cabinet minister and acting prime minister in Thompson's absence, Mackenzie Bowell (who himself felt he was in line for the premiership), should be given the opportunity of forming a government. The Governor General agreed and called on Bowell.

"The history of the Conservative party for the next eighteen months," according to Saywell, "is a study in the degeneration, moral and physical, of a political party." [13] To begin with, Bowell was regarded, like Abbott before him, as a temporary, compromise leader. But Bowell was suspicious, and this did not augur well for the party. According to Bowell's Minister of Finance, George Foster: "The general opinion expressed that this is a temporary arrangement naturally worries him [Bowell], and he sees a cabal in every two who converse together." [14] Additionally, as had been the case with Abbott, Bowell had no dedicated following in the party, his parliamentary seat was in the Senate, and he was seventy years of age. He was liked by his colleagues, but he was clearly not leadership material. Lady Aberdeen found

[11] Clark, "The Conservative Party," p. 62.
[12] John T. Saywell (ed.), *The Canadian Journal of Lady Aberdeen, 1893–1898* (Toronto: The Champlain Society, 1960), p. 166.
[13] Saywell, "The Crown and the Politicians," p. 319.
[14] As quoted in S. Morley Scott, "Foster on the Thompson–Bowell Succession," *CHR,* XLVIII (September 1967), 275.

him "rather fussy, and decidedly commonplace, also an Orange-man," [15] and Foster allowed that "B. is old, vain, and suspicious to a degree. What freak he may take no one knows, and this is really the most to be feared in the development of the thing." [16] All in all, it was a situation tailormade for the opposition, and the Liberals' confidence grew accordingly.

Bowell's leadership of the party and of the government proved to be so inept that by early 1896, less than a few months before the expiry of the five-year life of that parliament, seven prominent cabinet ministers resigned from his administration. The action has been unequalled in Canadian political history. Those who sub-mitted their resignation clearly lacked confidence in Bowell's leadership of the party and the government. Their spokesman, George Foster, made this clear in his statement to the House of Commons:

> Though with many misgivings we agreed to enter the Gov-ernment under Mr. Bowell in succession to Sir John Thomp-son, we have nevertheless unitedly and loyally striven to the best of our ability to make it strong and efficient, and it has been with growing regret that we have seen our efforts result in a measure of success less than that for which we had hoped and striven. We are of the opinion that the Liberal Conservative party ought to be represented by the strongest Government possible to be secured from its ranks, that the necessity therefore was never greater than under existing circumstances, and we believe that such a Government can be formed without delay. This we have repeatedly urged upon the Premier with the result that we found ourselves face to face with Parliament having a Government with its numbers incomplete, and with no assurances that the present Premier could satisfactorily complete it. Under these circum-stances we thought it our duty to retire, and in this manner to pave the way, if possible, for the formation of a Govern-ment whose Premier could command the confidence of all his colleagues, could satisfy the Liberal Conservative party, that its strongest elements were at its head and impress the country that it had a Government which was united and had power to govern. [17]

[15] Saywell (ed.), *Journal of Lady Aberdeen,* p. 161.
[16] Scott, "Foster on the Thompson–Bowell Succession," 275.
[17] Canada, *Debates of the House of Commons* (January 7, 1896), p. 10.

There was no question that the party was weak and divided under Bowell. There was also no question that the seven bolters (or "nest of traitors" as Bowell called them) wanted Sir Charles Tupper as their leader. Tupper had just arrived in Ottawa from England and had been well briefed about developments within the party. He was also willing to accept the prime ministership. Bowell judged the situation accurately and offered his resignation to the Governor General. Aberdeen, however, was determined not to call upon Sir Charles, nor was he prepared to accept the resignation of a prime minister whose government had just presented a throne speech to parliament and on which there had as yet been no vote. The following day Bowell again attempted to resign, but for a second time the Governor General would not yield. A stalemate had developed. The party could not continue without a change in its leadership, but the prime minister could not step down. Finally an understanding was reached which permitted both sides to save some face. Bowell was to stay on as prime minister, but Tupper was to enter the House of Commons through a by-election and assume effective leadership of the party. Bowell would step down as prime minister at the end of the parliamentary session (less than four months away) and Tupper would be named his successor, although on this last point the Governor General had his own views. He "refused to pledge himself in advance regarding any future change of Prime Minister." [18] Thus 1896 was, for good reason, a key year in Canadian party politics, in so far as the governing party asserted with some success a claim to choose its own leader (even though he may not, in fact, become prime minister) independent of vice-regal wishes.

As Bowell would soon be off the scene, the party's "temporary ills were borne with the patience which the instinct of self-preservation evokes." [19] The party tried desperately to paper over the cracks, but it was too late. "Even the commanding figure of Sir Charles Tupper could not restore the inward harmony or outward presence of the Conservative party." [20] The fact that Bowell was

[18] Saywell, "The Crown and the Politicians," p. 329. See also Longley, pp. 225-26.
[19] Longley, p. 226.
[20] Saywell, "The Crown and the Politicians," p. 331.

in the Senate enabled Tupper to assert his leadership over the party where it really counted, that is, in the Commons, but time was not on the Conservatives' side. The issues that had to be dealt with, notably the Manitoba school question, and the government's handling of them, proved to be too costly for the Conservatives. Tupper was asked to form a government when Bowell stepped down, with the retiring prime minister asking that he not be requested to give a recommendation to the Governor General about whom he should call. By that time the life of the seventh parliament had expired and the election date had been set. Tupper was shortly to become the only prime minister who, in that capacity, has never met parliament, for the Conservatives were defeated in the general election of June 1896.

The remaining leader to be chosen whilst his party was in office prior to the introduction of leadership conventions in his party was Arthur Meighen. On July 1, 1920, Sir Robert Borden informed the caucus of the Unionist party (the name of which was changed by the caucus that day to the National Liberal and Conservative Party) that because of failing health he was forced to step down as prime minister and party leader. His wish to relinquish the party leadership was respected when caucus unanimously adopted a "resolution of regret for [his] resignation and appreciation of [his] public service," [21] but it was ten days before Borden formally stepped down as prime minister. During that period there was rather faithful adherence to the British example of "soundings" and "consultations" within the parliamentary party — certainly more fully than had previously been the case within a governing party in Canada. Such an activity revealed a substantial difference between the opinions of the backbench supporters of the government on the one hand and those of the ministers on the other.

The depth of the party's differences of opinion was made more obvious to the retiring leader than to others by virtue of the

[21] Henry Borden, *Robert Laird Borden: His Memoirs,* 2 vols. (Toronto: Macmillan Company of Canada, 1938), II, 1031.

method adopted to canvass the opinions of the Government's parliamentary supporters. A unique plan to choose the new leader was devised by Sir George Foster and approved by caucus. According to Foster:

> The selection [is] ultimately to be made by Sir Robert. Each member of Parliament supporting the late government is to indicate by letter his first and other choices, and his reasons therefor. Sir Robert is to sift these out — ascertain the possibilities of each carrying the confidence and support of his colleagues, and using his long experience and knowledge of conditions, evolve the best from the number suggested.[22]

Although Borden referred to the members' letters as "ballots" he clearly understood that the role he was expected to play was something more than that of a returning officer. As the Montreal *Gazette* pointed out, "the selection of the new leader is . . . in Sir Robert Borden's hands, though he will be guided largely by the suggestions of his followers and colleagues."[23]

Borden's task was complicated by the division within the party over the succession. He and virtually the whole cabinet favoured as the new leader Sir Thomas White, the former Finance Minister. Others were mentioned as possibilities, but White was the clear favourite. The majority of the government backbenchers, on the other hand, supported the Minister of the Interior, Arthur Meighen.[24] Borden reported to Meighen that 90 per cent of the backbenchers preferred Meighen as their first choice. However this

---

[22] W. Stewart Wallace, *The Memoirs of the Rt. Hon. Sir George Foster* (Toronto: Macmillan Company of Canada, 1933), p. 205. Both Foster and Borden acknowledged the proposal as being Foster's, but years later H. H. Stevens claimed responsibility for it. See Ruth M. Bell, "Conservative Party National Conventions, 1927-1956: Organization and Procedure," (unpublished M.A. thesis, Department of Political Science, Carleton University, 1965), p. 18.
[23] R. MacGregor Dawson (ed.), *Constitutional Issues in Canada, 1900-1931* (London: Oxford University Press, 1933), p. 382.
[24] See Roger Graham, *Arthur Meighen*, 3 vols. (Toronto: Clarke, Irwin and Co. Ltd., 1960), I, 287-301, and Borden, II, 1030-40.

simply was not the case, for an examination of the "ballots" indicates that although Meighen received more than twice as much first-ballot support as White, he was the first choice of slightly less than 65 per cent of the backbenchers (see Table 3-1). Nonetheless, as over two-thirds of those preferring someone other than Meighen as their first choice gave him as their second choice, and as Meighen had a solid majority of the first-choice ballots, his support for the leadership was clearly of such a substantial nature that it could not be ignored.

Because of the uncertainty over the matter of the new leadership, there was considerable public speculation. This, in turn, led the prime minister to issue a statement outlining his interpretation

Table 3—1: *"Ballot" Totals Indicating to Borden Preferences, for His Successor, July 1920*

	First choice	Second choice	Third choice	Fourth choice
Arthur Meighen	65	28	4	
Sir Thomas White	27	27	4	
Sir George Foster	6	6	2	1
Sir Henry Drayton	2	5	4	
J. A. Calder	1	7	6	4
Sir James Lougheed	1	1	5	1
N. W. Rowell	1	1	4	
Hugh Guthrie		1	5	
C. C. Ballantyne			1	
Sir Arthur Currie			1	

Source: *Borden Papers*, private, in the possession of Mr. Henry Borden, Q.C., as provided by Professor R. C. Brown.

of the correct procedures to be followed in such a situation. A more exact phrasing of British constitutional practices could scarcely be imagined:

> Much confusion and misunderstanding seem to prevail in the press regarding the power and responsibility of a retiring Prime Minister in respect to the selection of his successor.
>
> The selection of a new Prime Minister is one of the few personal acts which, under the British constitution, a sovereign (in Canada the representative of the sovereign) is required to perform. A retiring Prime Minister has no right whatever to name his successor, nor has he any responsibility with respect to the selection of his successor, except as follows:
>
> The sovereign or his representative may not see fit to ask the view of the retiring Prime Minister with respect to the selection of his successor. For example, the Queen, on the final retirement of Mr. Gladstone, did not ask his advice or his views on that question. In such a case, the retiring Prime Minister has no right whatever to express his views or to tender any advice on the subject. If, however, the sovereign or his representative asks the views of the retiring Prime Minister, he has a right to express them, but they need not necessarily be followed. In expressing such views, he does not tender advice as a Prime Minister, because he has already retired from office. His advice is to be regarded simply as that of a person holding the position of Privy Councillor, who has acquired a wide experience in public affairs which would give a certain value to his opinion on the subject.[25]

As the weight of the cabinet ministers' opinions could not be ignored, the Governor General was informed of them by Borden, and White was issued an invitation to form a government. His refusal, on health and business grounds, left Borden free to recommend Meighen if he could persuade "the anti-Meighen faction in the Cabinet to accept Meighen's leadership and remain in the Government."[26] This was accomplished after much consultation. Meighen agreed to undertake the formation of a new government

[25] Dawson (ed.), p. 386.
[26] Graham, I, 292.

and he was sworn in as prime minister on July 10. The retiring leader's role had been a substantial one. He had determined satisfactorily the location and intensity of support for his various potential successors and his exhaustive consultations over a period of several days prepared the way for acceptance of the new leader within the parliamentary party.

Parties in Opposition

Those members of the Commons sitting in opposition to Macdonald's government following the 1867 election scarcely constituted a loosely knit coalition, much less a political party. There were Nova Scotia anti-confederationists, Quebec *Rouges,* and Ontario Reformers: each group anti-ministerialist, but with little else in common with the others that would seemingly enable rapid development of a parliamentary party. The most logical and, at the same time, the most acceptable, first leader for such a disparate group, George Brown, had been defeated in his attempt to get into the Commons in 1867. There was no better evidence of the apparent hopelessness of the opposition's plight than the fact that when parliament met after the 1867 election the opposition did not choose a leader, and it was the government, not the opposition, who assigned the leader of the opposition's seat to the Reform MP, Sandfield Macdonald. Yet within six years Sir John A. Macdonald's government had been replaced by the Liberals led by Alexander Mackenzie. By 1873-74, the party system had developed to the stage in Canada of fostering active inter-party competition as well as establishing within parliament a credible alternative to the party in power.

Alexander Mackenzie had clearly emerged as the chief opposition spokesman during the early post-Confederation years. Less than two years after the 1867 election he acknowledged this when he wrote:

> The newspapers call me the leader of the Opposition.
> I am nothing of the kind. I would not allow the party to

pass a vote naming me such when they proposed to do it last session. But at the same time, I am doing the work which devolves on the leader, until some one fit to be a political prophet shall arise to be a judge over them. Still, I feel a kind of obligation not to leave, without it is [*sic*] so agreed.[27]

The election of 1872 gave the opposition forces good reason to be encouraged for, although they had failed to defeat Macdonald's party, they had nonetheless narrowed the gap considerably between the numbers on the two sides of the House. The results convinced Mackenzie that the Liberals had to choose a leader as soon as parliament met, and he recorded in a letter to his brother the party's deliberations on this matter. The letter of March 1, 1873, describes fully the process utilized to choose the first leader of the Liberal party.

> We had a meeting of the Ontario members on Tuesday afternoon. I gave them my reasons for calling them together, and told them that Dorion had also called a meeting of the Quebec members, both meetings being with a view of forming a complete organization under one leader; that I had hitherto acted as leader, although not elected to that office; that I was now resolved to retire from the position; that we should have a friendly, open discussion on the subject, advising them to come to no decision until we could all meet together. I urged them to consider whether it would most advance the general interests of the party to make the choice from Quebec rather than from Ontario. I then said that my own impression was that the preponderating power Ontario held, would probably induce members from all sections to select one of the members from that Province, and in that case I thought Mr. [Edward] Blake should be chosen, as his splendid abilities and his standing in the country gave him many advantages, while his legal knowledge gave him additional power, placing him ahead of all others in the House. Blake then spoke, agreeing in the general plans I suggested, but protesting against my conclusions.

---

[27] William Buckingham and Hon. George W. Ross, *The Hon. Alexander Mackenzie: His Life and Times* (Toronto: Rose Publishing Company, 1892), p. 612. See Thomson, *Alexander Mackenzie: Clear Grit*, p. 119.

He spoke of my success during the last five years, and said the local Government was defeated through my efforts, and the late elections were carried by my influence and exertions, and consequently if an Ontario man were chosen, it must be me; and at any rate he could not listen to any proposal. One or two expressed themselves in favor of Blake in preference to me, all the others avoided any comparison, but discussed the matter fully. Finally it was delegated to a committee to consider. This committee was previously appointed to confer with a committee from Quebec, respecting the speakership and other matters. Our committee were Rymal, Young, Blake, Richards and myself, the others [from Quebec], Dorion, Holton, Letellier, Huntington and John Young. We had three long meetings, during which we arrived first at the conclusion that it was advisable to have the leader from Ontario, Blake and I agreeing that all Ontario would take Dorion freely if they considered that step advisable. They were unanimous against it. I then proposed to agree on Blake, each of us promising our utmost effort to support him. He would not listen to it. I also declined. The general meeting was adjourned till 4 o'clock this afternoon. The committee met again at 10, and I was pressed to yield which I reluctantly did. Dorion reported the result of the general meeting [to caucus]. Holton moved and Geoffrion seconded the motion to adopt the committee's report and declare me leader of the whole party. This was at once put by the chairman (John Young) and carried unanimously, seventy members being present.[28]

By early November the following year, Macdonald's government was so discredited by the Pacific scandal that its defeat appeared imminent. Macdonald resigned and Mackenzie accepted the Governor General's request to form a government. The changeover had been simplified by the opposition party's action of formally selecting a leader earlier in the life of that parliament.

Mackenzie's Liberals easily won the election of 1874 but they

---

[28] Buckingham and Ross, pp. 329-30. On the selection of Mackenzie in 1872 see also Thomson, pp. 146-48, and O. D. Skelton, *Life and Letters of Sir Wilfrid Laurier,* 2 vols. (Toronto: Oxford University Press, 1921), I, 172-74.

were defeated at the polls four years later. Mackenzie had failed to provide the leadership necessary to see the government successfully through a difficult economic period and he proved to be no match for Macdonald. Yet, following his government's defeat, Mackenzie chose not to offer his resignation to his party's caucus as might realistically have been expected. Macdonald had done this five years earlier when his government had resigned and his party was forced into opposition[29] and, although his resignation was not accepted, the gesture had established a precedent that would be followed by other leaders in both parties in the years ahead. Mackenzie's increasingly stubborn attitude toward the parliamentary group (he eventually stopped attending caucus meetings completely), as well as his unwillingness to bend on certain matters of policy, led to growing dissatisfaction with his leadership.

Although the details are unclear (there are two differing interpretations of the events immediately prior to his decision to retire), it is a fact that Mackenzie announced his resignation to a surprised House at 2:00 a.m. on April 28, 1880. The statement was as brief as it was to the point.

> Mr. MACKENZIE: I desire to say a word, or two with regard to my personal relations to the House. I, yesterday, determined to withdraw from the position as leader of the Opposition, and for [*sic*] this time forth I will speak and act for no person but myself.[30]

The background to Mackenzie's decision is clouded by contradictory accounts, but clearly Mackenzie had determined that in preference to forwarding his resignation to caucus he would make a simple announcement in the House of Commons. Laurier's biographer, O. D. Skelton, claims that a resolution was passed by the Liberal caucus "asking Mackenzie to consider the question of the

---

[29] In November 1873, Macdonald begged caucus to accept his resignation and choose a younger man, but his request was refused. See Donald Creighton, *John A. Macdonald: The Old Chieftain* (Toronto: Macmillan Company of Canada, 1955), pp. 180-81.

[30] Canada, *Debates of the House of Commons* (April 27-28, 1880), p. 815.

leadership," and that when this was put to him by a committee of five from caucus, Mackenzie reacted by stating he would shortly step down as Liberal leader. Mackenzie's version of his resignation was to the effect that a party conspiracy led by Edward Blake was determined to so undermine his position as leader that Mackenzie would resign and Blake would succeed him. Mackenzie stepped down even though, he maintained, a majority of his former cabinet colleagues assured him that they could "break down the compact" and "restore order" in caucus if he remained as leader.[31] In spite of the apparent contradictions, "it is not impossible," according to one of Mackenzie's biographers, "that both versions contain a large degree of truth."[32]

With Mackenzie out of the way, the Liberal caucus was free to choose a new leader, and there was no question who he would be. The man who had refused Mackenzie's offer of the leadership eight years earlier, Edward Blake, was the indisputable favourite. The Liberal caucus met (with Mackenzie not in attendance) the day following Mackenzie's resignation, and a brief account in the *Globe* summarized its activities.

> The Liberals of both Houses of Parliament met in caucus for the purpose of selecting a successor to Mr. Mackenzie in the leadership of the party. Scarcely a member was absent. . . . The utmost unanimity prevailed. The genial member for South Wentworth, Mr. Joseph Rymal, occupied the chair, a position to which he was entitled both by seniority and merit. After the object of the meeting had been explained it was moved by an Ontario Liberal, and seconded by a New Brunswick Liberal, "That the Hon. Edward Blake be elected leader of the Liberal party of Canada." Before the motion could be put every member present rose to his feet as if to emphasize his endorsation of the nomination, and amidst cheers the motion was declared carried. Mr. Blake, on being called upon, acknowl-

---

[31] Skelton, I, 220-21; also PAC, *Mackenzie Papers,* Reel M-199, Mackenzie to Charles Black, May 20, 1882, 2356-57, and *Mackenzie Letterbook,* vol. II, Mackenzie to L. H. Davies, May 20, 1880, 673-78.
[32] Thomson, p. 362.

edged in grateful terms the honour conferred upon him. . . . At the conclusion of Mr. Blake's speech a committee was appointed to convey to the Hon. Mr. Mackenzie the warm thanks of the Liberal party for his past valuable and untiring services during his long and useful parliamentary career, and their cordial appreciation of his integrity and usefulness to his party and country.[33]

Blake led the Liberals in two general elections, but both times the party was unsuccessful in its attempt to replace Macdonald's Conservatives. Following the 1887 election Blake, in poor health and dispirited by his party's electoral loss, determined to resign. Within two weeks of the election he sent a letter to all Liberals elected to the new House of Commons informing them of his intention to resign and reminding them that at the time of the opening of parliament "it will devolve on the liberals at once to choose their leader for the new Parliament."[34] In point of fact, Blake yielded to considerable pressure and agreed to stay on as leader but for the first parliamentary session only. Meeting in mid-April for the first time since the election, the caucus unanimously re-elected Blake to the party's leadership and at the same time set up an advisory committee of eight MPs to assist the leader in an attempt to ease his workload.[35] Blake's health did not permit him to continue much longer, however, and on June 2, 1887, he forwarded his resignation to caucus and it was accepted five days later.

During the period from June 2-7 several prominent Liberals were mentioned as potential successors to Blake. They included Sir Richard Cartwright and David Mills, both Ontario members of the House of Commons, and Oliver Mowat, the premier of Ontario. Little serious attention appears to have been paid to Wilfrid Laurier as a likely successor, but Blake was determined to see him as the next leader. Blake's opinion was that "there is

---

[33] *Globe,* April 30, 1880, p. 2.
[34] A copy of Blake's letter is to be found in Queen's University, *Douglas Library Notes,* vol. IV, no. 3 (August 1955), n.p.
[35] See Margaret A. Banks, "The Change in Liberal Party Leadership, 1887," *CHR,* XXXVIII (June 1957), 115.

only one possible choice — Laurier."[36] During their years together in the House, Blake had seen in Laurier a potentially great leader, and he argued that the party would be strengthened by choosing as its new leader a French-speaking Roman Catholic from Quebec. "To many members of the party the suggestion came as a surprise," Skelton records,[37] but it was equally true that "the knowledge of Mr. Blake's preference probably determined the action of the caucus."[38] When caucus met on June 7, Cartwright moved and Mills seconded Laurier's nomination, an action which effectively committed Laurier's major opposition to his support at the same time as it left him free to accept the leadership if he so wished with no substantial opposition. Laurier, however, took some time to deliberate the matter; it required much persuasion by Blake and others to bring him to the point of agreeing to accept the leadership. This was finally done on June 23, 1887, when Laurier announced his acceptance of the request contained in the Cartwright–Mills motion. Even then, Laurier was convinced that Blake would return to the leadership shortly, once his health had improved, in which case he would all too willingly step down. Others claimed that the selection of Laurier was understood to have been on a temporary basis only, making it possible for the selection of someone like Cartwright once Blake retired from politics.[39] If that were the case, then there is an element of irony in Laurier's service as Liberal leader, for he remained in that position until his death in 1919 — a term unequalled by that of any other party leader in Canadian history.

Prior to the introduction of leadership conventions, the only Conservative leader to have been chosen while the party was on the opposition side of the House was Robert Borden. Borden's selection as Conservative leader followed the party's poor showing in the November general election of 1900. In that election Sir Charles Tupper suffered personal defeat, a circumstance he seized upon

[36] Skelton, I, 341.
[37] *Ibid.*
[38] Sir John S. Willison, *Sir Wilfrid Laurier and the Liberal Party: A Political History*, 2 vols. (Toronto: George N. Morang, 1903), I, 34.
[39] See Banks, 122-25.

to tender his resignation to the party as its leader.[40] The most likely successor to Tupper would have been George Foster ("beyond question . . . the most outstanding figure in the party," according to Borden),[41] but Foster too had been defeated in the 1900 election. The absence of a parliamentary seat was not an impossible handicap, but it "had no doubt an influence in determining the choice of the Conservative caucus," observes Foster's biographer.[42] Sir Charles Hibbert Tupper was ruled out as a possible successor to his father because of strong "opposition to a dynastic succession" within the party.[43] With the opening of parliament in early February 1901, caucus met twice to choose a new leader. To Borden's surprise his name was proposed by Sir Charles Hibbert Tupper. Although he initially declined, Borden agreed under great pressure at the second meeting to accept, in his own words,

> the task for one year and coupled my acceptance with the stipulation that in the meantime a committee should be appointed to select a permanent leader of greater ability, experience and aptitude, one who would, perhaps, desire the position from which I shrank. This stipulation was accepted but "the Sons of Zeruiah were too hard for me." After the meeting some of the older members urged me to refrain from making public the temporary character of my leadership as any such announcement would tend to diminish my authority. I yielded to their persuasions. . . .[44]

Borden, in fact, remained at the head of his party for the next twenty years, and was the last leader to be chosen by a party in opposition prior to the introduction of national leadership conventions.

[40] A copy of Tupper's letter of resignation addressed to the "members of the Conservative party in the Senate and House of Commons" and dated January 17, 1901, is to be found in *The Times* (London), February 11, 1901, p. 6. The resignation was accepted by caucus at its first meeting of the new parliament, February 5, 1901.
[41] Borden, I, 73.
[42] Wallace, p. 114.
[43] Muller, "The Canadian Prime Ministers," p. 411.
[44] Borden, I, 73.

General Principles of Leadership Selection

Prior to any comparative analysis of the differences between leadership selection by parties in office and those out of office, what of the fact that without exception the leaders chosen in office were leaders of the Conservative party and, with one exception only, those chosen in opposition were leaders of the Liberal party? Can the differences, in other words, be explained as differences between the Liberals and the Conservatives rather than as differences in leadership selection techniques between parties in power and parties in opposition? It is, after all, one of the facts of Canadian political history that Liberal leaders right up to St. Laurent's selection in 1948 were chosen whilst the party was in opposition and that, with Borden's exception in 1901, it was sixty years after Confederation before the Conservatives had to choose a leader when they were out of office. Yet it seems highly improbable that the differences could be accounted for as a function of the specific parties rather than as a function of the party's position in parliament. The obvious point about Borden's selection in 1901 was that it was made in basically the same tradition is the preceding three opposition party selections: following considerable intra-party discussion a caucus motion on the party leadership was adopted by the members of that body (both Conservative MPs and senators) and accepted by the nominee (see Table 3-2). In office the Conservatives relied, when possible, on intra-party negotiations and agreements (1892 and 1896); but in the absence of such agreements or lacking an obvious successor the party relied, to an extent that varied with the particular situation, upon vice-regal consultations with party notables (1891, 1894 and 1920). There is no reason to believe that from the 1870s through to the early twentieth century the Liberal party would have acted differently had a leadership vacancy occurred when it was in power. Had the Liberals in 1873 been without a leader when the Macdonald government resigned (they in fact had chosen Mackenzie nine months earlier), the parliamentary party notables might well have participated in a consultative operation of some

Table 3—2: Leaders Selected Prior to the Introduction of Leadership Conventions in Their Party

	Year of selection	Name	Methods by which selections were made
In government	1867	John A. Macdonald	The exercise of the prerogative power of the Crown by the Governor General in naming the Prime Minister.[a]
	1891	J. J. C. Abbott	The exercise of the . . . Prime Minister.
	1892	John S. D. Thompson	The exercise of the . . . Prime Minister.
	1894	Mackenzie Bowell	The exercise of the . . . Prime Minister.
	1896	Charles Tupper	Agreement reached by various party notables in the cabinet.
	1920	Arthur Meighen	Retiring leader was instructed by caucus to play an influential role in discussions, negotiations and, finally, advice to the Governor General. Caucus members advised the leader individually by ballot of their first, second and third choices for their leader and their reasons therefor.
In opposition	1873	Alexander Mackenzie	Formal selection by unanimous vote of caucus acting on a recommendation of a ten-man caucus committee.
	1880	Edward Blake	Caucus vote on a motion from the floor.
	1887	Wilfrid Laurier	Caucus vote following the strong recommendation of the retiring leader.
	1901	Robert L. Borden	Caucus vote on a motion from the floor.

a The first four party leaders on the Government side were selected as a result of the use of the royal prerogative of the Crown by the Governor General. Depending upon the time and the circumstances of the appointment to be made, the Governor General usually sought the advice of and held consultations with various party notables.

kind with the Governor General to select from their midst an acceptable leader to head a new government. Laurier once remarked that it had been a mystery to him that on Macdonald's death Tupper had not been sent for immediately by the Governor General,[45] an interesting comment in that it questions only the decision arrived at in 1891, not the process used to make the decision. In short, the attitudes of personnel of both parties were not noticeably different on the matter of techniques used to select new leaders. The fact that neither the Liberals in opposition nor the Conservatives in office were critical of the techniques utilized by their opposites to choose their leaders would seem to indicate substantial acceptance of the processes used, even if the party itself had no occasion to use them.

For the party in power the Governor General did play an important role in many of the leadership discussions. The discretionary powers of the Crown were clearly exercised in the selection of Macdonald, Abbott and Bowell. A more formal consultative process, with the Governor General acting exclusively on the advice of the retiring leader, was followed when Thompson and Meighen were chosen. The contest between the governing party and the Governor General early in 1896 over the normally fused but potentially separate positions of party leader and prime minister made a rather special case of Tupper's selection, but it by no means challenged the continued existence of the Crown's discretionary power. It so happened that on this one occasion the selection of the party's leader did not coincide with the timing of the selection of the new prime minister. When Aberdeen did, in fact, accept Bowell's resignation and consider whom to ask to form a new government, he acknowledged an interest, if nothing more, in another prominent Conservative, Sir Donald Smith, and perhaps would have asked him in preference to Tupper to form a government had he not been previously informed that Smith would refuse such a request.[46] The prerogative power of the Crown had by no means died as a result of the intra-party activities of 1896;

[45] Canada, *Debates of the House of Commons* (February 7, 1916), p. 586.
[46] Saywell, "The Crown and the Politicians," p. 332.

it has remained to this day as one of the elements of Canadian constitutionalism. What had been established by 1920, and what did represent a break with earlier post-Confederation Canadian politics, was the decreasing involvement of the Governor General as one of the major participants in the search for new political leaders.

The caucus assumed greater importance when the party was out of power than when it was in power. In fact, in the Conservative party the parliamentary caucus' only opportunity to participate formally in the selection of its leader came when the party was in opposition. Yet what did such participation really mean? In all four instances of leadership selection in the opposition party the matter was handled by way of presentation of a motion to the caucus either on behalf of a caucus committee or by one or two party notables. Unanimity was a dominant feature of such meetings. As no motions proposing other members of the party for leader were presented, this would seem to suggest that much in the way of private discussions, of "soundings" within the party, had preceded the caucus meetings. In two cases (Borden, and more particularly, Laurier), a considerable amount of extra-caucus persuasion was needed to bring about acceptance by the nominee following the introduction of the motion in caucus. With such evidence it would be unfair to judge the caucuses' role as being anything more than a purely formal one, their powers more apparent than real.

The key to the leadership of a party obviously lay with the opinions and decisions of its most prominent and influential figures, regardless of whether or not the party was in power. The retiring leader might have been sufficiently able to judge the mood of his party to avoid protracted struggles and infighting and to ensure a relatively smooth leadership transition by timing his exit carefully. Such was the case with Abbott when he stepped down in Thompson's favour. A successful or a popular leader wishing to retire could virtually guarantee the succession to the man of his choice. Blake's support for Laurier (over Cartwright, Mills and Mowat) was sufficient to tip the scales in Laurier's favour, and

Macdonald was not exaggerating his own power within the Conservative party when he told Tupper in 1888 that he could designate Tupper as his successor if Tupper were agreeable.[47] In other cases of clear-cut succession, the leader, having lost his credibility in the party, was virtually powerless, and as a consequence was forced out when an attractive alternative supported by several prominent members of the party became available. Most certainly Bowell, and quite possibly Mackenzie, was removed in this way. On those occasions when no clearly acceptable individual stood out as the obvious successor, yet when a new leader had to be chosen (1887, 1891, 1894, 1901 and 1920), the party elite had no choice but to determine the amount of weight to be attached to the opinions expressed by various individuals within the party. The Borden–Meighen changeover best illustrates that point, for in 1920, if Borden and virtually the whole of the cabinet had had their way, the much more numerous backbenchers would have had to accept as leader a person other than the one a clear majority of them favoured.

The future of the party under various potential leaders was also a major consideration when leadership changeovers took place. *Party* was foremost in the minds of the participants as they attempted to judge its likely electoral success with different individuals at its head. The party whose future they were concerned with, of course, was the parliamentary party, for national organizations, party headquarters, staffs, elected executive officers, annual meetings and the other accoutrements of modern political parties were yet to come. Theirs, the parliamentary party, was in every sense of the word *the* party.

They were concerned, like any politicians, about timing. Entrances and exits to and from the leadership had to be so timed as best to preserve party unity. Had Thompson succeeded Macdonald directly, had the way not been prepared by Abbott, there would have been, in Lady Macdonald's words, "a stampede of Ontario

---

[47] Macdonald's offer to Tupper was recalled some years later by Tupper. See W. A. Harkin (ed.), *Political Reminiscences of the Rt. Hon. Sir Charles Tupper* (London: Constable and Co., 1914), p. 147.

supporters."[48] Had Mackenzie not resigned in 1880 when there was much displeasure with his leadership, he himself recognized that "any other course would have broken up the party more or less."[49] Had an arrangement not been made in January 1896, whereby Tupper could assume effective leadership of the party, the Conservatives knew all too well that they would be in a hopeless condition to fight the election of that year.

Political notables were interested as well in broadening the party's appeal when they searched for a leader whose qualities would quite possibly make the party more attractive in areas of electoral weakness. Blake was convinced in 1887 that by choosing Laurier as its leader the Liberal party would reap substantial benefits in future elections in Quebec and would not, at the same time, run the risk of losing its traditional support in Ontario. Blake's argument in favour of Laurier, therefore, was based on the likelihood of a net political gain for the party in forthcoming elections with such a man as leader. Macdonald's offer to Tupper in 1888 to name him as his successor was refused by Tupper in part because he knew Macdonald had previously promised it to Sir Hector Langevin and would not hear of Macdonald going back on his word, and in part because he felt the party would benefit more politically by having a French Canadian succeed Macdonald. Blake and Tupper acted in those circumstances with a primary interest in vote maximization for the party. They wanted not to reinforce areas of party strength so much as to effect an arrangement that would assist in improving the party's fortunes in areas of relative weakness. Mackenzie, on the other hand, argued in 1873 when he was chosen Liberal leader that the "preponderating power Ontario held" in the party left little choice but to select the leader from that province. As the Liberal party was in a somewhat earlier stage of development at the time than the Conservatives, and dominated as it was by its Ontario wing, Mackenzie's views were understandable. Eventually, however, at the end of Blake's leadership, the party was ready to be convinced that something other

[48] Clark, "The Conservative Party," p. 62.
[49] *Mackenzie Papers,* Mackenzie to Black, May 20, 1882.

than an Ontario Protestant leader was needed if the party were to stand a reasonable chance of regaining power.

Finally, there was no doubt but that experience in national politics and service in parliament as a private member, then as a cabinet minister, counted for a great deal when new leaders were to be chosen. Each of the leaders included in Table 3-2 had participated to some extent (most, quite fully), in parliamentary politics, and as a result it was not difficult to predict his likely success or failure as a leader. There were certainly genuine misgivings about Bowell when he was chosen as leader, and for good reason. Borden feared that his own period in parliament (less than five years) had not been sufficient time to prepare him for the leadership when he accepted it in 1901, and his first few years as Conservative leader seemed to confirm those fears. But it is also worth noting that George Foster, one of Borden's potential rivals for the leadership and a man with some eighteen years in the House, was effectively removed from the competition by virtue of his defeat in the 1900 election and his subsequent absence from parliament at the time Tupper's successor was chosen. How this feature of leadership selection would be altered in years to come with party conventions!

4

The Genesis of the National Leadership Convention

The Liberal Convention of 1919

A fundamental alteration in the system of selecting party leaders took place in 1919. In that year, the first national convention charged with the responsibility of selecting a party leader was convened, breaking the tradition of selection by a small circle of individuals: members of the parliamentary caucus, the retiring leader and, on occasion, the Governor General. For the first time, the extra-parliamentary wing of a national party participated in the selection of the party's leader, an activity not relinquished in subsequent selections and, eventually, copied by other national parties in selecting their leaders. Beginning in 1919, the parliamentary party was displaced as the body pre-eminent in the choice of party leader in Canada through the introduction of the leadership convention.

A peculiar combination of intra-party developments led the Liberal party into a convention in 1919. At the end of the First World War, Sir Wilfrid Laurier wanted to re-unite the Liberal party, so badly divided by the conscription issue and the election of 1917. He recognized that the party could never hope to regain

59

power without first healing the deep wounds resulting from the recent political battles. The future of the Unionist government was in doubt, now that the war was over, and it seemed an advantageous time to attempt to lure those who had abandoned him in 1917 back to the party fold. With this in mind Sir Wilfrid announced on November 19, 1918, that a national convention would be held sometime following the conclusion of peace to "examine the problems which have been laid before us when we know the full extent of the results of the war" and "to endeavor to settle them on the lines of Liberal principles."[1] In short, a party policy and organization convention was to be called.

Sir Wilfrid's only other experience with a national convention had convinced him of its worth as a vehicle for uniting and strengthening the party. A convention held in 1893, formally called by Laurier with the approval of the Liberal members of the House of Commons, had done much to bolster the morale of the party at large, and the parliamentary leadership in particular.[2] Suffering from four successive electoral defeats, and wishing to effect a "tactical withdrawal"[3] from the unrestricted reciprocity policy of 1891, the Liberals had been anxious to discover and to display publicly their strength. The disintegration of the Conservative government was increasingly evident and the Liberal opposition could sense victory with the right policies and the right people in the next election. What better way to define policy than through a policy convention? What better way to promote internal harmony

---

[1] *Globe,* November 20, 1918, p. 1.

[2] John W. Lederle, "The Liberal Convention of 1893," *Canadian Journal of Economics and Political Science* (hereinafter cited as *CJEPS*), XVI (February 1950), 42-52. Although referred to at the time, and since, as a "national" convention, in truth the overwhelming number of delegates to the 1893 meeting were from Ontario and Quebec. There were no delegates from British Columbia, and only one and five from the Northwest Territories and Manitoba respectively. See *Official Report of the Liberal Convention Held in Response to the Call of Hon. Wilfrid Laurier, Leader of the Liberal Party of the Dominion of Canada* (Toronto: Budget Printing and Publishing Co., 1893), p. 141. Hereinafter cited as *Official Report, 1893).*

[3] H. Blair Neatby, "Laurier and a Liberal Quebec: A Study in Political Management" (unpublished Ph. D. dissertation, Department of History, University of Toronto, 1956), p. 84.

than through a national assemblage of fifteen to eighteen hundred of the party faithful?

The idea for the 1893 convention had originated with J. S. Willison, editor of the *Globe*, and frequent correspondent with Laurier. At the time of the Democratic Party's convention of 1892 (which he covered for his newspaper), Willison wrote a series of editorials praising the convention system. "The system of government by party is not perfect," the *Globe* stated editorially. "It might be better if the electors of all shades of political opinions would meet together and discuss the questions of the day frequently and freely, but so long as parties exist and rule, the best we can hope for is the frequent holding of party conventions freely chosen and representing every diversity of opinion within the party."[4] In turn, the *Globe* carried several letters and comments favourably disposed to Willison's opinions on the subject.[5] On July 22, 1892, two days after the selection of Grover Cleveland as the Democratic candidate for president of the United States, Willison wrote to Laurier:

> I think you must have a convention in the late fall or early winter. . . . I look to a convention not so much for a policy as for a financial basis for a scheme of organization. Get your men from every constituency, point out that the party is supported by its leaders, members, and by Montreal and Toronto, and arrange for a plan of local collections or 3-year assessments in every part of the country. It would be easy to raise thousands of dollars. . . . There are other things, too, to be considered. . . . You of all men have no need to fear to meet the party in convention, any convention of Canadian Liberals will accept your policy, and a general meeting of the party will give the party an enthusiasm and a sense of responsibility that are needed.[6]

---

[4] *Globe*, July 15, 1892, p. 4.
[5] See *Globe* of July 19, p. 4, July 22, p. 3, July 23, p. 17, July 25, p. 4, and July 27, p. 3, 1892.
[6] PAC, *Laurier Papers* C-738, vol. 4-7 microfilm, pp. 2185-87. Several years later Laurier acknowledged the fact that it was Willison who gave him the idea for the convention of 1893. See PAC, *Willison Papers*, "Correspondence," vol. 48, file 179, pp. 17880-82, letter from Laurier to Willison of January 18, 1899.

The 1893 convention, according to Skelton, "proved an extraordinary success." It "revealed the personal assets the party possessed in Laurier, Mowat, Fielding. It linked up the local organizations. It gave an opportunity of framing a fighting platform." In addition, the convention "impressed the country and heartened the rank and file of the party."[7] In his biography of Laurier, Joseph Schull concludes that as a result of the 1893 convention "the party was both broadened and pulled together, and at last found the nerve it could not find for Blake."[8] Laurier had no reason to regret having called the 1893 convention for, at the time of the next election, his party defeated the Conservatives and he was asked to form the new government.

The 1893 convention had enabled the Liberals to enter the next election confidently, with a united and strengthened organization, and with attractive policy resolutions. The situation of 1918 was similar to that of the early 1890s, and the potential benefits to the party from a large, national gathering were too many for Laurier to resist. It was most essential that the doors of the party be opened to those who had left over the conscription issue. "When the convention takes place," Laurier wrote early in 1919, "all Liberals who are ready to subscribe to our programme will be admitted and no questions asked."[9] Thus the announcement was made that a convention would be called and held during 1919, but no date was fixed. Planning proceeded and preliminary arrangements were made for a policy and organization meeting to be attended by several hundred delegates from across the Dominion. However, Laurier's death on February 17, 1919, fundamentally altered the purposes of the convention.

Given the leadership selection processes that had obtained up to that time, the parliamentary wing of the Liberal party would normally have selected Sir Wilfrid's successor. Yet both the times and the parliamentary parties were anything but normal. The

---

[7] Skelton, *Laurier,* I, 458.
[8] Joseph Schull, *Laurier: The First Canadian* (Toronto: Macmillan Company of Canada, 1965), p. 269.
[9] PAC, *Laurier Papers,* vol. 728, Laurier to J. E. Adamson, January 11, 1919.

Conservatives and Unionist Liberals remained coalesced as the government but for how long, no one was certain. The Laurier Liberals, occupying the opposition benches, were overwhelmingly French-speaking members from Quebec: following the December 1917 election, 62 of the 82 MPs of the opposition caucus came from Quebec. Laurier's reflection in 1916 that it had been "a mistake for a French Roman Catholic to take the leadership" of the Liberal party because of the strength of "the forces of prejudice in Ontario"[10] was well known to members of caucus. These MPs saw the party's only hope for electoral success with a party united around an English-speaking leader.[11] No obvious successor on those terms was then a member of the opposition parliamentary group. Although not a member of the Liberal caucus at the time, Laurier's colleague for so many years, W. S. Fielding, would doubtless have been acceptable to many Liberal supporters. Yet Fielding was unacceptable to the Quebec MPs for his abandonment of Laurier in 1917, and numerically they controlled the caucus. Within a few days of Laurier's death, the *Globe* reported from Ottawa that "the objection still continues strong to having Mr. Fielding by many Quebec members, who are afraid it would be equivalent to making him a permanent choice. 'We don't want to be rushed,' they urge their leaders. 'Make some temporary arrangement for the session. Give us time.' "[12] Accordingly, strong pressures were exerted not to select a permanent leader at that time.

The elements of the selection were obvious. Laurier's successor

---

[10] Skelton, II, 484.

[11] "The break of 1917 cost me too much," said Laurier, "to build afresh with Fielding, or Rowell, or Sifton. . . . The new leader must be a Protestant. I'd ask no Catholic to go through what I have suffered!" W. T. R. Preston, *My Generation of Politics and Politicians* (Toronto: Rose Publishing Co., 1927), p. 382. *The Round Table* correspondent reported: "It is understood that the common feeling among Liberals is that Laurier's successor should be an English-speaking Protestant, not because a Frenchman or a Roman Catholic is objectionable, but in recognition of the Protestant element which for more than thirty years gave loyal support to a French and Catholic leader." "The Liberal Leadership," *The Round Table*, IX (June 1919), 593-94. See also the *Globe*, February 22, 1919, p. 1.

[12] *Globe*, February 22, 1919, p. 4.

would almost certainly have to be English-speaking, not from the province of Quebec, and Protestant. There was a distinct possibility that the new leader would not at the time of selection be a member of parliament, for of the four most frequently mentioned individuals as a successor to Laurier (G. P. Graham, Mackenzie King, W. M. Martin, and W. S. Fielding), only Fielding had a seat in parliament. What better way was there to select the new leader under such circumstances than by utilizing the "representative and democratic" national policy and organization convention soon to be held in Ottawa? The Liberal caucus considered the situation closely. Acting on the recommendation of a five-member subcommittee it approved, on April 1, 1919, the revised purposes of the convention including that of choosing the new party leader. The official call for the convention, issued by the parliamentary caucus of the Liberal party on May 6, 1919, recognized the additional task to be entrusted to the convention by stating:

> Pursuant to the announcement made by Sir Wilfrid Laurier in November, 1918, and in conformity with a resolution adopted by the Liberal members of the Senate and the House of Commons of Canada, a Convention of the Liberal party is hereby called to take place in the City of Ottawa, on August 5th, 6th and 7th next.
>
> The purpose of the Convention will be: *First* — to draft, discuss and adopt the platform of the Liberal party of Canada; *Second* — to deal with the question of party organization; *Third* — to select a leader in succession to Sir Wilfrid Laurier.[13]

The extra-parliamentary wing of a political party was being invited, for the first time, to participate in the selection of that party's national leader.

The caucus was prepared, in other words, to abdicate its responsibility for selecting Laurier's successor, a fact made immediately apparent by its decision not to name a permanent leader but to have such a leader "chosen by a general convention of the party."[14]

---

[13] *The National Liberal Convention, Ottawa, August 5, 6, 7, 1919: The Story of the Convention and the Report of its Proceedings* (Ottawa: n.p., n.d.), p. 6. (Hereinafter cited as *1919 Report*.)

[14] "The Liberal Leadership," *The Round Table*, 594.

For the first time in Canada a caucus selected a "temporary leader" to head the party. A member of parliament from Nova Scotia since 1904, D. D. McKenzie, was picked by his parliamentary colleagues to lead the opposition party until the convention made its choice. McKenzie, according to R. MacGregor Dawson, "was an anti-conscriptionist from outside Quebec, and his choice was thus designed to placate both Quebec and the other provinces. Beyond this, he had few assets."[15] To assist the temporary leader in the performance of his duties the caucus named an "Advisory Committee" of thirteen MPs and set about making plans for the forthcoming convention.

A surprising fact about the Liberal leadership convention of 1919 is that it was not regarded as being in any way unusual to select a leader in such a fashion. A thorough examination of the newspapers, journals and magazines of the time reveals that apparently no one in the Liberal party chose to make a public issue of or take exception to the decision to select the next leader by the new technique. If anything, there seemed to be an unquestioning acceptance of the inevitability of the convention. "Naturally, the choice of Sir Wilfrid's successor *must* lie with a convention representative of the Liberals of the country as a whole," wrote Mackenzie King in a letter from Ottawa a week following Laurier's death.[16] For his part, because of his unacceptability to

[15] R. MacGregor Dawson, *William Lyon Mackenzie King: A Political Biography, 1874-1923* (Toronto: University of Toronto Press, 1958), p. 283. One of the most perceptive of the twentieth-century commentators on Canadian politics, Arthur R. Ford, described McKenzie as "a dour Nova Scotian, who adored Laurier with all the earnestness of a Scottish clansman, hated Union Government and all its works, was uncompromising in his views, and had been raised on the Shorter Catechism and the Bible." *As the World Wags On* (Toronto: Ryerson Press, 1950), p. 107.

[16] PAC, *King Papers*, vol. 46, King to C. H. Higgins, February 24, 1919. (Italics added.) It is difficult to know with any certainty how "natural" a leadership convention really was to Mackenzie King, for less than a month before the convention he indicated a willingness to be picked by the caucus some time in the future if Fielding were selected as leader of the party at the convention. Writing to John D. Rockefeller, Jr., King stated: "From appearances at the moment, I should not be surprised if Hon. W. S. Fielding, who was Minister of Finance in Sir Wilfrid Laurier's Cabinet, were chosen as Leader of the Liberal Party at the forthcoming Convention. Mr. Fielding has the advantage of having a seat in Parliament,

the caucus, Fielding must have recognized that his only chance of capturing the party leadership lay in an opportunity to rally his extra-parliamentary support to his candidature for the leadership. Any opposition from Fielding to a leadership convention would, given these conditions, have been very unlikely. None of the major Canadian newspapers was prompted to comment editorially upon the change in selection procedures. They, too, apparently accepted the convention as a normal event. A Canadian Press despatch from Ottawa, written the day of Laurier's death, stated:

> The Leader of the Opposition *for the session* will be determined at a Liberal caucus which will be called at the earliest possible date, possibly on Thursday. It will be summoned by J. A. Robb, M.P., Chief Opposition Whip.
>
> In the *natural course of procedure* the caucus will be followed by a national convention at which a permanent Leader will be chosen.[17]

How was it that an event as fundamental as an alteration in the technique by which the leader was selected could be instituted without notice? Why was a leadership convention, the most unnatural of British and Canadian political procedures for that time, regarded as "natural" by politicians and newspaper correspon-

---

and the decision of the Government to hold a fall session almost immediately makes it more or less imperative that someone already in Parliament should be chosen. The objection to Mr. Fielding is, of course his years. He is now in his seventy-first year, and is not too robust in health. It is being said by some who favor my candidature that accepting Mr. Fielding for the present would afford opportunity for my getting into Parliament, and *succeeding in a natural way as the choice of the Party in the House,* once that necessary first step is accomplished. My own belief is that this is the trend events will take, and candidly, were I sure of obtaining a seat in the near future, I should be inclined to feel that succeeding to the Leadership in this way would be preferable in every way to acquiring immediately the responsibilities of leadership with my present lack of familiarity with the personnel of the Party in and out of Parliament." *Ibid.,* vol. 50, King to Rockefeller, July 25, 1919. (Italics added)
[17]*Globe,* February 19, 1919, p. 4. (Italics added.) In an editorial the following day the *Globe* stated: "It is to be assumed that the Opposition will use the best material available for the carrying on of its legitimate functions of criticism and amendment of Government measures during the period *that must precede the summoning of a Liberal convention and the choosing by that convention of a national leader." Globe,* February 19, 1919, p. 4. (Italics added)

dents alike? The very fact that the caucus was prepared to look outside the parliamentary party for a successor to Laurier obviously prepared the way for the acceptance of the *idea* that the *party outside parliament* should be involved in the task of leadership selection. The constituency delegates and provincial Liberal parties would scarcely have rejected the opportunity to exercise some influence over the choice of a national party leader. That a few provincial party leaders had been selected at so-called "conventions" no doubt helped to pave the way for a national leadership convention. From the turn of the century to 1919 conventions of some form or another had been held in every province, except Quebec, by various provincial parties to select their leaders. Certainly no firm pattern had been established in the provinces, for the caucuses, retiring leaders, party executives, and lieutenant-governors were still relied upon in the overwhelming number of cases to select the party leaders. Provincial leadership conventions were clearly the exception, and not the rule. That they were more popular in the four western provinces than elsewhere may have reflected the stronger populist-democratic and American influences in that part of the country. However, there could be no question but that conventions were being employed in other parts of the country with increasing frequency. Just prior to the August 1919 convention, for example, the Ontario Liberals chose their new leader (H. H. Dewart) in a convention with over three hundred delegates present.[18] Thus, although the provincial experience

---

[18] See the *Canadian Annual Review* (1919), pp. 651-52. An earlier convention worth noting is that of the Ontario Liberal party in 1911. On that occasion the choice of the party's leader was left to the parliamentary committee of legislative members working in concert with a four-member committee of the Liberal Association. This committee informed the delegates at the convention of its unanimous choice, N. W. Rowell, who had agreed to accept the leadership of the party when it was offered to him by that committee. The delegates, not having been party to the decision, accepted Rowell by "thoroughly approving of the tendering of the leadership to [him]." The legislative caucus was very much in control of the matter of leadership. In communicating to the delegates the news of the retiring leader's resignation and the acceptance of that resignation by the parliamentary group, the Liberal chief whip "made it clear that the message he bore to the meeting on behalf of the Legislative contingent was given as a matter of courtesy *and not by right*." *Globe*, November 1, 1911, pp. 1 and 8. (Italics added)

with conventions was limited, at Sir Wilfrid's death it could not easily have been ignored by the parliamentary Liberal caucus in a country as conscious of its federalism as Canada.

One additional explanation for the apparent "naturalness" of the convention of 1919 is to be found in the final act of the 1893 convention. Immediately prior to its adjournment, the delegates indicated their support for Laurier by adopting unanimously the following resolution: "This Convention desires to express its entire confidence in the leadership of the Hon. Wilfrid Laurier and its admiration of his brilliant eloquence, his endearing personal qualities and statesmanlike utterances upon the public questions of the day."[19] The leadership of the party had not been challenged at that time; if anything, quite the reverse was the situation, for not only had Laurier accepted the leadership reluctantly in 1887, he had tried without success to resign from his position on at least three occasions between 1888 and 1892.[20] The 1893 vote was taken as a courtesy and was intended to extend to Laurier the convention's appreciation and its pledge of support. Nonetheless, some members of the Liberal party have, over the years, seen the 1893 assembly as a "leadership" convention.[21] It is possible that a similarly mistaken understanding of the 1893 assembly may have been made in 1919 by some observers, leading them to believe a leadership convention was the natural way to select Sir Wilfrid's successor, even though the party's official *Report* of the 1919 meeting clearly recognized that the 1893 convention was not a

[19] *Official Report, 1893,* p. 141.
[20] See PAC, *Laurier Papers,* vol. 2, Laurier to Julius Scriver, May 1888; vol. 4, Willison to Laurier, June 30, 1890; and vol. 6, Laurier to Scriver, January 5, 1892.
[21] This view was expressed to the writer by Mr. Paul Lafond (now Senator Lafond) of the Liberal Federation of Canada in an interview on May 29, 1969, Ottawa. Mr. Lafond himself regards the 1893 convention as a leadership convention for it "confirmed" Laurier's leadership of the party. The call for the 1968 Liberal Convention erred when it referred to ". . . the four prior National Liberal Leadership Conventions . . . 1893–1919–1948–1958– . . . ." *Program of the National Liberal Convention, April, 1968,* p. 14. Similarly, the author of the publication recording the 1927 Conservative convention mistakenly identified the 1893 Liberal convention as one at which the "delegates elected [a] permanent National Leader." John R. MacNicol, *National Liberal-Conservative Convention Held at Winnipeg, Manitoba, October 10 to 12, 1927* (Toronto: Southam Press, 1930), p. 11. (Hereinafter cited as *1927 Report.*)

leadership convention. That *Report* referred to the 1919 assembly as "... the first political experiment of its kind in Canada."[22]

By late 1918 and early 1919, Laurier had given no indication publicly as to his own intentions, either with respect to his possible retirement, or with respect to the convention as a meeting suitable for selecting his successor. Yet Mackenzie King, in a letter written only weeks before Laurier's death, described one of the alternatives open to himself in the near future. It "is the possible leadership of the Liberal party in Canada." He continued:

> Sir Wilfrid himself and many of the Liberals in the House have spoken to me quite openly about the leadership once Sir Wilfrid retires. He, in fact, has gone so far as to say that if I were in the House to-day he would resign the leadership at once in my favor. I am not in the House and to get there means a bye-election, which it is by no means certain the Union Government will be willing to permit. They have it in their power to prevent anything of the kind. After the present session of Parliament, there will probably be a Liberal Convention, at which a leader will be chosen. If I am to go in for a political career, I ought to begin at once to deliver addresses in different parts of the country, and to come again before the public.[23]

Many years later King had more to say on this point:

> After the first Great War, Sir Robert Borden ... and Sir Wilfrid Laurier ... both felt that they should ask their followers to relieve them of continuing to carry the responsibilities and duties of leadership of their respective Parties. Though not stated at the time, this was one of the objects which Sir Wilfrid had in view when, in 1918, he issued the call for a convention in the following year. On more than one occasion, he so stated this intention to myself and others.[24]

King's statements raise several important questions relating to the 1919 convention. Was Laurier intending to resign sometime during 1919? If so, was he prepared to name Mackenzie King his successor? Did he, in fact, feel unable to name King because of

[22] *1919 Report,* p. 18.
[23] PAC, *King Papers,* vol. 48, King to Mrs. James Carruthers, January 28, 1919.
[24] *Report of the Proceedings of the National Liberal Convention, 1948* (Ottawa: National Liberal Federation of Canada, n.d.), p. 8.

King's absence from the House? Had Laurier intended to use the forthcoming convention as a vehicle for selecting the next Liberal leader? Was Sir Wilfrid of the opinion that a convention would be the best way of selecting, and winning approval for the selection of, a man not then in the parliamentary caucus?

King may have felt he had good reason to believe he was Laurier's choice for the leadership of the Liberal party as a result of various private conversations he had had with Laurier in Ottawa during the last year of Laurier's life. However, none of the correspondence between the two should have led King to conclude that he had been singled out as Laurier's choice or that Laurier necessarily intended to ask the convention to select his successor. For his part, Laurier stuck to his view (stated publicly in November 1918), that the convention was to be called for policy and organization purposes and to allow such recalcitrant Liberals to return to the fold as wished to, with "no questions asked." In one of his last letters, Laurier forcefully dismissed a newspaper report speculating that it was his view that a new Liberal leader should soon be selected. "The extract [from the newspaper] . . . is all news to me, and in so far as I am concerned there is not a word of truth in it. The question of leadership certainly is a subject of anxiety to me, but whenever I lay down the reins, the choice of the party will be absolutely unhampered."[25] In his only reference to the forthcoming convention in that same letter, Laurier gave no hint of having the convention select the new party leader.

> The National Liberal Convention cannot take place until late next fall. It should not be summoned until peace has been signed and the slate is clear for action. The first step should not be a National Convention, but provincial conventions all over, and after this has been done the field will be ready for the National Convention. This is my suggestion.[26]

[25] PAC, *Laurier Papers,* vol. 729, Laurier to W. R. Motherwell, February 11, 1919.
[26] *Ibid.* Laurier felt keenly about the necessity of holding provincial conventions before the national convention took place. Several provincial and regional conventions had been held in late 1918 and early 1919, two of

King's statements that Laurier "would resign the leadership at once" in his favour if he (King) were in the House, and that there would soon be a Liberal convention "at which a leader would be chosen," remain unsupported by Laurier's correspondence.

A comment by one of King's strongest supporters at the convention, a man who was one of the two nominators of King for the leadership, sheds some additional light on the events of that year, but adds no credence to King's interpretation of those events. Writing to Senator Charles Murphy in 1929, Senator A. B. Aylesworth gave his opinion of King's victory at the convention ten years earlier:

> There was, of course, a combination of causes for the election of MacKenzie [*sic*] King as Leader at the Convention ten years ago — Some men were influenced by one consideration — and others by other considerations — but I thought at the time — and I still think — that King could never have won if it had not been that both Fielding and Graham had deserted Laurier — In that sense I would think it not far wrong to say that it was "conscription that defeated Fielding" — For myself, at any rate, the one thing that *I* was bound to do everything *I* could to accomplish, was to prevent any man who had deserted Laurier in 1917 becoming our Leader in 1919 — because such a result I believed would have utterly disrupted and destroyed the Party — I know that a great many who were at the Convention had exactly the same feeling — and I think it was a very powerful factor in electing King —
>
> I know that in 1911 Laurier — fully intending to retire — thought Fielding was the man who ought to succeed him — and it is very likely that in 1919 Lady Laurier thought Fielding as Leader would be better qualified than any other man available, but she felt very keenly the defections of 1917 — I called to see her during the Convention week in 1919 — and we talked about the leadership — I told her what I was doing — and how I felt about it — and I believe that if she had voted at the Convention she would have marked her ballots exactly as I marked mine — but I agree entirely with what you say about its being pure newspaper "bunk" that

---

which Sir Wilfrid had himself attended: the Western Ontario Liberal Convention and the Eastern Ontario Liberal Convention.

Laurier himself ever designated King as his successor — He certainly never did it in any way to *my* knowledge[27]

Laurier's chief adviser on the convention arrangements, Charles Murphy, then a member of parliament, was better informed on Laurier's thoughts regarding the convention than any other person. Murphy had submitted a convention organization plan to Laurier in February 1919, which the leader approved hours before he suffered his stroke. It is doubtful if the matter of leadership had been included in those approved plans, given Laurier's views on the subject.[28] Less than a month earlier Murphy himself had dismissed the question of leadership as one "agitated principally from the West. . . . If people will only be patient, and will recognize that nature and Providence must soon combine to solve the leadership problem, there will be a natural solution to the problem, and no offence will be given to anybody."[29] That Laurier had been searching for an appropriate successor, there can be no doubt;[30] that he had intended to resign forthwith and have his successor picked by a convention, there can only be speculation.[31]

The Conservative Convention of 1927

In 1927 the Conservatives held the second national political convention charged with the selection of a party leader.

[27] PAC, *Murphy Papers,* vol. I, Aylesworth to Murphy, July 25, 1929. (Punctuation as in original.)

[28] No record could be located of the arrangements as approved by Laurier. Murphy's correspondence with McKenzie regarding the convention arrangements, as well as tentative and revised caucus memoranda in preparation for the call, are to be found in PAC, *Murphy Papers,* vol. 19, pp. 8021-25, and vol. 34, pp. 13967-73, 13987, and 14006-9.

[29] PAC, *Murphy Papers,* vol. 15, Murphy to W. E. Knowles, January 17, 1919.

[30] See Preston, pp. 382-83, and H. S. Ferns and B. Ostry, *The Age of Mackenzie King: The Rise of the Leader* (London: William Heinemann Ltd., 1955), pp. 287-88, for a discussion of two people Laurier appeared to consider acceptable successors in mid 1918.

[31] There is no evidence to support Dawson's claim that "Laurier had announced his coming retirement." Dawson, *Mackenzie King,* p. 287.

The political pressures and events leading to the decision to hold such a convention were strikingly similar to those which prompted the Liberals to hold the Ottawa convention of 1919. With the completion of the 1927 Conservative meeting, a convention judged to be highly successful at the time, it was clear that the leadership convention had replaced the earlier informal processes of choosing the party leader.

Following the 1926 general election (in which Meighen himself had been defeated in his Manitoba constituency), the Conservative party could not avoid a critical self-examination. How similar, in many ways, its position proved to be that of the Liberal party in 1918–1919! By late 1926 the Conservatives had been in opposition for five years, except for their three-month term of office in 1926 under Meighen; in 1918 the Liberals were entering their seventh year on the Speaker's left. The Conservatives had failed to retain or regain power in three successive elections (1921, 1925 and 1926), the Liberals in two (1911 and 1917). The Conservative parliamentary group was more overwhelmingly English-speaking Canadian than the Liberal caucus had been French-speaking, yet both groups were only too aware of the need to correct such imbalances and to appear as truly national political parties.[32] As the opposition Liberals were unmistakably identified with Laurier in 1918–1919, so the parliamentary Conservatives in 1926 were identified with Meighen. Within both parties some had reasoned that their party had suffered, electorally, from such identification. Both parties were divided on matters of policy and leadership, and intra-party harmony seemed possible only under new leaders.[33]

---

[32] The Conservatives had failed to have a single French-speaking Canadian elected from Quebec in the general elections of 1921, 1925 and 1926. Following the 1926 election and with the announcement of Meighen's retirement from politics, some Conservatives felt Meighen's successor should be a Roman Catholic who spoke French. One name mentioned prominently was that of R. J. Manion. See Graham, *Arthur Meighen*, II, 479.

[33] For examples of lack of unity in the Conservative party under Arthur Meighen see Graham, II, 24-32, 149-50, 175-80, 241-48, 263-67, 277-83, 356-61, 366-70 and 379-81. The *Gazette* of Montreal placed the blame unmistakably on the shoulders of Arthur Meighen: "French-Canadian Quebec has voted solidly against the Conservative party led by Mr. Meighen, and has done it thrice in succession, despite the admitted fact

The death of Laurier and the electoral defeat and voluntary retirement of Meighen presented the two parties with the opportunity to hold national conventions for the selection of new leaders and to heal the parties' wounds. Meeting for the first time since the 1926 election, the Conservative MPs, senators and defeated election candidates duplicated the acts of the Liberal caucus after the death of Laurier in 1919; the Conservatives named a "temporary" leader for "the approaching session of Parliament" and appointed a committee to organize a national convention to select the new leader.[34] A resolution presented to that meeting "that a convention of the Liberal-Conservative Party be held at the earliest possible date following the next session of Parliament, for the purpose of naming a *permanent Leader,* and for such other purposes as to the Convention may seem fit" was adopted unanimously.[35] The way had been prepared for a Conservative leadership convention.

Since their electoral defeat of 1921, various Conservative organizations and groups had called for a national convention — whether for leadership matters as well as policy, it was not always clear.[36] While re-electing Arthur Meighen as their leader in March 1922, the Conservative MPs, defeated candidates and senators adopted a motion calling for a national convention of the party. Prominent Conservatives in Winnipeg and Montreal who were dissatisfied with Meighen's leadership of the party spoke publicly of the need for a party convention "at which questions of policy and leadership could be settled and a little bone and muscle

---

that the Conservative policy conforms absolutely to the social and economic requirements of the Province. There was no accident about these votes; they were given deliberately upon each occasion by an overwhelming majority — and upon one issue — Mr. Meighen." Quoted in Graham, II, 478.

[34] Graham, II, 479.

[35] *1927 Report,* p. 15 (italics added). A copy of the resolution is to be found in PAC, *Bennett Papers,* K, Sec. D No. 10, p. 3261. Some useful material on the 1927 convention and its background exists in the *Meighen Papers,* MG 26, 1, vol. 67, and the *Bennett Papers,* MG 26, K, Sec. D.

[36] A movement had been afoot as early as 1920, a few months before Sir Robert Borden resigned as prime minister and party leader, to hold a national convention. See *1927 Report,* p. 13. Nothing, however, came of it at that time.

built onto the wasted frame of the party."[37] National Convention committees were established in two provinces, Manitoba and Quebec, and they passed resolutions calling for a National Liberal-Conservative convention. A similar proposal was endorsed by the annual meeting of the Liberal–Conservative Association of Ontario in 1923, as well as at a conference of provincial party associations attended by Arthur Meighen and other federal parliamentarians the following year.[38]

Yet why was no convention called until after Meighen's retirement in 1926? There was, quite clearly, no well-defined purpose for having a convention, and the differences of opinion on what a convention would accomplish produced something of a stalemate. Some who favoured holding a convention no doubt looked upon it as an honourable way of deposing Meighen as party leader, or at least of testing his popularity; others wanted to use a convention to defeat the anti-Meighen forces publicly and to strengthen Meighen's position as leader of the party. Meighen himself seemed to favour the view that a convention would weaken his control of the party and that before a convention could be called he would have to resign.[39] It must also be recognized that in the history of the party there was no precedent for summoning a national convention and, as a result, there was uncertainty about who had the authority to call such a meeting. If the leader did not favour the holding of a convention, if the vast majority of the parliamentary caucus supported the leader, and if the extra-parliamentary wing of the party could agree neither on the purpose to be served in summoning a convention nor on the way to summon it, then it is scarcely surprising no convention was convened.

Meighen's resignation in 1926, however, cleared the way for a leadership convention. Not only were there many parallels to the situation in which the Liberals found themselves in 1918–1919 to justify calling a convention, but there had been a growing number of provincial conventions called to elect party leaders in the period

[37] Graham, II, 176.
[38] *1927 Report,* p. 13.
[39] Graham, II, 247.

following the federal Liberal convention of 1919. The most significant of these was in 1920 when the Ontario Conservatives chose their new leader, G. Howard Ferguson, in convention. At the same time they had adopted an important resolution:

> It is hereby resolved, that when the permanent Leadership of the Liberal–Conservative Party in Ontario becomes vacant, the Liberal–Conservative Association of Ontario shall, at earliest convenience, summon a Provincial Convention, representative of all the Party forces, to select the permanent Provincial Leader.[40]

Electoral success followed the 1920 convention for the Ontario Conservatives and Ferguson became premier of the Dominion's most populous province. Ontario's experience with conventions, as well as that of other provinces, could not have been dismissed in 1926.[41]

So strong had the various precedents for leadership conventions become by the time Meighen resigned that the Toronto *Mail and Empire* commented editorially:

> No one has had the refusal of the leadership, because there is no one competent to offer it until the Conservative party has, through an all-Canada convention, come to a decision on the matter. . . . There can be no peddling of the leadership of the Conservative party by anybody. It is not in the gift of any coterie. The caucus of Conservative Senators, Conservative members-elect, and Conservative defeated candidates, which is to be held on Monday next may agree upon some one to lead in the House in the next session and until an *organic body of the party*, constituted for the purpose, appoints a permanent leader.[42]

Thus by 1926 a convention assembled to choose a new leader had become an "organic body of the party" and was expected to be summoned whenever a leadership vacancy might occur.

---

[40] *1927 Report,* p. 11.
[41] The *1927 Report* seems intent on justifying the 1927 convention on the basis of political precedent and historical progression. (See *1927 Report,* pp. 11-16.)
[42] Dawson (ed.), *Constitutional Issues in Canada, 1900-1931,* p. 389. (Italics added)

The provincial experience with conventions; the "unrepresenta-
tiveness" of the parliamentary group; the desire to replace the
elitism of the earlier informal selection processes by a more "democratic" and structured system; the need to develop a more effective
party organization; the hoped-for boost in party morale; the
vacancy in the party's leadership; the closing of the party's ranks:
such were the considerations in 1926 that led the Conservatives
to call their convention for the next year. Moreover, if Arthur
Meighen was right, the Conservatives could scarcely ignore in
1927 the precedent set by the Liberals *in opposition* seven years
earlier when they had selected their latest leader by an apparently
successful innovation in the Canadian political system. According
to Meighen:

> If the Liberals had formed the Government in 1919 instead
> of being in Opposition, the Parliamentary group would have
> chosen the leader. The adoption of the convention by the
> Liberals for the purpose of selecting a new leader *compelled*
> the Conservatives to follow the same method when in Oppo-
> sition.[43]

The Liberals had held their convention at the very time a political
party needs everything it can mobilize to its side — at the very time
a party has none of the advantages and all of the disadvantages of
being out of power. The Liberals had come out of the 1919 convention in appearance, if not in substance, a "democratic" and
"representative" national political party with a new leader, a new
platform, and a fighting organization. Appearance frequently being
as important in politics as substance, the Conservatives felt they
had no choice in the matter; in 1926–1927 they were "compelled,"
in Meighen's words, to follow suit. The mirror phenomenon of
Canadian political parties had manifested itself once again.

---

[43] John R. Williams, *The Conservative Party in Canada: 1920-1949* (Durham, N.C.: Duke University Press, 1956), p. 80. (Italics added.) Meighen's
comment was part of an interview with Williams in 1948.

Acceptance of the Change

The 1919 Liberal convention had not been designed, initially, as a "leadership" convention, but Laurier's death, combined with the peculiar internal conditions of the parliamentary Liberal party, made the convention appear to be a natural way of selecting the next leader of the Liberal party. The experience of the party with a convention in 1893, with the inspiration for that convention coming from Willison's favourable impression of the American Democratic convention of 1892, lent support to the caucus committee's decision to expand the purposes of the convention to include selection of a new leader. That the Liberals went on to electoral victory within little more than two years and formed the next government, reinforced the wisdom of the change. That is to say, the innovation could well have been less acceptable subsequently had it been followed by a series of electoral defeats.

In any event, the Conservatives found a national leadership convention suited their needs ideally when Arthur Meighen resigned in 1926. The selection of R. B. Bennett at the 1927 convention as leader of the revitalized Liberal-Conservative party was, in turn, followed by the Conservatives' electoral success in 1930. With the resignations of Bennett and Mackenzie King some years later, it would have taken exceptionally courageous caucuses to have urged a return to the methods of selecting party leaders used by Canadian parties prior to 1919. Leadership conventions had arrived, and they were to remain.

Conventions with several hundred delegates drawn together from across the Dominion were regarded as being both more "representative" of the party as a whole than the parliamentary caucus and more "democratic" as a means for selecting party leaders in 1919 and 1927. Such terms have been retained, over the years, as the very foundation for the philosophical justification of leadership conventions. To select their leaders by way of representative and democratic national gatherings has become a standard by which Canadian political parties like to be judged. Naturally the shift away from the members of caucus and the retiring leader as agents responsible for naming the party leader has been accompanied by a concomitant shift in intra-party power centres. By increasing the number of participants in the leadership selection process, the effect has been to transfer the locus of power from the parliamentary to the extra-parliamentary organization, giving rise to quite new and different commitments and relationships between the leader, his parliamentary group and the extra-parliamentary party than had hitherto existed.

The conventions of 1919 and 1927 made it abundantly clear that the man selected by caucus to serve as temporary leader had no pre-emptive claim on the party leadership when the delegates' votes were counted. D. D. McKenzie, the temporary Liberal leader named by caucus following Laurier's death, retired from the leadership race after tying for third place on the first ballot, and running fourth, of four candidates, on the second ballot. Of the six candidates at the Conservative convention, Hugh Guthrie, the party's temporary leader, fared better than had McKenzie at the Liberal gathering; he ran second on the two ballots needed to elect a new leader. Even then, however, his vote of 345 and 320 on those two ballots was never close to Bennett's 594 and 780 first and second ballot votes. Recognizing that caucus considerations at the time of naming a temporary leader would, almost invariably, be quite different from considerations affecting convention delegates' decisions, the fact remains the man chosen as temporary leader is by no means assured of gaining his party's permanent leadership. The conventions of 1919 and 1927 established that point conclusively.

The first two leadership conventions also proved that the winner of the leadership contest in convention need not be a man with much parliamentary experience. Mackenzie King had been a member of parliament for less than three years, and at that his parliamentary service occurred nearly a decade before the 1919 convention. Moreover, he had spent a good deal of the eight years since the first of his two successive electoral defeats out of the country altogether. Bennett, who had returned to the House two years previously after an eight-year absence, and whose parliamentary experience totalled eight years at the time he sought the leadership, defeated five other men who had served, on the average, eleven years in parliament. King's closest competitor for the leadership was Fielding, who at the time had been a member of parliament for nearly seventeen years; Bennett's closest competitor was Guthrie who at that time was serving his twenty-seventh uninterrupted year in parliament. The delegates, it would seem, were swayed by reference to considerations quite independent of parliamentary experience. Thus, another significant precedent had been established in 1919 and 1927 which, over the years, was to assume almost Parkinsonian proportions: the fewer the years a leadership candidate has served in parliament, the greater his chances of being elected a party leader. The value of political apprenticeships in Canadian politics was reduced with the introduction of the leadership convention. What in Britain has remained unmistakably essential, and what was also important in pre-convention Canadian politics, has now, in Canada, become relatively unimportant.

Both King and Bennett won the leadership of their respective parties by extremely close votes. For the Liberal and the Conservative conventions, the rule was established that the victor must receive at least a simple majority of the votes cast. King beat Fielding by 38 of the 914 votes cast on the third ballot; Bennett won by 6 votes over the combined opposition with 1,554 delegates voting on the second ballot. Obviously the closeness of the votes meant that neither winner could afford to ignore the views of the losing candidates and their supporters. For having inherited divided parties, and having many of those divisions sharpened by the leadership contests themselves, both King and Bennett were faced with the prospects of continued intra-party squabbles unless the ranks were closed. As it turned out, one of the best healing devices was the convention itself. The keen competition for policy and candidate support engendered considerable enthusiasm amongst the parties' rank-and-file supporters. If such enthusiasm could be marshalled into support for the new leaders, many of the parties' wounds would be healed. An overt, symbolic act of closing the party's ranks at the conclusion of the convention would help enormously. The 1919 and 1927 conventions did precisely that, by having the defeated contestants for the leadership in the final moments of the convention, with the name of the new leader just previously announced, move and second that the election of the new leader be made unanimous by the whole assembly. The general public as well as the rank and file of the party could not but be impressed by such enthusiastic support for the new leader and the apparent disappearance of previously existing internal party differences. The early conventions showed how diversity could give way to coalescence. This public display of intra-party harmony contributed a necessary degree of stability and confidence to the Liberals after their 1919 convention and to the Conservatives after their convention of 1927. That lesson, too, was not forgotten by Canadian parties in the years to come, for beginning with the 1919 and 1927 conventions through to the early 1970s, the two parties have, in total, used conventions on ten different occasions to select their leaders.

5

A Democratic and Representative Gathering

How Conventions Are Justified

Canadians have been subjected for over half a century now to the bold assertion that leadership conventions are "democratic and representative" assemblies — an assertion for which there has been a good deal of popular as well as learned support. Acceptance of conventions as the legitimate replacements for other forms of leadership selection has been aided by the ready credibility accorded the idea that Canadians have achieved in the party convention a leadership selection process more suitable to a modern, progressive democracy than any other process used in their past. The simplicity of the assertion, aided, no doubt, by its widespread repetition, has left Canadians convinced of its inherent truth. According to Dawson and Ward:

> The practice of making selections by the convention method
> is not likely to be repudiated in the foreseeable future; for to
> do so would be to show an open preference for a restricted

method of choice rather than one based on the representative and (so it is usually believed) the democratic principle. No party will willingly expose itself to the reproach that it is afraid to trust the judgment of its own representative convention.[1]

The tone had been set in 1919. An attitude typical of the time was expressed by one of the Quebec politicians active at the Liberal convention of that year: "Sir Wilfrid Laurier was the leader of a great democratic party, and it is fitting that his successor should be selected, not only by the parliamentary members of the party, but by the democracy, by the Liberals of Canada."[2] Newspaper editorialists quickly popularized the twin notions of the democracy and the representativeness of national conventions, so it was small wonder that Arthur Meighen felt the Conservatives were virtually compelled to hold a leadership convention when he resigned in 1926. Since the 1920s, the line taken by editorial writers has remained essentially the same. As if to lend authority to the claim, academic voices ultimately joined those of the journalists and politicians. To John W. Lederle, the national party convention stands "as a dramatic institution for the democratic marshalling of grass-roots' support in the management of party affairs,"[3] and to J. R. Mallory, "the leadership convention has now become an important element in democratic politics. It is [among other things] the summoning of an unusually large and representative 'parliament' of the party in order to ensure that the leader is the choice of the party as a whole."[4] It is clear, therefore, that the claims made regarding the democracy and representativeness of Canadian conventions are substantial; that conventions warrant such fulsome praise is, however, less certain.

[1] R. MacGregor Dawson, *The Government of Canada*, 5th ed., revised by Norman Ward (Toronto: University of Toronto Press, 1970), pp. 463-64.
[2] Ernest Lapointe, MP, in *1919 Report*, p. 88. A slightly different version of the statement appeared in the *World* (Toronto) on August 7, 1919: "Mr. Laurier had been leader of a democratic party and it was therefore fitting that his successor should be chosen not by a coterie of politicians but by a great democratic convention" (p. 7).
[3] Lederle, "The Liberal Convention of 1893," 43.
[4] J. R. Mallory, *The Structure of Canadian Government* (Toronto: Macmillan Company of Canada, 1971), p. 205.

"Democracy" is the chameleon of the political vocabulary. It is not easy to determine with certainty the meaning attached to that word, for it is undoubtedly used and interpreted in a variety of ways. However, a theory will be outlined so as to attempt an explanation as well as an assessment of Canadian leadership conventions as so-called democratic institutions.

Democracy, it is suggested, is vital to the belief system enveloping party conventions in Canada, important both to party participants and to the general population. The word carries with it favourable connotations and thereby serves a legitimating purpose. To refer to conventions as democratic entities is to suggest that within the whole selection process itself there is thought to be a substantial degree of *openness* as well as widespread *participation,* both of which are commonly regarded as procedural characteristics befitting modern political institutions. Likewise the word suggests that power within the party is not concentrated in the hands of a few but is dispersed in such a way as to permit meaningful *control* by the party membership over its leadership and its policies. Indirectly, a democratic convention even implies an acceptable level of competence of those chosen to select the new leader, for the delegates are thought to be carefully chosen and uniquely equipped so as to *represent* in some peculiar way the will of the people.

If there is common support for the belief that leaders are selected by an open process and that representatives are allowed substantial participation in and control over the party's affairs, then a societal norm has been established by which parties may be publicly judged. Given such a norm no party can afford the price of appearing to be undemocratic in the public's opinion by using some other procedure to choose its leader, even though the leader it might get as a result of a party convention might be less suitable to the party than one chosen by some other process. No party, in other words, can run the risk of being labelled "undemocratic" by its opponents, given a society in which the appearance of being "democratic" conforms to an acceptable belief. Furthermore, the parties will quite logically compete among themselves in their attempts to out-do, to "out-democratize," one another: regular and increasingly frequent conventions, "leadership accountability" sessions, leadership review mechanisms, widely publicized policy conferences, and sizable constituency delegations will be typical features of this aspect of inter-party rivalry. Furthermore, the general population and, more specifically, the party activists, will evince strong attachment to the norm and will reject, almost out of hand, as non-democratic any form of leadership selection that fails to meet what they conceive to be the standard applicable in their society.

Openness

How well do Canadian leadership conventions measure up to the norm? To begin with, *openness* implies relatively unrestricted access to the convention for those who wish to seek the leadership, public meetings for the purpose of selecting constituency delegates, and procedures designed to allow at least some public scrutiny of convention proceedings. (See Appendix B on p. 241 for one illustration of convention rules and procedures designed in an attempt to ensure equal and fair treatment for all candidates.) Because the public gets at least a partial glimpse of what is going on during the leadership campaign and convention, it is not difficult for a candidate to seek delegate support by implying that he is playing according to the rules and that other candidates are not. When a candidate declares that he will be party to no deals or arrangements and denounces his leadership opponents as "power brokers" and "wheeler-dealers," as John Turner did shortly before the voting day at the Liberal leadership convention in 1968, he is not only attacking those who have by-passed him with their arrangements, but also invoking the norm in the hope of gaining delegate support.[5]

[5] The issue that provoked Mr. Turner's outburst was Mitchell Sharp's withdrawal from the leadership race and his public declaration of support for Mr. Trudeau four days prior to the selection of the new leader. Mr. Turner's comments are from the *Telegram* (Toronto), April 4, 1968, p. 9.

Canadian leadership conventions have never used any system of open or declared voting, roll-call voting, unit rule or two-thirds rule to choose their leaders. They have, on one occasion, granted more than one vote to a delegate,[6] but they have avoided copying other American examples of convention voting. The delegates, subject as they are to pressure from various quarters to support different candidates, still retain the right to vote secretly and without any prior commitment to any delegating body. The example was set when, for reasons unexplained, the first national leadership convention committee decided in favour of the individual secret ballot, as the 1919 Liberal convention report points out:

> The procedure to be followed in the election of a leader for the Liberal Party by a popular Convention raised many questions, and one of them related to the form of ballot that should be used. There was no precedent in Canada to help solve the difficulty, and the method adopted by National Conventions in the United States, when nominating Presidential candidates, *was not regarded as meeting the case that had to be dealt with.* After many suggestions were considered and rejected, it was finally decided to print for the use of each delegate entitled to vote a book of ballots similar to a cheque book, containing 10 ballot papers, numbered from 1 to 10, inclusive, and detachable from stubs with corresponding numbers. . . . The ballots . . . designed for the first political experiment of its kind in Canada contributed in no small measure to the orderly conduct of the voting at the Convention.[7]

[6] In 1927 the Conservative convention committee decided that "where a constituency sent a full quota of delegates to the Convention, each delegate should have one vote on each ballot, and where owing to some insurmountable and unforeseen difficulty the entire number are not present, then those selected delegates present — in addition to polling one vote each — should be entitled to decide by a majority vote of those who were present how or in what proportion the votes of those selected to represent such riding who were not present should be polled. It was felt that far away constituencies which might find it impossible to get a full quota of delegates should have this safeguard." PAC, *R. B. Bennett Papers,* pp. 4094-95, March 22, 1927.

[7] *1919 Report,* p. 18. (Italics added.) In 1967 and 1968 voting machines replaced the paper ballots for the first time, but the fact that the balloting tended to take longer than it had with paper ballots may make their continued use less certain than had originally been hoped.

It is quite possible that in considering a convention floor roll-call vote by provinces the Liberal convention committee of 1919 rejected it for fear of splitting the convention on a Quebec and anti-Quebec basis. It was fairly certain that practically the entire Quebec delegation would support a candidate who had remained loyal to Laurier in 1917. Given rather strong support for Fielding (who, of course, had broken away in 1917) in other parts of the country, the convention committee might well have felt that it would run too high a risk of internal damage had a roll-call vote system been adopted. Moreover, it made sense for the convention committee to want to adopt something that the delegates would be both familiar with and disposed towards as a result of federal elections, namely the secret ballot. Many Liberals had unhappy recollections of the "soldiers' ballots" in 1917, which in some cases at least, were far from secret.

A recent suggestion that Canadian conventions abandon the secret ballot in favour of a roll-call vote has been made by a Manitoba politician. Basing his position "on the fact that no delegate is entitled to maintain the secrecy of his ballot, and as a corollary, every delegating body is entitled to know how [its] representatives vote," Sidney Green of the NDP believes that "from the point of view of drama, and also from the point of view of the proper selection of a leader, an open ballot, paged from the chair, as is done at the American conventions to choose the nominee for president" would be the best procedure to follow.[8] In a delegate situation a secret ballot is merely a sign of political immaturity, Mr. Green maintains. Mr. Green's suggestion is interesting insofar as it attempts to introduce a new dimension to the procedural characteristics of Canadian democracy, but little support is likely to be forthcoming for his proposal from other Canadian politicians, as the secret ballot is solidly entrenched as a feature of Canadian leadership conventions.

As leadership contestants have, in the past, been both few in

---

[8] Letter to the author from Mr. Sidney Green, then Minister of Mines and Natural Resources, Province of Manitoba, May 5, 1971. Mr. Green had originally presented his proposal to a meeting of the NDP federal council, but without success.

number and genuinely serious candidates, there has been no problem of access. Organizers of recent conventions, however, felt that they had to impose arbitrary barriers to nomination in the hope of discouraging potential "nuisance" candidates who sought nothing more than public attention. A "serious" candidate was one who for the Conservative (1967) convention had his nomination papers signed by twenty-five registered delegates and for the Liberal (1968) and NDP (1971), fifty delegates. The barrier, although in the Conservative and Liberal conventions not quite as successful as convention organizers had hoped, was an indirect result, the convention organizers argued, of national television coverage of conventions. With prime television time a major consideration in presenting the convention and the party in as favourable a light as possible, every party, according to one convention chairman, "has to cut these fellows off somehow even if it does run counter to the democratic ethos."[9]

It is worthwhile noting the attitudes of many of the serious candidates and their organizers toward nuisance candidates. On the whole, they are not displeased with or disturbed by the presence of one or two of them. Obviously, their presence lends credibility to the parties' claims of being "open" entities; the parties' images, therefore, more accurately fit the democratic norm when the candidatures of such people can be pointed to. But, more importantly, nuisance candidates also perform a vital service for the other candidates, their organizers, managers and floor staff,

[9] Interview with Senator John Nichol, co-chairman of the 1968 Liberal convention, Ottawa, June 9, 1969. The need to appeal to a television audience leads parties to do apparently strange things. On his retirement in 1968 as Liberal leader, Lester Pearson was presented on the platform of the convention with a dog. He later recalled the incident:

> I often wondered what inspired that particular unique gift to a retiring prime minister and leader, and what was the symbolism behind that. Now John Nichol told me that they were going to do this, and my wife and I, both of us, thought this was the silliest thing we ever heard of, and we told John: "We can't keep a dog." "Well," he said, "we want to do it." And I said, "Why?" He said: "It will be wonderful on television." There you are. . . . Can I give you a better example of the debasement of politics?

Transcript of the CBC television show "The Tenth Decade," Program 8, p. 17.

given the convention voting arrangements. Under a system in which the bottom candidate is automatically dropped if no one candidate receives a majority of the votes cast, candidates' staffs gain essential information from the first ballot without any of the serious contestants themselves facing removal when there is a token candidate present. Mrs. Mary Walker-Sawka's two votes in 1967 and the Rev. Lloyd Henderson's zero votes in 1968 on the first ballot of the Conservative and Liberal conventions respectively were obviously of no significance in themselves, but the candidacy of these two people was of great use to the various candidates' organizers. They were able to learn accurately both the ranking of the candidates and the absolute vote figures about which they had previously been able only to speculate. As well, they gained additional precious time to put this information to use by beginning preliminary discussions on likely courses of action to be followed by other candidates once their relative strength was known. All of this given without one serious candidate being removed! Convention officials may fear their presence, but candidates and their organizers realize the practical political worth of token candidates.

A more effective deterrent to keep nuisance candidates from widespread campaigning before the convention, and one which, unfortunately, hinders some serious candidates as well, is that of financing their own campaigns. Again, this is now a much more serious development, taking into account the apparent need of candidates to visit meetings of delegates across the country prior to the convention itself and the acceptance by so many candidates of the idea that to succeed they must excel in promoting their candidature through colourful, flashy, and costly campaigns. In the earlier leadership conventions time would not permit such visits, considering the distances involved, nor was the idea of campaigning for delegates' votes so popularly accepted. When he wrote to John D. Rockefeller, Jr., about his decision to travel abroad prior to the 1919 convention, Mackenzie King may have demurred at the thought of campaigning for the party leadership, but his attitude was not unlike that generally shared by others: it was unwise to appear too anxious to be chosen leader. "Each day," King wrote in his characteristic style,

> I am more satisfied with the decision made to go abroad. As
> you know, I should never be happy in seeking any position
> or manoeuvring for it; and in a position involving such grave
> responsibilities as that of leader of a political party, I should
> derive no happiness or satisfaction from the office, were it to
> come my way, did I feel that I had sought the position, rather
> than that the position had sought me. Except as an expression
> of confidence from the Liberal Party of Canada as a whole,
> I should decline altogether any offer of leadership were such
> to be made at the instance of any group. I realize only too
> well what the responsibilities and trials of political leadership
> are certain to be, to court them in any way. I am convinced,
> therefore, that, apart from the advantage from the point of
> view of my understanding of the industrial situation which a
> study of conditions in England at this time is certain to be,
> there is wisdom, as respects the political uncertainties and
> possibilities, in making the trip at this time; and I am only too
> grateful to you for making such a chance possible.[10]

Candidate attitudes towards campaigning changed markedly
during the 1940s and 1950s, and by 1967 and 1968 there was
no question that full-scale competitive campaigning had arrived.

---

[10] PAC, *King Papers,* vol. 50, King to Rockefeller, April 13, 1919. King
may, in fact, have been hoping for a draft. Writing to an acquaintance
following his return to Canada to urge no canvass by mail in his support,
King stated: "I have been most careful to avoid even the appearance of
attempting to influence, either directly or indirectly, the choice of Leader
of the Liberal Party to be made at the forthcoming Convention. . . . In
deciding to spend the last ten weeks in studying industrial conditions in
England and visiting the battlefields of Europe, I was not a little influenced by the belief that absence from Canada throughout this period
would enable the public to appreciate my desire to be wholly removed from
any movement with which my name might be directly or indirectly associated. My feelings remaining what they always have been, greatly as I
appreciate the kindness of my North York friends in offering to co-operate
in giving prominence to my name, you will readily understand that it is no
want of appreciation of their kindness, but only a sense of what is fitting
under the circumstances, which makes me feel that I should not care to
make any suggestion as to how their kindly intentions toward myself be
furthered." PAC, *King Papers,* vol. 43, King to W. H. S. Cane, July 24,
1919. To F. A. McGregor, Mackenzie King's secretary in 1919, King's
lack of interest in actively campaigning for his party's leadership was a
direct reflection of King's Calvinistic belief in predestination. McGregor,
The Fall and Rise of Mackenzie King: 1911-1919 (Toronto: Macmillan
Company of Canada, 1962), pp. 330-32.

It was estimated that some Conservative (1967) and Liberal (1968) leadership candidates may have spent at least $300,000 in their search for delegate support over a period of a few months, and even more modest campaigns were reported to have cost in the neighbourhood of $100,000 per candidate. Those candidates who were apparently seriously intent on winning the leadership but who were, at the same time, unable to raise substantial funds in their own support, suffered unnecessarily. Such, for example, was likely the fundamental problem with Michael Starr's campaign in 1967. (On a suggestion to limit the candidates' campaign expenditures, see Appendix C on page 244.)

In the call issued for their first leadership convention, the Liberal party stipulated that:

> A local convention shall be called in each Dominion Constituency not later than the 30th day of June, 1919, for the election of the said three delegates by a majority of the votes of those present at the meeting. To ensure a representative attendance at each of such conventions, sufficient advance notice shall be given by advertisement or otherwise and the date, hour and place of meeting shall be mentioned in such notice.[11]

The Liberal Federation has since adopted virtually the same statement in its constitution. The Progressive Conservative convention committee stipulated in 1967 that constituency meetings for that year's convention were to be open meetings. In the words of the party's national director:

> The meetings had to take place within the constituency; they had to provide copies of newspaper ads showing the meeting had been announced properly and was open; they had to waive party membership requirements so that no small groups could control the meetings.[12]

By calling for local public meetings the parties certainly invoke the democratic norm. Yet what do such requirements really mean? Despite the elaborate provisions stipulated by the parties, their

---

[11] *1919 Report,* p. 7. For the 1968 Convention Call see Appendix D.
[12] James Johnston, *The Party's Over* (Don Mills: Longmans Canada Limited, 1971), pp. 180-81.

hope of open, public meetings is not always realized; not all constituencies have party associations at the time of conventions, and not all constituency associations flourish as bountifully as party officials hope and pretend. In 1956, for example, the Progressive Conservative provincial executives, with the approval of the convention executive committee, could name riding delegates and alternates in the absence of a constituency association or a similar body. (See Appendix E, p. 251.) Constituency executive officers have, on occasion, appointed the delegates without an association election, sometimes even appointing themselves. With or without elections, the sitting member of parliament may in fact be in a sufficiently powerful position to choose all the constituency delegates himself, as Senator C. G. Power related in his memoirs, and those delegates would then "reflect his [the MPs] views and vote as he directs."[13] It is difficult to say with certainty that such practices are now a thing of the past. But it is not unreasonable to conclude that in 1967 and 1968, with the keen competition for delegate votes and the two parties' deliberate attempts to ensure constituency compliance with the convention requirements, there was less deviation from the norm than had been the case in the past.[14]

In the vast majority of constituencies open meetings in fact are the rule, although constituency conventions attended by delegates from various parts of the riding are not unknown to Canadian politics. The Quebec Conservatives resorted to the local convention system in 1948 as one newspaper reported at the time:

> In Quebec, where riding organization is almost unknown, another method is being used. Next Sunday and the following two Sundays small groups of Progressive Conservatives will meet after church in hundreds of parishes.
> They will appoint three or four members each to attend central meetings for the constituency and these meetings will in the main send Quebec's quota of delegates to Ottawa.[15]

---

[13] C. G. Power, *A Party Politician: The Memoirs of Chubby Power,* ed. Norman Ward (Toronto: Macmillan Company of Canada, 1966), p. 371.
[14] On this point, see D. V. Smiley, "The National Party Leadership Convention in Canada: A Preliminary Analysis," *Canadian Journal of Political Science* (hereafter cited as *CJPS*), I (December 1968), 377.
[15] *Globe and Mail,* August 10, 1948, p. 4.

Typically, however, open invitations are extended to interested members of the public. Newspaper advertisements announce the time and place of the meetings and party memberships are usually sold at the door for those who wish to vote. Given such arrangements it is not at all difficult for supporters of a particular candidate to "pack" a constituency meeting so as to ensure the election of delegates favouring the candidate. In 1968, in the Toronto constituency of St. Paul's allegations of packing were made against Mr. Trudeau's organizers (and denied) but the president of the constituency Liberal association admitted that in the three days before the cut-off of membership applications more than two hundred and fifty new members had joined the association. "I don't know where these people came from," he said. "We had never seen any of them before."[16] In the various Winnipeg constituency meetings prior to the 1968 Liberal convention, keen competition between supporters of several leadership candidates led to the presentation of slates of potential delegates to constituency meetings by organizers for those candidates. Invariably there were charges of packing. One meeting with five hundred people in attendance was described by the press as "solidly packed by the organizers for Mr. Martin and Mr. Turner," the latter's supporters having arranged, among other things, for two busloads of "members" to attend the meeting: one with sixty students from a local university, the other with fifty habitués from the Indian-Métis Friendship Centre.[17] Instances of such practices are, on the whole, rare. The much more characteristic constituency meeting is the one attended by the local party faithful, and few others.

At such meetings, the delegates are typically chosen from amongst the local party notables. And among these, the tendency to favour past or present executive officers of the local constituency, women's and youth associations is most pronounced. By way of illustration, of the 2,442 delegates to the 1968 Liberal convention, 68 per cent either had been or were at the time of the convention elected officers in a constituency association. In

[16] *Ibid.,* March 4, 1968, p. 11.
[17] *Winnipeg Free Press,* February 6, 1968, p. 3

fact, excluding past or present federal, provincial and municipal legislators or candidates, only 6 per cent of the delegates at that convention had never served or were not then serving in some executive capacity for the party.[18] The usual argument given in support of constituency executive officers serving as delegates is that convention delegate status is a fitting way to recognize and reward their service to the party. Such an argument aside, it must be remembered that constituency officers would stand an excellent chance of being selected in any event for, as Robert Michels and others have argued convincingly, the marked tendency of parties is towards governance by an oligarchy.[19] Such oligarchical characteristics seem to result naturally from a combination of the deference paid by the party rank and file to the occupants of particular executive positions, and familiarity with the names of the party elite when elections are held to choose conventions delegates.

Participation

A second element essential to the democratic norm is the notion of widespread *participation* by the delegates in their own party's affairs. In announcing the 1969 Harrison Liberal Conference as "the inaugural event in a 3-phase program of policy formulation and renewal that affects and seeks to involve all Canadians interested in questions of public policy," the president of the Liberal Federation stated that

> the Liberal Party firmly believes effective policy decisions cannot be made by a few individuals in one or a series of weekend meetings, but rather that the involvement of many

---

[18] Figures taken from the author's mail questionnaire to delegates to the Liberal convention of 1968. (N = 1,335, or 54.7 per cent of convention delegates.)
[19] See, for example, Robert Michels, *Political Parties* (New York: Dover Publications, Inc., 1959), pp. 11 and 377-92.

over a considerable period of time is the only way open to
a modern mass political party.

Accordingly, the Liberal Party's 3-phase policy formulation program is also being carefully designed as a major
'participation' program and techniques and procedures are
or will be built into each phase of the program to ensure the
widest possible participation of all Canadians interested in
questions of public policy.

The Liberal party is or will be seeking increased participation in each of the three phases of its program of policy
formulation. . . .

In actively seeking the involvement of the greatest number
of Canadians possible the Liberal party is not only fulfilling
the historic role of liberalism but also giving substance to
Prime Minister Pierre Elliott Trudeau's belief that only
through increased participation can decisions on questions
of public policy be a reflection of the hopes and aspirations
of individual Canadians for their society in the 70's.[20]

Such repeated use of "participation" and "involvement" suggests
that strong positive values are associated with both words, and
that the parties anticipate favourable public reaction and membership response when they refer to their own proceedings in those
terms. In this respect the value of debates on party policy was
clearly understood by Senator Power:

It leaves the impression with the rank and file that they
have had their say in the formulation of party views and the
advancement of party ideals and ideology. . . . The members
of the party have at least the satisfaction of being able to
say they did have some influence, and that they have a stake
in the party's fortunes. This enables them to return home
with the feeling that they have a personal interest in the
success of the party, and to dissipate the idea that decisions
are handed down from the hierarchy. They have had an
opportunity of expressing their views in a democratic way.[21]

Thus, not only the fact of formal participation through voting

---

[20] Liberal Federation of Canada, press release, "Policy Formulation and
Participatory Democracy," October 8, 1969.
[21] Power, pp. 370-71.

on leadership, policies, and organization, but the delegates' impression (whether or not it is in accord with the actual facts) of being meaningfully involved in the work of the party are vital components of this part of the belief system.

Although the idea of participation is no less a component of leadership selection through convention balloting than it is of policy formulation through party conferences, the nature of the participatory act is somewhat different. In leadership conventions, the delegate is fully conscious of the fact that, unlike the case of policy debates, a final decision *has* to be made, a winner *has* to be declared. He knows that the leadership decision is one that the party has no choice but to live with for the next few years at least. To that extent, his participation in the decision on his party's leadership gives an immediacy to his actions that does not obtain to the same extent in the debates and votes on party policies. Not surprisingly, the delegate who attends conventions at which both policy resolutions and leadership selection require his attention will, in all likelihood, be less able to concentrate on policy matters than he might like, given the overriding importance of the party's decision on leadership. Some politicians are convinced that delegates cannot play the two roles well in a single convention and that policy considerations invariably suffer. Senator Power shrewdly observed:

> The obsession of conventions with the choice of leaders has resulted in the adoption of platforms that as a rule contain items that, through want of full discussion by delegates who often have fundamental differences of opinion, are a conglomeration of verbose language and ponderous phrases with little substance or meaning, calculated only to meet the divergent and often uninformed views of those who participated in the discussion.[22]

Not surprisingly, therefore, some convention organizers now favour

[22] *Ibid.*

separating the two tasks so that they might be dealt with at different party meetings.[23]

Control

Robert Dahl has pointed out that "at a minimum . . . democratic theory is concerned with processes by which ordinary citizens exert a relatively high degree of control over leaders."[24] One of the processes by which the "ordinary citizens" of Canadian political parties attempt to exert some control over their leaders and policies is, of course, the national convention, but it is doubtful if the results would be regarded as entirely satisfactory by a democratic purist. For one thing, the rank and file have had few chances for testing their power within the party until the past decade, given the infrequency and irregularity of national conventions. The Liberals were quite remarkable in this regard, having held no national party convention from the time Mackenzie King was chosen leader in 1919 until he retired in 1948. For another, the parliamentary parties, and more specifically, their leadership, have staunchly and, so far at least, successfully maintained that policy suggestions may come from the party in convention, but final policy commitments remain the prerogative of the group in parliament.

Party leaders may be chosen by party conventions but they have maintained successfully that their policy positions need not necessarily be based on, or agree with, their party's policy resolutions and platforms. The Progressive Conservative platform hammered out at the 1956 convention was shortly thereafter ordered suppressed by the new leader, John Diefenbaker, so as to allow the

---

[23] Interviews with Senator John Nichol, co-chairman of the 1968 Liberal convention, Ottawa, June 9, 1969; Senator Paul C. Lafond, former associate general secretary, Liberal Federation of Canada, Ottawa, May 29, 1969; and Mr. Clifford A. Scotton, federal secretary, New Democratic Party, Ottawa, May 16, 1969.

[24] Dahl, *A Preface to Democratic Theory* (Chicago: University of Chicago Press, 1956), p. 3.

party room for tactical manoeuvrability in the policy suggestions it intended to lay before the electorate during the 1957 election campaign.[25] Piqued by a resolution on bilingualism in the federal civil service passed by the Liberal Policy Conference and National Meeting of October 1966, the prime minister (Mr. Pearson) made it clear that the government's policy on this matter had already been determined and would not likely be changed. He informed the House of Commons that:

> resolutions serve as a guide, and we on this side take them very seriously as a guide to policy. But resolutions themselves do not establish policy, and in respect of the resolution on bilingualism, which we undoubtedly will consider, I would like to point out that the policy of the government on that matter was laid down in the house on April 6.[26]

It is worth noting that at that same convention the Liberals had previously approved an amendment to their constitution aimed at specifying the importance of the convention's policy role and the responsibility of the parliamentary group to implement policies approved in convention. The parliamentary party was to be held directly accountable to the party in convention for its policy decisions:

> The basic policies of the Party shall be established by the Party assembled in policy conferences at least every two years.
>
> At each Convention a member of the caucus appointed by the Leader, and when the Party forms the government a member of the cabinet appointed by the Leader, shall attend and report upon the consideration given, the decisions made and the reasoning therefore regarding resolutions passed at the previous Convention, which decisions shall be presumed to be ratified unless there is a contrary decision by the Convention.[27]

---

[25] See John Meisel, *The Canadian General Election of 1957* (Toronto: University of Toronto Press, 1962), pp. 39-44 and 170-71.
[26] Canada, *Debates of the House of Commons,* October 14, 1966, p. 8656.
[27] Liberal Federation of Canada, *Constitution* (as amended October 1966), clause 9 (I, 1-2).

A more embarrassing conflict between government policy and party policy developed in the aftermath of the FLQ crisis in Quebec in the fall of 1970. In parliament, Mr. Trudeau's government had defeated an opposition proposal to establish a review board designed to safeguard individual rights under the Public Order (Temporary Measures) Act, 1970, yet his party's national convention, meeting shortly afterwards, voted overwhelming approval for the establishment of just such a board. The prime minister noted his dilemma: "If I listen to the convention, I may be in contempt of Parliament. If I don't, I may be in contempt of this convention."[28] The government's position did not change, however, and it soon defeated yet another opposition amendment aimed at establishing a review board. Writing to all Liberal delegates to thank them for their contribution to the convention as well as for their "involvement" in party affairs, Mr. Trudeau allowed that "although the government may not be able to accept and act upon *all* your resolutions, my Colleagues and I cannot and do not intend to ignore any of them." The prime minister concluded his letter by assuring the party that "the delegates' resolutions do and will retain the government's attention, and that we will study them — all of them — as soon as arrangements for this can be made."[29] A special issue of the party newspaper summing up the achievements of the 1970 Liberal meeting noted that those who had attended the convention were now aware of the fact "that participatory democracy is more than a catch phrase."[30]

Until recently neither the Liberals nor the Conservatives had any provision in their party constitutions for the periodic review of their leadership. In the history of both parties, leaders were chosen without term — a feature of leadership selection unchanged with the switch to national leadership conventions. It had been a generally accepted principle of party politics in Canada (as in many other parliamentary countries) that the leader who was successfully directing his party would remain in that position

[28] *Star-Phoenix* (Saskatoon), November 23, 1970, p. 7.
[29] Letter from Mr. Trudeau to Miss Denise Howe (but sent to all policy convention delegates), December 18, 1970, pp. 2 and 4. (Italics in original)
[30] *The Canadian Liberal*, extra post-convention issue, n.d., p. 1.

for as long as he wished, whereas the leader who was clearly an electoral liability or who had lost the confidence of his parliamentary colleagues would, perhaps with some urging, realize that the time had come for his resignation. The timing of the leader's withdrawal, in other words, was very substantially a matter of his own personal judgment. The situation closely paralleled that of the British parties although, of course, while in opposition the Parliamentary Labour Party has chosen to elect its leader annually.

Within one month in 1966 that tradition of Canadian politics was swept aside. The Liberal party's national meeting in Ottawa in October of that year approved a significant addition to the party's constitution:

> A resolution calling for a Leadership Convention shall be placed automatically on the Agenda of the Biennial Convention next following a Federal General Election. If such resolution is duly adopted by secret ballot the Executive Committee shall call a Leadership Convention to take place within one year.[31]

In all, the party had received twenty-five resolutions (from constituency and provincial associations) calling for amendments to the party's constitution to establish some mechanism for the review of the party's leadership. The resolutions were not aimed specifically at the then Liberal leader and prime minister, Lester Pearson, for it was widely assumed that within a year or two at the most Mr. Pearson would step down as Liberal leader. Rather the resolutions rested clearly and simply on the premise that a party was not "democratic" if it lacked regular opportunity to vote on the desirability of calling a leadership convention. Mark MacGuigan, a supporter of a stronger resolution than that finally adopted, one which called for an automatic leadership convention within two years of every federal election, told the convention: "Democracy must be complete. The party must have its checkreins to keep the leader close to the party. Leadership

[31] Liberal Federation of Canada, *Constitution* (as amended October 1966), clause 9 (H).

conventions should be a matter of course."[32] The mover of the amendment finally adopted argued before the convention that it was necessary to reserve "to the members of the party at large the essential control over leadership."[33] Mr. Pearson indicated support for the idea of leadership accountability sessions, following which a vote of confidence would test the leader's support in the party, but he was opposed to the MacGuigan proposal for automatic leadership conventions:

> It is quite reasonable that the leader should give an account of his stewardship to [a] biennial convention. I think it is equally reasonable that, if a majority of the members are not impressed by his report, they should be able to vote their lack of confidence in him. But I do not think the leader of our party should have to appear automatically every two years at a formal leadership convention and compete with other candidates. The responsibilities and labors of a prime minister are already sufficiently crushing — at times they seem almost unbearable. I hope he would not have to run a leadership campaign for the last year of every two.[34]

The first occasion on which the Liberal party's new constitutional provision applied was at the party's biennial meeting of November 1970, when by a secret ballot vote of 1,064 to 132 the party rejected the resolution calling for a leadership convention within a year and thereby indicated its continued support for Mr. Trudeau's leadership.

The Progressive Conservative party at its annual meeting of November 1966, handled the issue of leadership review differently and in such a way as to create deep divisions within the party. The Conservatives characteristically display the best intentions of dealing with the principle of a matter, but so often end up quarrelling over the personalities involved. To a certain extent this results from the frustrations created within a power-oriented party

---

[32] *Star-Phoenix* (Saskatoon), October 11, 1966, p. 1.
[33] *Globe and Mail,* October 12, 1966, p. 29.
[34] Mr. Pearson's opening speech to the 1966 annual meeting. Note the assumption that the Liberal party will be in office. *Globe and Mail,* October 11, 1966, p. 33.

which is scarcely ever in power. But it also results from a dilemma which is peculiar to the Conservative party. As the Conservatives are not a sufficiently major force to succeed in competing on their own terms, they so often must adopt the terms dictated by their opponents. Appearing not to be "democratic" would be a stigma difficult for the Conservatives to overcome; therefore, they feel they must partake in the democratic exercise even though some of the traditions and loyalties felt more keenly by a Conservative than by a Liberal are, in and of themselves, not fully compatible with the democratic ethic. As not all Conservatives are capable of playing the game on the other party's terms, the party remains highly susceptible to injurious in-fighting. Thus it was in 1966.

John Diefenbaker's leadership of the Conservative party was at the very core of the dispute. Since his government's defeat in the 1963 election, Diefenbaker's leadership had been loyally accepted by most members of the parliamentary caucus (although there were certainly pockets of opposition), but dissatisfaction with Diefenbaker was evident in several quarters outside parliament. In early 1965 the national executive of the party narrowly defeated a motion calling for a leadership convention, the request for which had come formally to the party's executive in the form of a letter from Leon Balcer, the leader of the Quebec caucus of Conservative MPs. In 1966, for some two months before the party's annual meeting in November of that year, Dalton Camp, the party's national president then seeking re-election to that post, spoke publicly in various parts of Canada of the dual need to "democratize" the Conservative party and to "re-assess" its leadership, handy terms that in fact were widely interpreted as meaning removal of Mr. Diefenbaker. Camp staked his re-election to the party presidency on a pledge that a leadership convention would be held before the end of 1967. The Diefenbaker forces entered a presidential candidate in the person of Arthur Maloney, a former member of parliament. But with Maloney's defeat by Camp by a vote of 564 to 502, and with the subsequent approval by the meeting of a motion calling for a leadership convention in 1967, the removal of Mr. Diefenbaker from the party leadership was virtually assured.

The bitter struggle within the Conservative party in 1966 had been so centred on the immediate issue of John Diefenbaker's leadership that the more fundamental question of constitutional procedures for reviewing party leadership was left unresolved. Not until their annual meeting of March 1969 did the Conservatives formally consider amending their constitution to enable periodic review of the leadership by party convention. A party constitution committee under the chairmanship of Heath Macquarrie, MP, recommended the following:

> The Association shall hold a General Meeting every two years, and the Executive Committee shall make all procedural arrangements in respect thereto. The National Executive shall have the authority to call a Special Meeting at any time, or to postpone the General Meeting in any calendar year in which there may be a General Election, Leadership Convention of the Party, or other reason which justifies such postponement.
>
> At every General Meeting the following question shall be put, without debate, and voted on by ballot or voting machine: "Should the Party hold a Leadership Convention within twelve months?" If a majority of registered delegates vote in the affirmative, the Executive Committee shall proceed to call a Convention to be held within twelve months from the taking of such a vote.[35]

The committee's proposal met with strong opposition from the conference floor. The chief spokesman against the committee's recommendation argued that re-assessment of leadership ought to take into account whether or not the Progressive Conservative leader happens also to be prime minister at the time, and ought to come at the most opportune time for the party, that is after an election, not before it. The party and its leader could both be handicapped going into an election if the leader had just previously been sustained in a convention vote by only a slight

---

[35] Progressive Conservative Association of Canada, *Report of the Constitution Committee* (March 11, 1969), proposed article XII. The wording of the proposal left much to be desired. There need *never* be a general meeting, for example, for under the parliamentary system there *may* be a general election any year.

margin. In addition no review, it was argued, need take place if the party has had at least a modest increase in its parliamentary support at the last general election.[36] No member of the constitution committee spoke in support of its own recommendation, the above arguments apparently proved persuasive, and the following, rather awkwardly phrased, amendment was approved in place of the constitution committee's second paragraph:

> When we are the government party no resolution calling for a leadership convention may be put unless the office is then vacant through death or resignation or unless the chairman of caucus shall certify that the leader has lost the support of that body by a regular vote of caucus on the question of confidence.
>
> When we are in opposition the question shall be put to the first general meeting following an election "Do we wish to have a leadership convention next year?" No such question may be put following any election where the party increased its standing in the House by more than 20 per cent and the leadership office is not presently vacant.
>
> The vote, which shall be taken by ballot or voting machine, shall be announced to the meeting as to result only and not with statistics.[37]

As the matter now rests, the Conservative leadership review provision is a peculiar mixture of both traditional (specifically assigning, unlike the Liberal party constitution, a role to the parliamentary group), and "democratic" elements.

---

[36] Progressive Conservative Association of Canada, tape recording of proceedings of annual general meeting (PC Headquarters, Ottawa, March 10-12, 1969).

[37] Progressive Conservative Association of Canada, *Constitution* (as amended March 1969), article XII. The Macquarrie committee proposal had included an important proviso that was omitted from the amendment finally adopted stipulating that approval for a leadership convention to be called had to come from a majority of the delegates *registered* at the meeting, not simply those voting on the question. Given the Conservatives' penchant for intra-party disputes this is an oversight that should be rectified.

Representation

The biggest single claim made in defence of conventions in Canada is that they are representative bodies. Indeed, it would not be an overstatement to say that conventions *qua* representative gatherings has become one of the clichés of Canadian politics. Politicians and other party activists readily associate conventions with "representativeness" and the association repeated often enough publicly (as it has been) has led to its acceptance by the general public.

Yet there is no clear agreement on what conventions are supposed to be representative of. Undoubtedly the convention is looked upon as being more representative of the various demographic components of the entire population than the parliamentary group — a consideration, as was noted previously, that counted heavily in both 1919 and 1927, when the Liberals and Conservatives switched to leadership conventions. Support for such a claim is easily demonstrated. Table 5-1 makes it clear that conventions are useful in reducing some of the demographic imbalances that obtain in the parliamentary groups of both parties and in making the bodies responsible for selecting the Conservative and Liberal leaders noticeably less biased toward the areas of the parties' electoral strengths. Generally the conventions are more inclusive of the age, sex, occupation and religious categories than the caucuses, but glaring deficiencies nonetheless remain when compared to the total population. However, it is certainly worth noting that the two Canadian conventions of 1967 and 1968 fared considerably better in including young people, and somewhat better in including women than either the Republican or Democratic conventions of 1968 (see Table 5-2).

That both parties in convention embraced more of the Canadian mosaic than did their respective membership in the House of Commons must certainly be regarded as a positive contribution in a country so conscious of its linguistic, religious, cultural and regional differences. But surely convention representation involves something more than simply reducing the demographic imbalances of caucus. Are delegates expected to be representative of the population as a whole? At the time of their first convention in 1927 the Conservatives were told so: "the convention delegation must be thoroughly representative of all divisions of the people. Agriculture, the trades, the professions, business life,

---

Table 5—1: Comparison of Certain Basic Demographic Characteristics of Canadian Population with Liberal and Conservative MPs and Convention Delegates
(%)

	Canadian Population	Progressive Conservative (1967)		Liberal (1968)	
		MPs at time of convention	All convention delegates	MPs at time of convention	All convention delegates
Sex					
Male	50	99	81	98	82
Female	50	1	19	2	18
Age*					
24 and under	49	—	11	—	12
25 – 34	12	1	10	4	18
35 – 44	13	20	20	26	29
45 – 54	10	35	26	37	25
55 – 64	7	28	18	24	12
65 – 74	5	16	11	8	4
75 and over	3	—	4	1	1
Major Religious Affiliations					
Anglican	13	23	26	8	12
Baptist	3	2	3	3	2
Jewish	1	—	3	2	3
Lutheran	4	3	1	—	1
Presbyterian	5	9	—	9	4
Roman Catholic	46	11	24	56	43
United Church	20	44	27	16	24
Selected Occupations					
Managerial	8	14	21	20	16
Lawyer	0.2	24		33	20
Professional other than lawyer	10	22	34	26	14
Clerical	13	4	2	1	2
Sales and Service	19	13	9	15	7
Farmer	10	20	4	2	5

	Canadian Population	Progressive Conservative (1967)		Liberal (1968)	
		MPs at time of convention	All convention delegates	MPs at time of convention	All convention delegates
Provinces					
Nfld.	2	—	3	5	3
P.E.I.	0.5	4	3	—	3
N.S.	4	10	7	2	5
N.B.	3	4	5	5	5
Que.	29	7	22	44	25
Ont.	35	26	32	38	30
Man.	5	10	7	0.7	6
Sask.	5	18	6	—	6
Alta.	7	16	7	—	7
B.C.	9	3	8	5	9
Yukon	0.1	1	0.9	—	0.4
N.W.T.	0.1	—	0.8	0.7	0.5

Sources: Lists of delegates provided by the Progressive Conservative and Liberal parties; the author's mail questionnaire to delegates to the Liberal convention of 1968; H. G. Thorburn, "An Approach to the Study of Federal Political Parties in Canada," paper read to the First Colloque sponsored by the Canadian Political Science Association and la Société Canadienne de Science Politique, Ottawa, November 10, 1968, *passim;* additional information provided by Professor Thorburn, Queen's University; DBS, *1961 Census of Canada,* Occupation and Religion, Series 3.1-3 and 1.2-6, and *1966 Census of Canada,* vol. 1, 92-602, 609, 610; and Table 3 of J. Lele, G. Perlin and H. Thorburn, "Leadership Conventions in Canada: the Form and Substance of Participatory Politics," in D. I. Davies and Kathleen Herman (eds.), *Social Space: Canadian Perspectives* (Toronto: New Press, 1971), p. 208. For the Progressive Conservative Convention delegates, no information was available on the Presbyterian religious category and on the Lawyer Category as distinct from the Other Professional Category.

*The age categories for the Progressive Conservative delegates differ from those listed above. They are: 25 and under; 26–30; 31–40; 41–50; 51–60; 61–70; and 70 and Over.

women's interests, youth and age — all should be there."[38] Or are delegates to be representative of the party rather than the general population? To Senator Power and most other politicians, national conventions have been looked upon as vehicles designed to obtain "the fullest possible representation of party views."[39] But delegates

[38] *Calgary Herald,* editorial, May 25, 1927, p. 12.
[39] Power, p. 371.

who are expected to represent the views of the party, or of particular units of the party, are likely to find that they receive little in the way of direction either from the party membership or the unit itself. Instructions to delegates or pledges from delegates to their constituency associations to support a particular leadership candidate (at least on the first ballot) are virtually unknown in Canadian convention politics, and in any event are of questionable value to the delegating body, given the secrecy of balloting. To allow their delegates greater independence and freedom of choice, constituency associations may even, in the extreme, deliberately *not* discuss the party leadership race at the meeting called to select the constituency delegates to the convention, as was the case with the Lisgar Liberal Association in 1968,[40] or they may instruct their delegates *not* to reveal their leadership choices publicly, as was done by the St. Boniface Liberal Association in 1968.[41] Furthermore, the flow of information to the delegate

Table 5—2: Women and Young Delegates at Recent Canadian and United States Conventions

(%)

Convention	Women Delegates	Delegates Thirty Years of Age and Under
Progressive Conservative 1967	19	19
Liberal 1968	18	25
Democratic 1968	13	4
Republican 1968	17	1

Sources: For the Progressive Conservative and Liberal parties, sex determined from the parties' delegate list. Age information provided by Professor Hugh Thorburn, Queen's University. For the Democratic and Republican parties, the Democratic party's Commission on Party Structure and Delegate Selection, *Mandate for Reform* (Washington: Democratic National Committee, 1970), pp. 26 and 28. Substantial changes within the Democratic party were slated for the 1972 convention when specific "minority" groups (women and blacks, in particular) were to be guaranteed a fairer share of each state's total delegation than had been the case in the past.

[40] *Winnipeg Free Press*, February 12, 1968, p. 4.
[41] *Ibid.*, February 19, 1968, p. 3.

tends to be more from the direction of the candidates and the media than from the general population or the party membership. Such attitudes and practices substantially determine the nature of representation in Canadian conventions and their net impact, not surprisingly, is to leave the delegates very much on their own. The delegates may choose to wait, and some of them do, until the last few days before the leadership voting, when they have had an opportunity to hear all the candidates speak, before they decide whom to support. According to two newspaper polls, one week before the Progressive Conservative convention of 1967 30 per cent of the delegates had not decided for whom they would vote, and within two days of the 1968 Liberal convention 11 per cent of the delegates had still not decided for whom they would vote.[42]

Table 5—3: Categories of Delegates: Liberal Conventions, 1919-1968

Category	Year			
	1919	1948	1958	1968
Constituency Delegates (Number per Constituency)	3	3	3	6
Ex-Officio Delegates				
Privy Councillors			x	x
Senators	x	x	x	x
Members of Parliament	x	x	x	x
Candidates defeated at last election	x	x	x	x
Candidates nominated for next election		x		x
Provincial Legislature Members + Candidates[1]	x	x	x	x
Provincial Party Leaders	x	x	x	x
Provincial Association Presidents	x			
National Executive Officers[2]		x	x	x
Provincial Executive Officers[3]		x	x	x
University Liberal Delegates[4]		x	x	x

[1] The number equivalent to 1/4 the size of the provincial legislature.
[2] National executives of the Liberal Federation of Canada, Women's Liberal Federation, Young Liberals, and as of 1958, Canadian University Liberal Associations.
[3] Provincial Liberal executive, Women's, Young Liberals and University Club executives. As of 1948 the Provincial Association Presidents are included in this category.
[4] In 1968 Regional Associations were included.

Sources: Official Convention Calls for each of the four conventions.

Are the delegates "representatives" then? In the sense of acting as instructed agents of the delegating body, or as elected officials who will subsequently be held directly accountable to the group responsible for their election, they clearly are not. But in the best Burkean sense, with its heavy emphasis on individual judgment, on representation of interests, and on rational deliberation, they are. Thus, by virtue of the transaction of being given the *authority* to act, Canadian convention delegates are considered "representatives," even though such use of the term "can tell us [nothing] about what goes on *during* representation, how a representative ought to act or what he is expected to do, how to tell whether he has represented well or badly."[43]

But who, in fact, are the delegates? To begin with, the Liberal and Progressive Conservative parties differ to some extent in their estimation of acceptable delegate categories. Both have, of course, always had delegates from each federal riding, the Liberals having varied the number from three to six per constituency, and the Progressive Conservatives from three to five per constituency (see Tables 5-3 and 5-4). Privy councillors, members of parliament, senators, provincial party leaders and various national party executive officers have, in both parties, been automatically granted delegate status *ex officio,* and Liberal and Conservative university political clubs have consistently been entitled to select delegates since 1948. But there the similarities end.

---

[42] *Gazette* (Montreal), September 2, 1967, pp. 1 and 25, and *Telegram* (Toronto), April 5, 1968, p. 1.
[43] Hanna Fenichel Pitkin, *The Concept of Representation* (Berkeley: University of California Press, 1967), p. 58. (Italics in original.) In her excellent study of representation Dr. Pitkin also makes the point that "the basic features of the authorization view are these: a representative is someone who has been authorized to act. This means that he has been given a right to act which he did not have before, while the represented has become responsible for the consequences of that action as if he had done it himself. It is a view strongly skewed in favor of the representative. His rights have been enlarged and his responsibilities have been (if anything) decreased. The represented, in contrast, has acquired new responsibilities and (if anything) given up some of his rights. The authorization view concentrates on the formalities of this relationship; it is what I shall call a 'formalistic' view. It defines representing in terms of a transaction that takes place at the outset, before the actual representing begins. To the extent that he has been authorized, within the limits of his authority, anything that a man does is representing" (pp. 38-39).

Table 5—4: Categories of Delegates: Conservative Conventions, 1927-1967

Category	Year					
	1927	1938	1942	1948	1956	1967
Constituency Delegates (Number per Constituency)	4	4	3	3	3	5
Ex-Officio Delegates						
Former Lieutenant-Governors	x	x				
Privy Councillors	x	x	x	x	x	x
Senators	x	x	x	x	x	x
Members of Parliament	x	x	x	x	x	x
Candidates defeated at last election	x	x				
Candidates nominated for next election						x
Members of Provincial Legislatures	x	x	x	x	x	x
Provincial Party Leaders	x	x	x	x	x	x
Provincial Ex-Cabinet Ministers	x	x				
Newspaper Representatives and others	x	x				
Convention Committee + Chairmen Sub-Committees	x		x			
Executive officers + Chairmen Sub-Committee	x			x	x	x
Delegates-at-Large						
Provincial	x	x	x	x	x	x
Dominion	x	x	x			
Special			x			
University Delegates	x			x	x	x

Sources: Ruth M. Bell, "Conservative Party National Conventions, 1927-1956: Organization and Procedure" (unpublished M. A. thesis, Department of Political Science, Carleton University, 1965), Table IV, and *Report of the Executive Committee of the Executive Officers of the Progressive Conservative Association of Canada Being the Convention Committee of the Progressive Conservative Centennial Convention to the Convention* (presented to the Progressive Conservative Convention, Toronto, September 7, 1967).

The Liberals have traditionally recognized the right of provincial party officers to delegate status. This category has included since 1919 provincial association presidents and, since 1948, two, three or four executive officers of the provincial association, the provincial Women's Association, the provincial Young Liberals' organization, and University Clubs. The emphasis has been clearly placed on the federated nature of the Liberal Party of Canada, whose members are not individuals (as is the case with the Progressive Conservative party) but the ten provincial and two territorial associations. Despite the emphasis on the provincial units, however, Liberal members of provincial legislative assemblies have not automatically been named delegates. From their first convention in 1919, Liberal candidates (whether elected or not) in the last provincial election have been empowered to choose as delegates from their midst a number equal to 25 per cent of the size of the provincial legislature. A strong provincial party is likely to find itself in a no more favoured position than a weak provincial party, for, given such a provision, the only possible differences among the provinces can stem from the number of candidates nominated in the preceding provincial election and the number of seats in the legislature. The Liberal parties in Saskatchewan and Alberta illustrate this point well. At the time of the 1968 convention, the Liberals were in office in Saskatchewan, having won almost 60 per cent of the fifty-nine legislative seats in the provincial election the preceding year. According to the party regulations they were entitled to send fifteen delegates. The Alberta Liberals, who had not won office since 1917, had been successful in taking only three of the forty-five seats they contested in 1967. Yet they were entitled to one more delegate than the Saskatchewan provincial caucus because of the slightly larger size of the Alberta legislature.

The Conservatives, reflecting the non-federated nature of the party itself, have granted delegate status to no provincial party officers outside of the provincial leader.[44] They have, however, en-

---

[44] The Conservative National Executive includes as *ex officio* members all provincial presidents of the general, women's, YPC's and student associations and they, naturally, have been given delegate status; but the Conservatives have never gone so far as the Liberals in allowing their provincial bodies to name delegates as representatives of those bodies.

titled all members of provincial legislatures who support the Progressive Conservative party of Canada to become delegates. This is an interesting provision, for it naturally has the effect of rewarding those organizations in provinces in which the Progressive Conservatives are strong in provincial elections, and in principle is similar to the system of "bonus" votes used by both the Republicans and Democrats in United States' conventions.[45] The Liberal party has no such category. Indeed, had the Liberal provision applied to the Conservatives in 1967 Duff Roblin and Martin Pederson would, as Manitoba and Saskatchewan party leaders respectively, have each led a fifteen-man provincial delegation. As it was, Roblin had a provincial caucus of thirty-one MLAs accompanying him, and Pederson none.

Delegates-at-large have been named to every Conservative convention. There has been no such category of delegates in the Liberal conventions, although certainly in 1919 some pressure was exerted on convention officials to make it possible to have "at-large" delegates appointed. The Montreal MP, S. W. Jacobs, wrote to the convention organizer, Charles Murphy, shortly before the August convention:

> I have been asked to write you to see whether it is possible for the Convention Committee to arrange for the selection of a restricted number of delegates at large, say two from each Province. This you will see, would not in any way affect the numerical supremacy of any of the Provinces.
>
> My reason for making the suggestion, is that we have a number of sterling men who have not been selected at the various conventions, and whose inclusion in the general Convention is highly desirable. For instance, the President of the Montreal Reform Club, one of the best men in the Province of Quebec, finds that he is not named, and I am sure the same obtains in other parts of the country.
>
> You will remember that on our National Liberal Advisory Committee, the late Sir Wilfrid had the right to name delegates at large, and in that way men of the stamp I referred to were included.[46]

---

[45] On apportionment and the voting structure, including bonus votes, see David, Goldman and Bain, *The Politics of National Party Conventions*, chap. 7.

[46] PAC, *Jacobs Papers*, vol. 2, Jacobs to Hon. Charles Murphy, July 15, 1919.

The reason cited by Mr. Jacobs is, of course, the classic defence of delegates-at-large: people prominent in party affairs not otherwise selected or eligible to attend the convention should be taken care of. In addition, noticeable deficiencies in representation from certain important groups in society might also be corrected through the appointment of such delegates. The chairman of the 1927 Conservative convention was informed by the secretary *pro tem* that:

> Generally, from the correspondence and questionnaires received, it would seem advisable that there should be an increase in the delegates-at-large, with a view to taking care of women, labour representatives and big men of the party. From information at hand, unless some special provision is made, there will be very few women at the convention.[47]

Some criticism has come from the press of the Conservative party's use of such a delegate category, and from members of the party against the way in which it has been used. A controversy raged within the Conservative party shortly before the 1967 convention over two matters both relating to appointment of delegates-at-large. The chairman of the 1967 convention executive committee, E. A. Goodman, informed the participants at the Montmorency Policy Conference that they would all be eligible for appointment as voting delegates to the party convention one month later.[48] As many of the participants at the policy conference were invited from outside the ranks of the party, and as a few were known supporters of other parties, there was, not unexpectedly, some hostility over the use to which the convention executive committee had put its power. Although the number of Montmorency participants eligible to attend the September convention as delegates was reduced to sixty-eight from eighty-four, the party's national director (James Johnston) disagreed at the time with the whole practice:

> I . . . disapproved of a convention committee's assuming the right not only to set the rules of the game but then to try to play in the game itself. I also disapproved of the "estab-

[47] PAC, *Bennett Papers,* pp. 4130-31, July 2, 1927.
[48] Address by E. A. Goodman at the opening of the Montmorency Conference, August 7, 1967, p. 4.

lishment" of the party having this power to perpetuate itself and to thwart the will of the constituency delegates. But what I really wanted to stop was the open-ended nature of appointments. I was afraid that the numbers could run to 130 or 150 with virtually no control. I also disputed the whole idea that people who had never supported the party before could suddenly be given delegate status — something which was being hard fought for in constituency after constituency across Canada. "Why not ask David Lewis or Tommy Douglas to appoint our delegates?" I challenged at one point.[49]

Other objections were raised at the same time by one of four members of the Ontario committee charged with the responsibility of naming the province's ninety delegates-at-large. Miss Laura Mann resigned from the committee claiming that its choices tended to favour one or two of the leadership candidates and maintaining that it was "not the least bit democratic to have four people choose ninety delegates."[50]

Any system which sanctions the appointment by a few people of up to 25 per cent of the delegates (see Appendix F, p. 252) appears in the eyes of the public to be running counter to the democratic ethos. It presents itself as a natural target for charges of "elitism" and "anti-democratic actions" even though the party operates under the impression that it is correcting a number of representational imbalances and is no less democratic for it. However, attempts by the Progressive Conservative party's constitution committee under the chairmanship of Heath Macquarrie to abolish the category failed when the committee's report came before the annual meeting of the party in 1969. Influential party organizers, such as E. A. Goodman and Elmer Bell, argued effectively against the removal of the delegate-at-large category (citing the traditional reasons) and succeeded in getting approval for the following amendment to the party constitution:

> Delegates appointed by the recognized Progressive Conservative Association of each province equal in number to one half of the number of federal electoral districts in the provinces; provided that there shall not be less than five such

[49] Johnston, p. 221.
[50] *Globe and Mail*, August 29, 1967, p. 2.

delegates for each province and provided that at least twenty per cent of such delegates from each province must be members of the Young Progressive Conservative Association or Progressive Conservative Student Federation and provided that at least twenty per cent of such delegates from each province must be women. Where a fraction occurs the next highest number shall apply.[51]

If future controversies such as those of 1967 continue in the Conservative party (and the new constitutional provision by no means eliminates that possibility) it will likely be only a matter of time before the Progressive Conservatives will have to abandon the delegate-at-large category so as to avoid being branded as "undemocratic."

The fact that the Liberals have never had delegates-at-large and that the Conservatives have never been without them presents a rather marked contrast between two parties that so often are described as simply mirror images of one another. What the Conservatives want to achieve by way of appointment of such delegates must either (a) be regarded as unimportant by the Liberals and therefore needs not be taken into account in delegate representation, or (b) is compensated for by the Liberals in some way other than by appointments at the discretion of one individual or a small group. One suspects the latter. And surely there is rather significant compensation in the Liberals' *ex officio* delegate status granted (as in 1968, for example) to four members of the executive of each provincial association; the president and two other officers of each of the ten provincial organizations of Liberal Women and of the ten provincial organizations of Young Liberals; as well as two representatives of each of the University Liberal Clubs and of the four regional organizations of the Canadian University Liberal Federation. The feeling the Conservatives experience of needing to have available a mechanism whereby party notables might be appointed as delegates is understandably less pronounced in the Liberal party, for at least some of the very sort of people who would almost assuredly be appointed as delegates-

---

[51] Progressive Conservative Association of Canada, *Constitution* (as amended March 1969), article III (j).

at-large in the Conservative party attend the Liberal conventions as *ex officio* delegates.[52]

Between 52 and 64 per cent of the total number of Liberal delegates since 1919 have been constituency delegates. The range for the Conservatives since their first convention has been between 54 and 61 per cent for the same category (see Tables 5-5 and 5-6). Through to 1958 the percentage of constituency delegates was diminishing at successive Liberal conventions as a result of

Table 5—5: Delegate Allotment by Category: Liberal Conventions, 1919-1968

Category	Year			
	1919	1948	1958	1968
Potential Number of Delegates	1135	1302	1534	2472
Constituency Delegates (%)	62	56	52	64
Ex-Officio Delegates (%) (including University Delegates)	38	44	49	36

Sources: *Proceedings* for each of the Liberal Conventions in 1919, 1948 and 1958, as well as list of potential delegate registration provided by the Liberal party headquarters for the 1968 convention.

Table 5—6: Delegate Allotment by Category: Conservative Conventions, 1927-1967

Category	Year					
	1927	1938	1942	1948	1956	1967
Potential Number of Delegates	1620	1764	1258	1312	1472	2411
Constituency Delegates (%)	61	56	58	58	54	55
Ex-Officio Delegates (%)	23	25	17	18	20	22
Delegates-at-Large (%) (including University Delegates)	16	19	25	24	26	23

Sources: Bell, *op. cit.*, Table V, and list of potential delegate registration provided by the Progressive Conservative party headquarters for the 1967 convention.

[52] Since the 1968 convention the Liberal constitution has been amended so as to reduce the number of provincial *ex officio* officers eligible to attend the convention as delegates.

the steady growth in the number of *ex officio* delegates and in spite of the increase in the number of constituencies over that period from 235 to 265. No such clearly discernible pattern developed in the Conservative party. In fact, the Conservative constituency delegates have never regained the relative position they occupied in 1927, something due initially to a reduction in the number of delegates per constituency as part of an intra-party austerity move in both 1938 and 1942, then to a healthy increase in the delegates-at-large category beginning in 1942. It is certain that in both parties, had there not been an increase in the number of constituency delegates in 1967 and 1968, (Tables 5-3 and 5-4), the *ex officio* and at-large delegates (the so-called "party brass") would have been in a clear majority. Because of the nature of their federal and provincial legislative delegate representation, the numbers in the Conservatives' *ex officio* category depend very much upon the timing of the convention. "For example," it has been noted, "in 1935 the [Conservative] Party had 40 seats in the House of Commons, and did not control a single provincial government. In 1960 they had over 200 federal seats and con-

Table 5—7: Comparison of Total Potential Delegate Registration at Progressive Conservative Convention (1967) and Liberal Convention (1968)

	Progressive Conservative		Liberal	
	N	%	N	%
Constituency Delegates	1320	54.8	1584	64.0
Ex-Officio Delegates*	428	17.8	620	25.1
Delegates-at-Large	452	18.7	—	—
University Student Delegates	116	4.8	138	5.6
Members of Parliament	95	3.9	130	5.3
Total	2411	100.0	2472	100.0

*Excluding MPs but including 68 Montmorency Policy Conference Delegates.

Sources: Lists of categories of delegates prepared by the headquarters of the two parties.

trolled four provinces. If conventions had been called at these times, the numbers of Ex-Officio delegates would have differed considerably."[53] Thus, although it is a feature more pronounced in the Conservative than the Liberal party, the relative strength or weakness of the parties both nationally and provincially at the time of the convention has a direct bearing on the number of privy councillors, senators, members of parliament, and members of provincial legislatures, and indirectly affects the proportionate voting strength of constituency delegates. For the 1967 and 1968 conventions specifically, Tables 5-7, 5-8, and 5-9 compare the parties' total potential delegate registration by category and by province and reinforce many of the forementioned points regarding the nature of convention representation in the Liberal and Conservative parties.

As might be expected, and as Table 5-1 has already suggested, convention delegates are not a true cross-section of Canadian society. Table 5-1 indicates that in 1967 and 1968 better than four out of five delegates were men, that over half were between thirty-five and fifty-four years of age, and that managerial and professional occupations (and within this last group, the lawyers in particular) predominated in both the Liberal and Conservative conventions. The one respect in which the parties differed most from one another was in that of religious denominations. Anglicans were more than twice as numerous in the Conservative convention as in the Liberal, with the Roman Catholics in substantially greater numbers at the Liberal convention. Other than that, in the remaining religious categories and in terms of age, sex and occupations, the two parties had virtually identical types of delegates.

What else is known of delegates at recent Canadian conventions? Table 5-10 presents some useful data gathered from two different sets of mail questionnaires of delegates attending the recent conventions. Not only were the parties' delegates amazingly similar in the characteristics presented in Table 5-10; they were also noticeably atypical of Canadian society. Over 40 per cent of the delegates had at least one university degree and over two-

---

[53] Bell, "Conservative Party National Conventions, 1927-1956," p. 100.

Table 5—8: Total Potential Delegate Registration —

Ex Officio

National

Province	Constituency Delegates	Privy Council	Senators	M.P.s	New Candidates	Executive Officers*	Women's Executive*
British Columbia	115	4	—	3	—	7	2
Alberta	95	—	1	14	—	7	—
Saskatchewan	65	—	2	17	—	7	—
Manitoba	65	—	4	10	—	8	—
Ontario	440	14	9	25	4	11	2
Quebec	370	6	5	7	1	8	—
New Brunswick	50	—	2	4	—	6	—
Nova Scotia	55	—	4	10	—	9	—
Newfoundland	35	1	1	—	—	8	—
P.E.I.	20	—	2	4	—	8	—
Yukon	5	—	—	1	—	5	—
N.W.T.	5	—	—	—	—	4	1
Totals	1320	25	30	95	5	88	5

*Excluding those persons included in other Ex Officio Delegate categories.
**Not all Montmorency Policy Conference participants accepted delegate status to the September convention. No provincial breakdown is available.
†Total actual registration was 2205.

Progressive Conservative Convention — September 5-9, 1967

Delegates			Provincial	Provincial Delegates-At-Large			University Clubs		
Y.P.C. Executive *	*P.C.S.F. Executive* *	*Montmorency Policy Conference Delegates* **	*M.L.A.s*	*General*	*Women's Association*	*Y.P.C.*	*P.C.S.F. Delegates*	*Total*	*%*
–	–		–	30	3	3	8	175	7.5
1	–		6	25	3	3	4	159	6.8
–	1		1	25	3	3	4	128	5.5
–	–		31	25	3	3	8	157	6.7
2	2		77	90	9	9	44	738	31.5
2	3		–	90	9	9	14	524	22.4
1	–		20	20	3	3	10	119	5.1
1	1		40	20	3	3	18	164	6.9
–	–		3	15	3	3	2	71	3.0
–	–		15	10	3	3	4	69	2.9
–	–		–	3	3	3	–	20	0.9
–	–		–	3	3	3	–	19	0.8
7	7	68	193	356	48	48	116	2343†	100.0

Table 5—9: Total Potential Delegate Registration

Ex Officio

National

Province	Constituency Delegates	Privy Council	Senators*	M.P.s	1965 Defeated Candidates**	L.F.C. Executive	W.L.F.C. Executive	Y.L.F.C. Executive	C.U.L.F. Executive
British Columbia	138	2	6	7	15	1	3	1	2
Alberta	114	1	5	1	16	1	4	1	—
Saskatchewan	78	—	3	—	17	1	3	1	—
Manitoba	78	2	2	1	12	1	3	2	3
Ontario	528	3	15	50	33	2	8	3	3
Quebec	444	8	20	55	18	2	6	—	3
New Brunswick	60	1	6	6	4	1	4	2	2
Nova Scotia	66	—	5	2	9	1	4	1	—
Newfoundland	42	—	4	7	—	—	3	1	—
P.E.I.	24	—	2	—	3	1	4	1	—
Yukon	6	—	—	—	1	—	—	—	—
N.W.T.	6	—	—	1	—	1	—	—	—
Totals	1584	17	68	130	128	12	42	13	13

*Includes eight retired Senators.
**Includes three newly nominated candidates: two in B.C.; one in Sask.
†Total actual registration was 2442.

— *Liberal Convention* — *April 4-6, 1968*

Delegates   *University Clubs*

Standing Committees Co-chairmen	Affiliated Federation Reps. on Standing Committees	Legislative Assembly Delegates	Prov. Leaders	Prov. Senior Executive	Prov. Young Liberal Executive	Prov. Reps. on Standing Committees	Prov. Women's Executive	University Liberal Clubs	University Regional Assoc.	Total	%
—	2	14	1	4	2	5	2	12	2	219	8.9
—	2	16	1	4	2	5	2	6	—	181	7.3
—	—	15	1	4	2	5	2	4	—	136	5.5
—	2	14	1	4	2	5	2	12	2	148	6.0
2	3	29	1	4	2	5	2	36	2	731	29.6
5	3	27	1	4	—	5	2	22	2	627	25.4
—	2	15	1	4	2	3	2	14	—	129	5.2
1	—	12	1	4	2	5	2	16	1	132	5.3
—	—	11	1	4	2	5	2	2	—	84	3.4
—	—	8	1	4	2	5	2	4	1	62	2.5
—	—	—	—	4	—	—	—	—	—	11	0.4
—	—	—	—	4	—	—	—	—	—	12	0.5
8	14	161	10	48	18	48	20	128	10	2472†	100.0

thirds were from families with total incomes in excess of $10,000. In fact the total family income for one out of every four delegates was $20,000 or more. These figures stood in sharp contrast

Table 5–10: Social, Economic and Political Variables of Progressive Conservative and Liberal Delegates at 1967 and 1968 Conventions
(%)

	Progressive Conservative (1967)	Liberal (1968)
Education		
Elementary	5	5
Secondary	31	29
University started	10	14
University degree	33	37
Postgraduate degree	10	7
Post Secondary/Non-university	9	7
Total Family Income		
$4,999 or less	7	7
$5,000 – 9,999	22	23
$10,000 – 14,999	22	26
$15,000 – 19,999	17	16
$20,000 and over	27	25
Organizational Membership		
Charitable	31	27
Service Club	26	27
Fraternal	31	20
Business or Professional	51	48
Other Occupational	14	18
Civic	21	24
Sport and Social	41	40
Religious	17	18
Years of Party Membership		
less than one year	1	2
1 – 3 years	5	9
3 – 5 years	5	9
5 – 10 years	10	14
10 – 15 years	16	9
over 15 years	58	55
Candidate at Any Time[1]		
Federal		14
Provincial		16
Municipal		22
Party Officer at Any Time[1]		
University		16
Constituency		68
Provincial		37
National		15
Young Liberal		20

Delegate at Previous Convention[1]

1958	16
1948	5
1919	0.2

[1] Information unavailable for the Progressive Conservative Convention.

Sources: Thorburn, "An Approach to the Study of Federal Political Parties in Canada"; additional information provided by Professor Thorburn; and the author's mail questionnaire to delegates to the Liberal convention of 1968. For education through years of party membership categories Progressive Conservative N = 895 and Liberal N = 920. For remaining three categories Liberal N = 1335. For comparative purposes see also C. R. Santos, "Some Collective Characteristics of the Delegates to the 1968 Liberal Party Leadership Convention," *CJPS*, III (June 1970), 229-308.

to the Canadian population as a whole; at the time of the 1961 census only slightly better than 3 per cent of those twenty years of age and over had university degrees and the mean family income was $5,449.[54] Liberal and Conservative delegates were typically active (many serving as elected officers) in various local and national voluntary organizations, a characteristic noted as well among delegates to the Liberal party convention of 1958.[55] The majority of delegates claimed party membership of not less than fifteen years, and within the Liberal party at least (but there is no reason to believe it would have been different in the Conservative party), two-thirds had held an elected office within the party at the constituency level. Some, naturally, had run for federal and provincial office, but even more had stood for election to a municipal body. Sixteen per cent of the Liberal delegates had attended the 1958 convention and 5 per cent had been delegates at the convention ten years prior to that. In fact there were even some (3 of 1,335 respondents) who had been present at the Liberals' first leadership convention in 1919.

The picture of the typical Liberal or Conservative convention delegate in 1967 or 1968 (and, it is fair to assume, at earlier conventions as well) is not difficult to describe. He is well above-

[54] Dominion Bureau of Statistics, *1961 Census of Canada,* "School Attendance and Schooling," Bulletin 1.2-10, and "Family Incomes by Size, Type and Composition of Family," Bulletin 4.1-3. For more on the socioeconomic characteristics of the convention delegates of 1967 and 1968, see J. Lele, G. Perlin and H. Thorburn, "Leadership Conventions in Canada: The Forms and Substance of Participatory Politics," in D. I. Davies and Kathleen Herman (eds.), *Social Space: Canadian Perspectives* (Toronto: New Press, 1971), pp. 205-11.

[55] See Paul T. Larocque, "Leadership Selection in the Liberal Party," (unpublished B.A. thesis, Department of Political Science, Carleton University, 1968), pp. 57-68.

average in both income and education. The chances of his being a middle-aged manager, or a lawyer (or some other professional), are extremely good, but the chances of his being employed in a clerical position, or as a labourer, or a skilled worker are very slight. He is an activist in community affairs in general and, in common with a small percentage of the total population, in political affairs in particular. He is in fact a party devotee. And this, more than anything else, distinguishes him from the general population. There are, after all, thousands of above-average income managers and professionals (and even some lawyers) who never become actively involved in politics. But those who do, those who choose to work assiduously for a party and who, in so doing, establish something of a reputation in local political circles as a leader, or an organizer, or a fund-raiser, or a campaigner, are turned to as the obvious choices of the selecting body. Furthermore, the relatively greater occupational freedom and financial independence of such people heightens their chances of being chosen, for delegates are expected to travel some distance to attend a convention lasting several days. In short, local party notables are clearly favoured as constituency delegates.

The Value of the Norm

Every political system needs some sustaining myths. Over time, considerable importance may be assumed by such myths if the political institutions they support fulfill at least minimal societal requirements. They may assume, in the form of beliefs, or norms, or symbols, a perhaps immeasurable value to the society and thereby make a substantial contribution as stabilizing and satisfying forces, and they may do so even if they diverge from the actual practice. After all, a norm

> which is violated wholesale . . . still can be an important ingredient in the functioning of the political system. Should that norm wither or vanish, it would be much easier for unscrupulous elites to seize power and tyrannize ordinary citizens. Elites believing in that norm are more likely to welcome new recruits, are more likely to relinquish office easily

when defeated in an election, are more likely to try to inform
and educate their followers, are more likely to keep communication channels open and listen to the desires of the
people, than are elites not believing in that norm. Perhaps
one of the reasons the norm remains viable is that elites
realize a decline of the norm could spell their own doom
as they compete for the power to govern.[56]

The fact that actual practice may miss the mark, then, is of little
import so long as that practice remains within the loosely defined
bounds of acceptability, and so long as there are recognized and
accepted customs built into the social system to compensate for the
divergence between theory and practice.

Canadian party conventions and the myths surrounding them
should be understood that way. References to "open" political
conventions, or to widespread "participation" by the delegates and
delegate "control" over the parties' affairs through the convention
mechanism, or to conventions as "democratic and representative
gatherings," surely stand as evidence of the acceptance of, indeed
the vicarious satisfaction with, such rhetoric by both the general
population and the politically committed, even though the terms
themselves fail to describe either fully or precisely the political
reality of the convention system itself. Canada's partaking of the
populist tradition has been sufficient to enable ready deployment
of much of the vocabulary of progress and reform, and the terms
have in this instance become ideal tools for justifying the existence
of and generating the needed respect for party conventions.

It is neither obvious nor certain that conventions are necessarily
more democratic than the informal processes used by Canadian
parties prior to their adoption. Parliamentarians are professional
politicians and are abundantly aware of the likely consequences of
their political acts. Only an impolitic legislator would consciously
ignore opinions and advice expressed to him by interested members of the public and by party supporters on the matter of party
leadership. If soundings, or informal consultations, or caucus deliberations and votes were currently the order of the day in
choosing the leader of the party, then the Canadian legislator

[56] Lester W. Milbrath, *Political Participation* (Chicago: Rand McNally and
Company, 1965), pp. 152-53.

would, like his nineteenth and early twentieth century predecessors, and like his British contemporaries, accept as one of his tasks that of participating in the work of the parliamentary group in choosing a new leader for that body. He would look upon that task as part of his job as an elected representative and he would seek advice from extra-parliamentary sources to guide him in reaching his decision. After all, he might argue, he had been chosen to sit in parliament by way of a democratic, public election — an election far more open and with much greater and more widespread participation than any party convention could hope for. He would regard himself as a representative not in any narrow sense — not simply of those who had voted for him, or of his constituency, or of some particular group or interest. He and his fellow MPs would know that their parties could justify their claims of being truly "national" only by taking into account the great variety of interests in the Canadian polity in choosing their leader. Furthermore he would be faced with the ultimate test of which convention delegates know little: accountability or answerability to the electorate for the decision made.

For his part the leader chosen in convention may find that he enjoys more power over his parliamentary colleagues than would otherwise be the case because of the widespread acceptance of the idea of conventions as democratic and representative bodies. Mackenzie King was known to have

> placed great stock in the fact that he was selected by a democratic convention and not by the parliamentary caucus. On those rare occasions when the parliamentary caucus [had] begun to growl . . . he . . . more than once silenced the parliamentary wolves by emphasizing that he [was] the representative and leader of the party as a whole, not merely of the parliamentary group. What the parliamentary group did not create it may not destroy, at least not without ratification by the "grass roots." The leader may appeal beyond the caucus to the party membership.[57]

Or the leader may find that he and his parliamentary colleagues

---

[57] John W. Lederle, "The Liberal Convention of 1919 and the Selection of Mackenzie King," *Dalhousie Review*, XXVII (April 1947), 86. Lederle's appraisal was confirmed by the Hon. J. W. Pickersgill in an interview with the author, June 3, 1969.

are virtually powerless in the face of a determined extra-parliamentary association. It now seems that John Diefenbaker in 1967 felt he had no choice but to allow his name to stand once again in nomination for the party leadership, given what he felt to be the absence of an honourable course of withdrawal prior to the convention. To Diefenbaker:

> Only a party convention had the right to undo what a similar convention had done eleven years earlier. If Diefenbaker were to be thrown out as leader, he would be thrown out by a party convention, and the entire party would be responsible for it. . . .
>
> . . . Diefenbaker had never questioned the legal power of the convention, but he had questioned the legality and the logic of a political party's allowing its president to attack its leader, and allowing its non-elective wing, the party association, to overpower its elected wing, the Members of Parliament, who had received their authority from the Canadian electorate.[58]

As a final comment it is worth noting that many Progressive Conservative members of parliament felt that Robert Stanfield's position as Diefenbaker's successor and as the new leader of what had been a few months earlier a "pro-Diefenbaker caucus" was clearly strengthened, indeed legitimized, by virtue of Stanfield's selection by the party in convention. The convention, in other words, had created a climate of opinion within the party favourable to Stanfield's acceptance by the parliamentary group. Why? Because, the MPs argued, the decision was made in a democratic way by a body they thought was representative of the party's views.[59]

[58] Johnston, p. 238.
[59] In November 1966, following the decision of the Progressive Conservative Association's annual meeting to call a leadership convention before the end of 1967, seventy-one of the party's ninety-five MPs signed a "Declaration of Loyalty" supporting Mr. Diefenbaker and asking him to continue as leader of the party. For a copy of the declaration listing the names of those who supported and those who did not support Mr. Diefenbaker's leadership, see Robert C. Coates, *The Night of the Knives* (Fredericton: Brunswick Press, 1969), pp. 200-203. For the Diefenbaker loyalists in the caucus the declaration brought the issue between caucus and the party association to a head and led to a caucus purge of anti-Diefenbaker MPs from the party's 140-member national executive. See *Globe and Mail*, December 1, 1966, p. 10. The argument regarding Stanfield's strengthened position was presented to the author by several PC members of parliament during interviews in May and June, 1969.

6

Who Is Chosen, and Why?

Demographic Characteristics

Many a minor party politician in Canada has won nodding approval from his audience by painting, with colourful imagery, a word-picture of the Liberal and Conservative parties as mirror-images of one another. The parties are characterized as identical twins — as Tweedledum and Tweedledee — as having policies, candidates, leaders, interests, and support bases so similar that they are virtually indiscernible one from the other. T. C. Douglas was probably not the first and most certainly will not be the last Canadian politician to have quipped that "the only difference between the Conservatives and Liberals is that when one party is in office, the other is not." Certainly in so far as the two groups' ideologies and their attitudes toward major issues of public policy, authority, democracy and the exercise of political power are concerned, such a characterization may well be an accurate one. Yet, at least with respect to demographic attributes of the parties' leaders, it is, in fact, misleading. Some rather marked differences do exist between the two parties in this area.

130

Table 6—1: Demographic Characteristics of Conservative Leaders Chosen Prior to Leadership Conventions *

Name	Age	Religion	Occupation	Province
John A. Macdonald	52	Presbyterian	Barrister	Ontario
J. J. C. Abbott	70	Anglican	Barrister	Quebec
John S. D. Thompson	48	Roman Catholic	Barrister	Nova Scotia
Mackenzie Bowell	70	Methodist	Journalist	Ontario
Charles Tupper	74	Anglican	Physician	Nova Scotia
Robert L. Borden	46	Anglican	Barrister	Nova Scotia
Arthur Meighen	46	Presbyterian	Barrister	Manitoba

*Naturally the demographic variables referred to in Tables 6—1 to 6—6 are only some of the personal characteristics of leaders that could be compared. Unfortunately, reliable information on such particulars as father's occupation, rural, small-town or urban background, and ethnic ancestry on both sides of the family, could not always be obtained for all candidates. Therefore those characteristics, important as they would be to a full comparison of the demographic variables of party leaders, have been omitted of necessity.

The Conservatives have shown a greater tendency to select lawyers as leaders and to have lawyers as leadership candidates than have the Liberals. Three out of every five Conservative leadership candidates and nearly seven out of every ten Conservative leaders have been lawyers, whereas the same has been true with less than three-fifths of the Liberal leaders (see Tables 6-1 to 6-5).[1]

[1] Arthur Meighen's selection as Conservative leader in 1941 is not included in the statistics and tables of this chapter (with the exception of Table 6-8), as it quite clearly represented an exception to the then general practice within the Conservative party of choosing a leader by leadership convention. It was recognized at the time as being exceptional and was carried out under unusual circumstances. Although Meighen might well have been selected by a party convention had a convention been held, he was in fact named leader by a meeting of the Dominion Conservative Association executive, MPs, privy councillors, and defeated parliamentary candidates from the 1940 election, a body heavily weighted in favour of the parliamentary party. Meighen was the only leader of either the Liberal or Conservative parties to have been selected from 1921 on by a means other than a party convention. Within thirteen months of his 1941 selection, Meighen stepped down as leader of the party. On Meighen's selection see Graham, *Meighen*, III, 84-107, and J. L. Granatstein, *The Politics of Survival: The Conservative Party of Canada, 1939-1945* (Toronto: University of Toronto Press, 1967), pp. 82-94.

Table 6–2: Demographic Characteristics of
Liberal Leaders Chosen Prior to Leadership Conventions

Name	Age	Religion	Occupation	Province
Alexander Mackenzie	51	Baptist	Journalist	Ontario
Edward Blake	46	Anglican	Barrister	Ontario
Wilfrid Laurier	45	Roman Catholic	Barrister	Quebec

Statistically significant differences exist between the two parties in terms of the age of leaders at the time they were chosen, the religious affiliations of those who sought the leadership, and the home provinces of both the leaders and leadership candidates (see Table 6-6). The spread between the average Liberal and average Conservative leader's age at the time of election was six years, with the average Conservative leader the older at 57.4 years of age (see Table 6-7). Yet the averages obscure the fact that each of the Conservative leaders chosen in convention has closely approximated the party's mean leadership age, whereas of all the Liberal leaders chosen since 1867 only one has been in his fifties, the rest being either in their forties or in their sixties when they were selected. The same data show that the high variability in ages of Conservative as opposed to Liberal leaders in the pre-convention period (standard deviation of 11.76 as opposed to 2.62 years) has been reversed in the convention period with the Liberals showing much greater variance than the Conservatives (standard deviations of 8.87 and 2.75 years respectively). Since leadership conventions have been used, the mean ages of Conservative and Liberal leaders have moved closer together, and although the average age of Liberal leaders has been less than that of that parties' convention candidates, the reverse has been true within the Conservative party (see Table 6-7).[2]

---

[2] Also of interest is the fact that the Conservative and Liberal parties have moved in different directions *over time* with respect to the actual age of their leaders at the time of their selection. By way of a regression analysis a negative relationship between age and time was found to exist for the Conservatives (slope $= -.40$), whereas for the Liberal party a positive relationship was discovered (slope $= 1.42$). As the change in direction has been slight, however, no statistical significance could be attached to it.

Table 6—3: Demographic Characteristics of Conservative Leadership Candidates, 1927-1967*

Year	Candidates in order of Rank on First Ballot	Age	Religion	Occupation	Province
1927	R. B. Bennett	57	United Church	Barrister	Alberta
	Hugh Guthrie	61	Presbyterian	Barrister	Ontario
	C. H. Cahan	66	Presbyterian	Barrister	Quebec
	R. J. Manion	46	Roman Catholic	Physician	Ontario
	R. Rogers	63	Anglican	Merchant	Manitoba
	Sir Henry Drayton	58	Anglican	Barrister	Ontario
1938	R. J. Manion	56	Roman Catholic	Physician	Ontario
	M. A. MacPherson	47	Presbyterian	Barrister	Saskatchewan
	Joseph Harris	49	Presbyterian	Businessman	Ontario
	Denton Massey	38	United Church	Businessman	Ontario
	J. E. Lawson	46	United Church	Barrister	Ontario
1942	John Bracken	59	United Church	Professor	Manitoba
	M. A. MacPherson	51	Presbyterian	Barrister	Saskatchewan
	John G. Diefenbaker	47	Baptist	Barrister	Saskatchewan
	H. C. Green	47	United Church	Barrister	British Columbia
	H. H. Stevens	64	United Church	Businessman	British Columbia
1948	George Drew	54	Anglican	Barrister	Ontario
	John G. Diefenbaker	53	Baptist	Barrister	Saskatchewan
	Donald M. Fleming	43	United Church	Barrister	Ontario
1956	John G. Diefenbaker	61	Baptist	Barrister	Saskatchewan
	Donald M. Fleming	51	United Church	Barrister	Ontario
	E. Davie Fulton	40	Roman Catholic	Barrister	British Columbia
1967	Robert L. Stanfield	53	Anglican	Barrister	Nova Scotia
	Duff Roblin	50	Anglican	Businessman	Manitoba
	E. Davie Fulton	51	Roman Catholic	Barrister	British Columbia
	George Hees	57	Anglican	Businessman	Ontario
	John G. Diefenbaker	70	Baptist	Barrister	Saskatchewan
	Wallace McCutcheon	61	United Church	Businessman	Ontario
	Alvin Hamilton	55	Protestant	Teacher	Saskatchewan
	Donald M. Fleming	62	United Church	Barrister	Ontario
	Michael Starr	56	Ukrainian Orthodox	Clerk	Ontario

*Excluding John MacLean and Mrs. Mary Walker-Sawka in 1967.

*Table 6—4: Demographic Characteristics of Liberal
Leadership Candidates, 1919-1968**

Year	Candidates in order of Rank on First Ballot	Age	Religion	Occupation	Province
1919	W. L. Mackenzie King	44	Presbyterian	Indust. rel. advisor	Ontario
	William S. Fielding	70	Baptist	Journalist	Nova Scotia
	George Graham	60	Methodist	Journalist	Ontario
	D. D. McKenzie	60	Presbyterian	Barrister	Nova Scotia
1948	Louis St. Laurent	66	Roman Catholic	Barrister	Quebec
	James G. Gardiner	64	United Church	Teacher	Saskatchewan
	C. G. Power	60	Roman Catholic	Barrister	Quebec
1958	Lester B. Pearson	60	United Church	Civil servant	Ontario
	Paul Martin	54	Roman Catholic	Barrister	Ontario
1968	Pierre E. Trudeau	48	Roman Catholic	Barrister	Quebec
	Paul Hellyer	44	United Church	Businessman	Ontario
	Robert Winters	57	United Church	Businessman	Ontario
	John Turner	38	Roman Catholic	Barrister	Quebec
	Paul Martin	64	Roman Catholic	Barrister	Ontario
	J. J. Greene	47	Anglican	Barrister	Ontario
	A. J. MacEachen	46	Roman Catholic	Professor	Nova Scotia
	Eric Kierans	54	Roman Catholic	Economist	Quebec

*Excluding Reverend L. Henderson in 1958 and 1968.

Only two of the thirteen Conservative leaders (each of whom led the party for only two years) have been Roman Catholics, whereas three of the Liberals' seven leaders have been Roman Catholics. Since 1919 nearly as many Roman Catholics have run for the Liberal leadership as Protestants, a statistically significant factor differentiating that party from the Conservatives. Moreover, the parties differ markedly respecting the provinces and regions from which their leaders have been recruited. The Liberals are unquestionably associated with central Canada, for every one of their leaders and all but four of their convention candidates has been from either Quebec or Ontario. For their part, the Conservative leaders have come from six different provinces, with Ontario and Nova Scotia equally represented as the most common. Only

Table 6—5: Leaders and Leadership Candidates from the Legal Profession (%)

	Liberal	*Conservative*
Leaders (1867-)	57	69
(Liberal N = 7)		
(Conservative N = 13)		
Leadership Candidates		
(1919 and 1927-)	47	61
(Liberal N = 17)		
(Conservative N = 31)		

Table 6—6: Significant Difference Between the Liberal and Conservative Parties at 5% Level of Confidence*

	All Convention Candidates (1919 and 1927-)	*All Leaders* (1867-)
In terms of:		
Age (difference between two means)	No (t test = 1.54) df = 46	Yes (t test = 3.39) df = 48
Religious affiliation (Roman Catholic as opposed to all others)	Yes (χ^2 = 6.58) df = 1	No (χ^2 = 1.72) df = 1
Province (likelihood of coming from Quebec or Ontario or all other provinces combined)	Yes (χ^2 = 7.42) df = 2	Yes (χ^2 = 6.81) df = 2

*Yates' Correction for Continuity used for all χ^2.

Table 6—7: Mean Age of Liberal and Conservative Leaders
(in years)

	Conservative	Liberal
All leaders since 1867	57.4	51.4
	(S.D. = 8.85)	(S.D. = 7.78)
	(N = 13)	(N = 7)
All pre-convention leaders	58.0	47.3
	(S.D. = 11.76)	(S.D. = 2.62)
	(N = 7)	(N = 3)
All convention period leaders	56.6	54.5
	(S.D. = 2.75)	(S.D. = 8.87)
	(N = 6)	(N = 4)
All convention period candidates	53.9	55.1
	(S.D. = 7.6)	(S.D. = 8.9)
	(N = 31)	(N = 17)

one Conservative leader has been from the province of Quebec, and at that he was a Protestant, English-speaking senator. The Conservative weakness in the province of Quebec is further illustrated by the fact that of the thirty-one Conservative candidates who sought their party's leadership since 1927, only one has come from Quebec and he, too, was an English-speaking Protestant. In one Conservative convention (1942) not one candidate was from either Ontario or Quebec: one was a Manitoban, two were from Saskatchewan, and two were from British Columbia.

Yet another difference between the two parties is worthy of note. Liberal candidates, having once run for the party's leadership and having lost, seem content not to run again. Only Paul Martin and the Rev. Lloyd Henderson have sought their party's leadership more than once (1958 and 1968). Not so with the Conservatives. Three Conservatives have contested the leadership twice (R. J. Manion, M. A. MacPherson, and E. Davie Fulton), one has sought the leadership three times (Donald Fleming), and John

Diefenbaker has been a candidate in four leadership contests. Indeed, it is a Conservative (Arthur Meighen) who holds the distinction of being the only Canadian politician to have been chosen on two different occasions to lead his party: 1920 and 1941. The greater frequency of Conservative conventions (the Conservatives have averaged a leadership convention every seven years, whereas the interval between Liberal conventions has averaged 12.5 years) no doubt makes it easier for politically ambitious men to stand more than once for the leadership of their party, but a fuller explanation of such behaviour would have to take into account the motives of such men, their positions within the party, and their party's position within the political system.

The typical Conservative leader, therefore, might be described as being a lawyer and a Protestant, who at age 57 was selected from a pool of men whose average age was less than his, whose home province was almost assuredly not Quebec, and whose chances of being from some province other than Ontario were twice as great as being from Ontario. His Liberal counterpart, on the other hand, was younger by six years, was less likely to have been a lawyer, was more likely to have been a Roman Catholic, and was from either Quebec or Ontario but from no other province. Differences, in other words, have existed between the two parties in terms of a number of demographic characteristics of their leaders and their leadership candidates, and it would be a mistake to claim otherwise.

Political Experience

However, in one important respect, the parties have not been unlike one another. With the adoption of the leadership convention, the same became true in both the Liberal and Conservative parties as had earlier proved to be the case in American parties after the switch from congressional to convention selection of presidential candidates: a major alteration took place in the type of person chosen as party leader. From Tables 6-8 and 6-9,

Table 6–8: Parliamentary, Legislative and Ministerial Experience of Leaders of the Conservative Party of Canada, 1867-1967

Name	Term as Leader	Parliamentary Experience	Parliamentary Ministerial Experience	At the Time of Selection		M.P. or Senator
				Provincial Legislative Experience	Provincial Ministerial Experience	
John A. Macdonald	1867-1891	nil	nil	23 yrs.[a]	12 yrs.[a]	neither
J. J. C. Abbott	1891-1892	13 yrs. 3 mo. Commons 4 yrs. Senate	4 yrs.	10 yrs.[a]	1 yr.[a]	Senator
John S. D. Thompson	1892-1894	7 yrs. 2 mo.	7 yrs. 2½ mo.	4 yrs. 7 mo.	3 yrs. 9 mo.	M. P.
Mackenzie Bowell	1894-1896	20 yrs. Commons 2 yrs. Senate	16 yrs. 2 mo.	nil	nil	Senator
Charles Tupper	1896-1901	18 yrs.	10 yrs. 3 mo.	12 yrs.[a]	7 yrs.[a]	Not in parliament at time of selection.
Robert L. Borden	1901-1920	5 yrs.	nil	nil	nil	M.P.
Arthur Meighen	1920-1926	12 yrs.	5 yrs.	nil	nil	M.P.
R. B. Bennett[b]	1927-1938	8 yrs. 2½ mo.	5½ mo.	8 yrs.	nil	M.P.
R. J. Manion[c]	1938-1940	17 yrs. 10 mo.	5 yrs. 2½ mo.	nil	nil	Not in parliament at time of selection.
Arthur Meighen[d]	1941-1942	17 yrs. Commons 9 yrs. Senate	10 yrs. 4 mo.	nil	nil	Senator
John Bracken[e]	1942-1948	nil	nil	20 yrs. 2 mo.	20 yrs. 4 mo.	Not in parliament at time of selection.
George Drew	1948-1956	nil	nil	9 yrs. 7½ mo.	5 yrs. 1½ mo.	Not in parliament at time of selection.

| John G. Diefenbaker | 1956-1967 | 16 yrs. 8½ mo. | nil | nil | nil | M.P. |
| Robert L. Stanfield | 1967- | nil | nil | 18 yrs. | 11 yrs. | Not in parliament at time of selection. |

aPrior to July 1, 1867.

bFrom Meighen's resignation in 1926 to Bennett's election as party leader in 1927 Hugh Guthrie served as "temporary" leader of the party in the House of Commons.

cThe post of the national party leader was vacant from the time of Manion's resignation in May 1940, to November 1941, when Meighen was chosen to lead the party.

dFrom 1940-1943, R. B. Hanson was leader of the party in the House of Commons. Meighen was chosen in 1941 by a meeting of the Dominion Conservative Association executive, MPs, privy councillors, and defeated parliamentary candidates from the 1940 election.

eFrom 1943 to 1945, Gordon Graydon was leader of the party in the House of Commons. Bracken did not enter the House until the general election of 1945.

Table 6—9: Parliamentary, Legislative and Ministerial Experience of Leaders
of the Liberal Party of Canada, 1873-1968[a]

Name	Term as Leader	Parliamentary Experience	Parliamentary Ministerial Experience	At the Time of Selection		
				Provincial Legislative Experience	Provincial Ministerial Experience	M.P. or Senator
Alexander Mackenzie	1873-1880	5 yrs. 8 mo.[b]	nil	7 yrs.[c]	10 mo.[d]	M.P.
Edward Blake	1880-1887	11 yrs. 7 mo.[e]	2 yrs. 10 mo.	5 yrs. 3½ mo.[f]	10 mo.[g]	M.P.
Wilfrid Laurier	1887-1919	13 yrs.	1 yr.	3 yrs.	nil	M.P.
W. L. Mackenzie King	1919-1948	3 yrs.	2 yrs. 4 mo.	nil	nil	Not in parliament at time of selection.
Louis St. Laurent	1948-1958	6 yrs. 6 mo.	6 yrs. 8 mo.	nil	nil	M.P.
Lester B. Pearson	1958-1968	9 yrs. 3 mo.	8 yrs. 9 mo.	nil	nil	M.P.
Pierre E. Trudeau	1968-	2 yrs. 5 mo.	1 yr.	nil	nil	M.P.

[a]Not until 1873 did those members of the House sitting in opposition to Macdonald's government formally select a leader, although certainly by 1870 Mackenzie had begun to emerge as chief Liberal spokesman.
[b]One year of this period (October 1871— October 1872) overlapped with membership in the Legislative Assembly of Ontario.
[c]Occurred both before and after Confederation, 1861 to 1867 in the Legislative Assembly of the Province of Canada, and October 1871 to October 1872, in the Legislative Assembly of Ontario. The last term in the Legislative Assembly of Ontario overlapped with service in the House of Commons.
[d]Occurred between December 21, 1871, and October 1872, overlapping with membership in the House of Commons.
[e]Five years, three and a half months of this period (July 1867 to October 1872) overlapped with membership in the Legislative Assembly of Ontario.
[f]Overlapped with membership in the House of Commons.
[g]Occurred between December 20, 1871, and October 15, 1872, overlapping with membership in the House of Commons.

as well as from the information presented in Chapter 3, it is evident that prior to the introduction of leadership conventions Canadian party leaders typically were men of parliament. They had several years' experience as members in the House of Commons (in two instances, the Senate as well), and even though there were, understandably, differences between the long-term governing and opposition parties, nearly all had served as ministers in the cabinet. The typical career pattern also included some seasoning in government and politics by way of membership in provincial legislatures and cabinets, though at the time of selection as party leader a more important consideration was undoubtedly membership in parliament and experience in federal government and politics. Although they tended to fall short of the standard of parliamentary and ministerial experience established by the leaders of British parties (compare Tables 6-8 and 6-9 with Tables 1-1 and 1-2), Canadian party leaders in the late nineteenth and early twentieth centuries had, nonetheless, as a minimum requisite for the leadership of their respective parties, some (and in most cases, considerable) practical experience in federal parliamentary politics.

Since the change to leadership conventions, however, the mean parliamentary experience of Conservative and Liberal leaders at the time of their selection has been nearly half of what it had been in the pre-convention period (see Table 6-10). The same table also reveals a sizable drop in prior parliamentary ministerial experience for Conservative leaders but more than a threefold increase in the same category for Liberal leaders. The explanation for the differences between the two parties is simple. Until their first leadership convention in 1927, the Conservatives had been in power intermittently for 34 of the 60 years from the date of Confederation, a fact which gave rise to a sufficiently large pool of men with at least some previous cabinet experience who were available to serve as leader when a vacancy occurred. In this respect the party has suffered from being out of office for all but 11 of the 40 years between 1927 and 1967, so much so that the average number of years of ministerial experience dropped to 1.7 for leaders chosen during that period. Alternatively, the Liberals tended to be the out-of-office party at the time of the pre-convention system (32 of

Table 6–10: Mean Parliamentary, Legislative and Ministerial Experience of Leaders at the Time of Their Selection, Canada and Britain (in years)

	Parliamentary Experience	Parliamentary Ministerial Experience	Provincial Legislative Experience	Provincial Ministerial Experience
CANADA				
Pre-convention period				
Conservative party[a] (N = 6)	13.5	7.0	4.4	2.0
Liberal party[b] (N = 3)	10.1	1.3	5.1	.6
Convention period[c]				
Conservative party (N = 6)	7.1	1.7	9.3	6.2
Liberal party (N = 4)	5.3	4.7	0.0	0.0
BRITAIN				
Conservative party, 1885-1965 (N = 12)	25.0	8.1	—	—

Labour party, 1922-1963 (N = 6)	15.2	2.9	—	—

[a] John A. Macdonald is not included, for at the time of his selection as prime minister and party leader (1867) Macdonald's considerable legislative and ministerial experience (23 years and 12 years respectively) had taken place prior to the existence of the Parliament of Canada and within a colonial legislature. To have included Macdonald would have unnecessarily inflated the "Provincial Legislative Experience" and "Provincial Ministerial Experience" means and deflated the "Parliamentary Experience" and "Parliamentary Ministerial Experience" means.

[b] Overlapping membership in the federal parliament and the provincial legislature of Ontario should be noted for Alexander Mackenzie and Edward Blake.

[c] For the Conservatives, the convention period dates from 1927, and for the Liberals, it dates from 1919.

Table 6–11: Liberal Convention, August 5-7, 1919, Ottawa, Ontario

Leadership Balloting: August 7

Candidates in order of rank on first ballot	First ballot	Second ballot	Fifth ballot[a]	Parliamentary experience		Provincial experience	
				House or Senate	Cabinet	House	Cabinet
W. L. Mackenzie King	344	411	476	3 yrs.	2 yrs. 4 mo.	—	—
William S. Fielding	297	344	438	16 yrs. 7 mo.	15 yrs. 2½ mo.	14 yrs.	13 yrs. 5 mo.
George Graham	153	124		9 yrs. 10 mo.	4 yrs. 1½ mo.	9 yrs.	2½ mo.
D. D. McKenzie	153	60		13 yrs.	—	4 yrs.	—
Total Number Voting	947	939	914				

[a]The third and fourth ballots were destroyed after being partially taken because of Mr. Graham's and Mr. McKenzie's withdrawals.

those 52 years were spent in opposition) and those who were chosen to lead the party, as a result, had had little opportunity for prior ministerial experience. The four Liberal leaders selected since 1919 have averaged 4.7 years in the cabinet at the time of their selection, a figure markedly higher than the pre-1919 average simply because the Liberal party had been the governing party for 36 of those 49 years from 1919 to 1968. That the Liberal means for parliamentary experience and for parliamentary ministerial experience are not *higher* than 5.3 and 4.7 years respectively is surely surprising, given the electoral dominance of that party over the past fifty years. Judged by the standards of the Conservative party, by the pre-convention period Conservative and Liberal parties, and by those applied in Great Britain, the Liberal convention period figures are low. That the Liberal parliamentary and parliamentary–ministerial figures are so close bears witness to the propensity of the Liberal party to co-opt notables into parliament and into the cabinet at almost the same time, and to choose, within a relatively short period of time, the leaders of the party from among those who were co-opted. Furthermore, Table 6-10 makes abundantly clear a pronounced shift by the Conservatives toward the provinces and by the Liberals away from the provinces as areas in which the newly selected leaders had previously been politically active.

Not only has the convention system made it easier for men with little in the way of parliamentary and ministerial experience to be selected as party leaders, it has made it more difficult for those politicians with considerable experience in federal politics to be chosen by the convention delegates as leaders of their parties. Herein lies the supreme irony of the switch to the leadership convention in Canada. Without exception the four Liberal leaders chosen by party conventions since 1919 had been in both parliament and the cabinet for much shorter periods of time than any of their chief competitors (see Tables 6-11, 6-12, 6-13, and 6-14). Mackenzie King and Pierre Trudeau are extreme but nonetheless important illustrations of this fact. King, having sat in parliament for just under three years, having failed to be elected in the two most recent federal elections he contested, having been out of

Table 6–12: Liberal Convention, August 5-7, 1948, Ottawa, Ontario

Leadership Balloting: August 7

Candidates in order of rank on first ballot	First ballot	Parliamentary experience		Provincial experience	
		House or Senate	Cabinet	House	Cabinet
Louis St. Laurent	848	6 yrs. 6 mo.	6 yrs. 8 mo.	–	–
James G. Gardiner	323	12 yrs. 7 mo.	12 yrs. 9½ mo.	21 yrs. 4 mo.	8 yrs. 8½ mo.
C. G. Power	56	30 yrs. 7½ mo.	9 yrs. 1 mo.	–	–
Total Number Voting	1227				

Table 6–13: Liberal Convention, January 14-16, 1958, Ottawa, Ontario

Leadership Balloting: January 16

Candidates in order of rank on first ballot	First ballot	Parliamentary experience		Provincial experience	
		House or Senate	Cabinet	House	Cabinet
Lester B. Pearson	1074	9 yrs. 3 mo.	8 yrs. 9 mo.	–	–
Paul Martin	305	22 yrs. 3 mo.	12 yrs. 2 mo.	–	–
L. Henderson	1	–	–	–	–
Total Number Voting	1380				

Table 6—14: Liberal Convention, April 4-6, 1968, Ottawa, Ontario

Leadership Balloting: April 6

Candidates in order of rank on first ballot	First ballot	Second ballot	Third ballot	Fourth ballot	Parliamentary experience House or Senate	Cabinet	Provincial experience House	Cabinet
Pierre E. Trudeau	752	964	1051	1203	2 yrs. 5 mo.	1 yr.	—	—
Paul Hellyer	330	465	377a		17 yrs. 4 mo.	5 yrs. 1½ mo.	—	—
Robert Winters	293	473	621	954	14 yrs. 5 mo.	10 yrs. 10 mo.	—	—
John Turner	277	347	279	195	5 yrs. 10 mo.	2 yrs. 4 mo.	—	—
Paul Martin	277a				32 yrs. 6 mo.	17 yrs. 2 mo.	—	—
J. J. Greene	169	104	29b		5 yrs.	2 yrs. 4 mo.	—	—
A. J. MacEachen	165	11c			10 yrs. 5½ mo.	5 yrs.	—	—
Eric Kierans	103a				—	—	5 yrs.	5 yrs.
L. Henderson	0b				—	—	—	—
Total Number Voting	2366	2364	2357	2352				

a Withdrew after this ballot.

b Eliminated as a result of this ballot.

c Withdrew after the first ballot but his name remained on the ballot because formal notification failed to reach the chairman of the convention in time and eleven supporters missed the notification of his withdrawal. Subsequently eliminated as of this ballot.

parliament for the preceding eight years, and lacking a seat in the House at the time of the convention, was selected over three other men who had served as members of parliament for a combined total of thirty-nine years. Trudeau's experience as a parliamentary politician, as a cabinet minister and, indeed, as a supporter of the Liberal party itself, could scarcely have been shorter; yet he defeated for the party leadership such men as Paul Hellyer, Robert Winters, Paul Martin, and Allan MacEachen, whose terms in parliament and in the cabinet approximated or exceeded those of the pre-convention party leaders. When he held his first press conference following his election as Liberal leader, Trudeau admitted, not surprisingly, that he felt very much an "outsider" and a "new-comer" in the party of which he had just been made head.[3] The other two Liberal leaders chosen by party convention (St. Laurent in 1948 and Pearson in 1958) had both been appointed to senior cabinet portfolios before either had represented a parliamentary constituency. Both men were widely regarded, soon after their entry into parliament, as strong contenders for their party's leadership if they chose to seek it in convention, even though such conventions would undoubtedly be several years away. Both men were easily elected as leader on first ballots, defeating others who had made a career of politics. How accurate was Norman Ward's comment of several years ago to the effect that "it would appear to be established that one excellent way of ensuring that one will not rise to the top of the Liberal party is to start at the bottom."[4]

But the Liberal leaders are by no means alone in having short parliamentary careers at the time of their selection. Of the six Conservative leaders chosen by conventions since 1927, all but two defeated several other leadership candidates whose years in the parliamentary party comfortably surpassed their own. Of those two (Manion and Diefenbaker), Manion resigned shortly after the 1940 election, having served as leader for less than two years and having

---

[3] Transcript of press conference with Pierre E. Trudeau, National Press Building, Ottawa, April 7, 1968, pp. 7 and 8.
[4] "The Liberals in Convention: Revised and Unrepentant," *Queen's Quarterly,* LXV (Spring 1958), 1.

Table 6–15: *Liberal-Conservative Convention, October 10-12, 1927, Winnipeg, Manitoba*

Leadership Balloting: October 12

Candidates in order of rank on first ballot	First ballot	Second ballot	Parliamentary experience		Provincial experience	
			House or Senate	Cabinet	House	Cabinet
R. B. Bennett	594	780	8 yrs. 2½ mo.	5½ mo.	8 yrs.	—
Hugh Guthrie	345	320	27 yrs.	2 yrs. 9 mo.	—	—
C. H. Cahan	310	266	2 yrs.	—	4 yrs.	—
R. J. Manion	170	148	9 yrs. 10 mo.	6 mo.	—	—
R. Rogers	114	37	7 yrs. 1 mo.	5 yrs. 10½ mo.	12 yrs.	11 yrs.
Sir H. Drayton	31	3	8 yrs. 6 mo.	2 yrs. 8 mo.	—	—
Total Number Voting	1564	1554				

Table 6–16: *National Conservative Convention, July 5-7, 1938, Ottawa, Ontario*

Leadership Balloting: July 7

Candidates in order of rank on first ballot	First ballot	Second ballot	Parliamentary experience		Provincial experience	
			House or Senate	Cabinet	House	Cabinet
R. J. Manion	726	830	17 yrs. 10 mo.	5 yrs. 2½ mo.	—	—
M. A. MacPherson	475	648	—	—	9 yrs. 5½ mo.	5 yrs. 2 mo.
Joseph Harris	131	49	16 yrs. 7 mo.	—	—	—
Denton Massey	128	39	2 yrs. 9 mo.	—	—	—
J. E. Lawson	105[a]	—	9 yrs. 9 mo.	2 mo.	—	—
Total Number Voting	1565	1566				

a Withdrew after first ballot.

Table 6–17: Progressive Conservative Convention, December 9-11, 1942, Winnipeg, Manitoba

Leadership Balloting: December 11

Candidates in order of rank on first ballot	First ballot	Second ballot	Parliamentary experience		Provincial experience	
			House or Senate	Cabinet	House	Cabinet
John Bracken	420	538	—	—	20 yrs. 2 mo.	20 yrs. 4 mo.
M. A. MacPherson	222	255	—	—	9 yrs. 5½ mo.	5 yrs. 2 mo.
John G. Diefenbaker	120	79	2 yrs. 8½ mo.	—	—	—
H. C. Green	88[a]		7 yrs. 2 mo.	—	—	—
H. H. Stevens	20[a]		28 yrs. 5½ mo.	4 yrs. 8½ mo.	—	—
Total Number Voting	870	872				

[a] Withdrew after first ballot.

been personally defeated in his first election as party leader, and Diefenbaker was defeated in all but one of his four convention attempts to gain his party's leadership (see Tables 6-15, 6-16, 6-17, 6-18, 6-19, and 6-20). The Conservatives have evidenced a strong predilection for provincial party leaders. Bracken, Drew, Stanfield and Roblin were all provincial premiers at the time they sought the national leadership. Not one of these men had ever sat in, or run for, parliament before pursuing the leadership of the Conservative party. In fact, of the Conservative leaders chosen since the party began using leadership conventions in 1927, only two (Bennett and Diefenbaker) had seats in the House of Commons when they were selected. Parliamentary apprenticeships may have been important at one time in Conservative party politics, but that seems no longer to be the case.

Why should such features of leadership selection be characteristic of the convention phase of Canadian politics? There are a number of reasons, different for each of the two parties, for the established proclivity of the Liberals and the Conservatives in convention to favour leadership candidates with little or no federal political experience. In the case of the Liberals they have been, save for eleven years, Canada's governing party since 1921. Liberal supporters have become accustomed to looking upon their party as the governing party, anticipating that it will control governmental power over time. The party is accurately described as being attractive to

> those who wish to share in power, or to be close to those in power. Policy becomes . . . a device to be manipulated to achieve and maintain power. As a result the party becomes cohesive and united — because only so can it sustain itself in power. Its elite therefore becomes committed to the maintenance of the party in power.[5]

---

[5] H. G. Thorburn, "An Approach to the Study of Federal Political Parties in Canada," paper read to the First Colloque sponsored by the Canadian Political Science Association and la Société Canadienne de Science Politique, Ottawa, November 10, 1968, p. 4.

Table 6–18: *Progressive Conservative Convention, September 30-October 2, 1948, Ottawa, Ontario*

Leadership Balloting: October 2

Candidates in order of rank on first ballot	First ballot	Parliamentary experience House or Senate	Parliamentary experience Cabinet	Provincial experience House	Provincial experience Cabinet
George Drew	827	—	—	9 yrs. 7½ mo.	5 yrs. 1½ mo.
John G. Diefenbaker	311	8 yrs. 6 mo.	—	—	—
Donald M. Fleming	104	3 yrs. 3½ mo.	—	—	—
Total Number Voting	1242				

Table 6–19: *Progressive Conservative Convention, December 12-14, 1956, Ottawa, Ontario*

Leadership Balloting: December 14

Candidates in order of rank on first ballot	First ballot	Parliamentary experience House or Senate	Parliamentary experience Cabinet	Provincial experience House	Provincial experience Cabinet
John G. Diefenbaker	774	16 yrs. 8½ mo.	—	—	—
Donald M. Fleming	393	11 yrs. 6 mo.	—	—	—
E. Davie Fulton	117	11 yrs. 6 mo.	—	—	—
Total Number Voting	1284				

Table 6–20: Progressive Conservative Convention, September 5-9, 1967, Toronto, Ontario

Leadership Balloting: September 9

Candidates in order of rank on first ballot	First ballot	Second ballot	Third ballot	Fourth ballot	Fifth ballot	Parliamentary experience		Provincial experience	
						House or Senate	Cabinet	House	Cabinet
Robert L. Stanfield	519	613	717	865	1150	—	—	18 yrs.	11 yrs.
Duff Roblin	347	430	541	771	969	—	—	17 yrs. 10 mo.	9 yrs. 5 mo.
E. Davie Fulton	343	346	361	357[a]		19 yrs. 8 mo.	5 yrs. 10 mo.	—	—
George Hees	295	299	277[a]			14 yrs. 9 mo.	5 yrs. 8 mo.	—	—
John G. Diefenbaker	271	172	114[a]			27 yrs. 5½ mo.	5 yrs. 10 mo.	—	—
Wallace McCutcheon	137	76[a]				5 yrs. 1 mo. (Senate)	8 mo.	—	—
Alvin Hamilton	136	127	106	167[b]		10 yrs. 3 mo.	5 yrs. 8 mo.	—	—
Donald M. Fleming	126	115	76[b]			17 yrs. 10 mo.	5 yrs. 10 mo.	—	—
Michael Starr	45	34[b]				15 yrs. 3½ mo.	5 yrs. 10 mo.	—	—
John MacLean	10[a]					—		—	—
Mary Walker-Sawka	2[b]					—		—	—
Total Number Voting	2231	2212	2192	2160	2119				

[a] Withdrew after this ballot.
[b] Eliminated as a result of this ballot.

The recruitment practices of the Liberal party would be expected to reflect the party's intense interest in appealing as successfully as possible to a heterogeneous electorate, thereby helping it to stay in power. A hierarchical career pattern within such a political context would be inconsistent with the party's desire to maintain power, for such a pattern would inhibit the party's ability to co-opt appropriate leaders at the appropriate times.

When such a power orientation is combined with a parliamentary system in which there is a high turnover of members in a relatively short period of time, then the likelihood of repeatedly co-opting extra-parliamentary notables into parliament, into the cabinet, and into the leadership of the Liberal party, is heightened. The evidence provided in Tables 6-21 and 6-22 suggests that the House of Commons fares poorly as a reservoir of members with considerable political experience. In each of five of the eight elections from 1949 to 1968 over one-third of the House of Commons was newly elected.[6] Of comparative interest is the fact that the highest Canadian figure of mean years of service in the House of Commons was still below the lowest United States' House of Representatives' figure. The extent to which such a markedly high turnover of parliamentary politicians contributes to the practice of co-optation of leaders is, of course, difficult to establish. But it seems reasonable to assume that some relationship exists between these two features of Canadian politics whereby it becomes easier

[6] High turnover of members of the House is not, of course, new. It has been a feature of Canadian politics since the 1870s. See Norman Ward, *The Canadian House of Commons: Representation* (Toronto: University of Toronto Press, 1950), pp. 115-18. There is some evidence to suggest that the turnover may in fact be higher in the Liberal party than in either the Progressive Conservative or the New Democratic parties, which, among other things, serves to support the claim that the two opposition parties are in fact more parliament-oriented than the party which tends to be the governing party. Of those members elected in the 1968 election, only 7 per cent had been first elected prior to the 1957 general election. However, for the Liberals, less than 4 per cent of their caucus had been elected prior to 1957, whereas for the PCs and NDP the figures were 12.5 per cent and 17.4 per cent respectively — in reverse order to the size of the three parties in the House of Commons.

Table 6–21: U.S. House of Representatives and Canadian House of Commons

	% First Term Members, 1949-1968 House of Representatives	House of Commons
1949	22.3	35.1
1950		
1951	14.9	
1952		
1953	19.5	25.7
1954		
1955	11.7	
1956		
1957	9.9	34.3
1958		39.6
1959	18.2	
1960		
1961	12.6	
1962		36.6
1963	15.2	18.9
1964		
1965	20.9	17.7
1966		
1967	13.8	
1968		36.4

Source: Data for U.S. House of Representatives from 1949 to 1965 are from Nelson W. Polsby, "The Institutionalization of the U.S. House of Representatives," *American Political Science Review*, LXII (March 1968), 146, Table 1. Data for 1967 are calculated from *Congressional Directory* (90th Congress, 1st session, 1967). Data for Canadian House of Commons are calculated from *Reports of the Chief Electoral Officer, 1949-1968* and *The Canadian Directory of Parliament, 1867-1967* (Ottawa, 1968).

Table 6—22: U.S. House of Representatives and Canadian House of Commons

Mean Years of Service in House at Time of Election of Members Elected, 1949-1968

	House of Representatives	House of Commons
1949	6.8	6.1
1950		
1951	7.5	
1952		
1953	7.4	6.7
1954		
1955	8.4	
1956		
1957	9.2	6.4
1958		3.8
1959	8.7	
1960		
1961	9.3	
1962		5.0
1963	9.3	4.9
1964		
1965	8.6	5.6
1966		
1967	8.9	
1968		4.5

Source: Data for U.S. House of Representatives from 1949 to 1963 are calculated from Polsby, Table 2, and from *Congressional Directories*. Data for Canadian House of Commons are calculated from *Reports of the Chief Electoral Officer, 1949-1968* and *The Canadian Directory of Parliament, 1867-1967*.

for the party (in this case, the Liberals) to justify continued co-optive practices and whereby, at the same time, the arguments are strengthened of those MPs who see little point in remaining in a House in which slight value is placed on political apprenticeship.

Between 1921 and 1970 no fewer than a third of the Liberal ministers were brought into the cabinet having served less than a

Table 6—23: Years in Parliament before
Appointment to Cabinet
(%)

	Number of Years	CANADA Liberal Party (1921-1970)	BRITAIN Conservative Party (1922-1960)	Labour Party
House of Commons	20 +	1.5	11.9	11.5
	15—19	4.5	15.6	16.4
	10—14	14.2	23.9	27.9
	5—9	19.4	12.8	22.9
	1—4	23.1	4.6	6.6
	0—1	33.6	5.5	1.6
Upper House		3.7	25.7	13.1
Total		100.0	100.0	100.0
N		134	109	61

Source: For the British Data: Joseph A. Schlesinger, "Political Careers and Party Leadership," in Lewis J. Edinger (ed.), *Political Leadership in Industrialized Societies* (New York: John Wiley and Sons, 1967), Table 9.6, p. 287. Data for Liberal party of Canada calculated from *Reports of the Chief Electoral Officer, 1921-1970,* and *The Canadian Directory of Parliament, 1867-1967*

year in the House of Commons; during that same period over a half of the Liberal cabinet ministers had spent fewer than five years in the House when they were first appointed to the cabinet. A comparison with the British Conservative and Labour parties makes this feature of the Canadian Liberal party even more pronounced (see Table 6-23). "When a significant proportion of a party's cabinet members has spent less than five years and some even less than one year in the legislature," one scholar has commented,

> it is hard to accept the legislature as the base for their advancement. The legislature may be the formal last step, but the routes to the top begin to look much like those in the presidential system: government administration, state or provincial offices, posts in industry or with other pressure groups.[7]

A party interested in maintaining power requires leaders who are capable of keeping it in power, or at least seemingly capable of accomplishing that feat. The evidence suggests that in such a situation no amount of parliamentary experience is sufficient to overcome the attractiveness of a relatively new face on the political scene if the novice seems to be the most certain way of leading the party to power. No amount of parliamentary experience can successfully counter the image of the candidate who, being least tarnished from political wars, is best able to appear as the man most in keeping with his times, most likely to solve the pressing problems of the day. These lessons the Liberal party has learned well.

The Conservatives, for their part, have been plagued by problems typically faced by out-of-office parties in a political system with little class politics, and with relatively flexible attitudes toward policy both on their own part and on the part of the long-term governing party. To attempt to match the Liberals' success, the

---

[7] Joseph A. Schlesinger, "Political Careers and Party Leadership," in Lewis J. Edinger (ed.), *Political Leadership in Industrialized Societies: Studies in Comparative Analysis* (New York: John Wiley and Sons, 1967), pp. 286-88.

Conservatives have found that they too must select leaders who appear to have the qualities necessary to carry the party into power, or they will have no opportunity to govern. The Conservatives have no less an interest in political power than the Liberals. But the nature of that interest is necessarily different. Whereas the Liberals' concern is generally with maintaining power, the Conservatives' is with getting power. The usually small size of their parliamentary party[8] suggests that the Conservatives actually have a better reason for adopting co-optive practices than the Liberals. But co-optation is made more difficult for the Conservatives because the Liberals have succeeded in dominating most of the predictable areas from which the Conservatives might attempt to co-opt their parliamentary notables: the civil service, universities, businesses and corporations.

As a result, the Conservatives have little alternative but to recruit from a source in which the party is, at the same time, moderately successful electorally: provincial politics. Indeed, it could well be that one of the reasons why Conservative MPs are at a disadvantage when the time arrives to select a new leader for their party stems from the fact that the group with which they are so closely associated (the parliamentary caucus) bears the marks of electoral defeat. Provincial premiers do not. They offer something few federal Conservatives are able to offer: a record of electoral successes. In addition, there is no doubt but that the political base, the public image and the governing experience of a provincial premier would be superior to that of all but the most exceptional of the Conservative MPs sitting in opposition. To co-opt provincial leaders into federal politics should be understood, then, as a highly rational act performed by the Conservative party when meeting in convention. A provincial premier with a record of electoral victories to his credit is obviously difficult for the convention delegates to resist; on each of the three occasions

---

[8] Excluding their membership in the House of Commons following the elections of 1930, 1957, 1958 and 1962 (at which times they formed the government), the Conservatives' average House membership from 1921 to 1968 was 69. The average size of the House for that period was 255 members.

on which premiers have sought the leadership (1942, 1948 and 1967), they have been elected leader over men with considerable federal political experience. Thus Conservative convention delegates, when given the opportunity, apparently prefer as party leader someone relatively unscathed by federal political battles who, based on his past political accomplishments at least, is seemingly more capable of leading the party to electoral victory than anyone in the parliamentary group.

The Interaction Theory and Four Examples

Numerous studies have identified several different variables which, individually and collectively, help to explain why certain types of persons tend to be recruited into political roles.[9] Socio-economic status, skills and talents appropriate to the functional needs of society, as well as patterns of political socialization, are three such factors.[10] Other studies have shown that leadership should be understood as an interactional phenomenon:

---

[9] Of the many general and comparative works on leadership, the following were found to be the most useful: James MacGregor Burns, *Roosevelt: The Lion and the Fox* (New York: Harcourt, Brace and World, Inc., 1956), "A Note on the Study of Political Leadership," pp. 481-87; Lewis J. Edinger, "Political Science and Political Leadership; Reflections on the Study of Leadership," *The Journal of Politics*, XXVI (May and August, 1964), 423-39 and 648-76; Edinger (ed.), *Political Leadership in Industrialized Societies;* Alvin W. Gouldner, *Studies in Leadership* (New York: Harper and Brothers, 1950); "Philosophers and Kings: Studies in Leadership," *Daedalus* (Summer 1968); Lester G. Seligman, "The Study of Political Leadership," in Heinz Eulau, Samuel J. Eldersveld and Morris Janowitz (eds.), *Political Behavior: A Reader in Theory and Research* (Glencoe, Ill.: Free Press, 1956), pp. 177-84; and David B. Truman, *The Governmental Process* (New York: Alfred A. Knopf, 1950), pp. 188-210.

[10] Kenneth Prewitt has quite correctly suggested that the study of political socialization patterns should, given the necessary data, be more useful than either of the other two variables in helping to understand why certain types of people are selected as leaders. According to Prewitt, political socialization "can account for findings generated by other theories of

"leadership is a function of personality, and of the social situation, and of these two in interaction."[11] According to supporters of the interactional theory, the once popular notion that leadership could be explained simply by determining the traits or characteristics distinguishing those who lead from those who follow has been replaced by a theory stressing the situational or cultural context within which leaders are recruited and selected, the attributes of those chosen as leaders, the needs and attitudes of those in the group responsible for the selection, and the interaction of these variables.[12] Although it is necessarily both speculative and

---

leadership selection. For instance, upper-strata, more than average or lower-strata, groups not only provide political leaders, they also contain a larger proportion of persons frequently exposed to political matters. . . . It is reasonable to expect that different groups contribute to the leadership class not relative to their absolute size or to their status but relative to the percentage of their membership 'overexposed' to politics. . . .

"Similar reasoning can be employed to account for tendencies of persons with appropriate skills to be recruited into political posts. Ignoring causal direction, it is apparent that skills needed by society are, almost by definition, skills possessed by persons in roles tangential to the polity. For instance, in the normal course of events, artists are more isolated from political matters than lawyers; they are also less frequently recruited into public leadership, *and* their skills, comparatively speaking, are less needed for political management." Prewitt, "Political Socialization and Leadership Selection," *Annals of the American Academy of Political and Social Science*, 361 (September 1965), 109-110. (Italics in original.) As satisfactory data are unavailable on the political socialization of Canadian party leaders and their leadership convention opponents, no attempt can be made to test Prewitt's theories in a Canadian context.

[11] Cecil A. Gibb, "Leadership," in Gardner Lindzey and Elliott Aronson, (eds.), *The Handbook of Social Psychology,* 2nd ed., 5 vols. (Don Mills: Addison-Wesley Publishing Co., 1969), IV, 268.

[12] Enormous difficulties beset any attempt to explain why certain people are chosen as leaders, and others not, for recruitment and selection of leaders are unbelievably complex events involving innumerable societal, cultural, political and personal variables. To test merely one aspect of the interactional theory as fully as possible, for example, it would be necessary to present, if this were possible, the most unashamedly ideological of analyses: what were the needs of the Canadian political system at each point in time in which a leader was chosen? How were they perceived? Did the leader selected fit those needs better than any other? These would be difficult questions to attempt to answer, and it is by no means certain that they could be answered properly. Kenneth Prewitt and Heinz Eulau draw a useful distinction between "leadership selection" and "leadership recruitment." "The latter term identifies practices and processes that are

inferential, the interactional theory may, nevertheless, help to shed some light on leadership selection in Canada through its emphasis on the relationship between events and personality. Two examples from each of the two political parties have been selected to illustrate how the theory might be applied: King and Trudeau in the Liberal party, and Bracken and Diefenbaker in the Conservative party.

The Winnipeg general strike as well as labour disturbances in other Canadian cities were fresh in the minds of the Liberal delegates as they assembled in Ottawa to choose Laurier's successor. Accounts of labour unrest on two continents vied with reports of the Liberal convention for space on the Ottawa newspapers' front pages during the week of the 1919 convention. The mood of the country was one of profound unease, an unease resulting largely from a combination of the labour discontent and the rapidly rising post-war cost of living.

Mackenzie King had, less than a decade earlier, figured prominently in the work of the Department of Labour. Almost immediately after entering the new department in 1900 as a civil servant, King had been appointed its deputy minister and within eight months of his election to parliament in 1908, he had been named the first minister of a separate Labour Department. King had established a not inconsiderable reputation as a conciliator, as a labour adviser to John D. Rockefeller, Jr., and, generally, as an industrial relations counsellor, by the time he came to seek the Liberal leadership in 1919. Furthermore, King's address to the convention dealt in part with the need to improve labour–management relations and included the resolution of the party's com-

---

a subset of those identified by the former. Leadership selection refers to the processes that determine which few men from any generation will come to hold political office, and thus include political socialization patterns, socio-economic bias, the formation of the politically active stratum, and the political opportunity structure. Political recruitment refers to the intramural sorting and screening processes among those persons already members of the active stratum. Primarily this means advancing from being politically active to becoming a candidate for political office." Prewitt and Eulau, "Social Bias in Leadership Selection, Political Recruitment and Electoral Context," *Journal of Politics*, XXXIII (May 1971), 293, note 1.

mittee on labour and industrial relations — a committee of which he served as chairman. A. W. Roebuck, in seconding the committee's resolution following King's speech, first noted that "there is great labour unrest in this country, and unless that unrest is met in a reasonable and statesmanlike way, there is going to be greater unrest," then seized the opportunity to make a plea on King's behalf. "On the one hand, my friends," Roebuck pointed out, "you have the spiked-helmet class of legislation of such men as Arthur Meighen and N. W. Rowell, and on the other you have the broad and sympathetic statesmanship of Mackenzie King."[13] King's reputation as an expert on labour relations could scarcely have helped but work to his advantage in such a situation and his supporters, quite naturally, made the most of it on his behalf.

Moreover, King's speech to the delegates (which, in retrospect, must have been one of the most brilliant of his career) dealt with more than industrial relations. It had to, for as one Ottawa newspaper properly noted four days before the convention balloting:

> The chances of Mr. Mackenzie King depend upon his making a strong oratorical impression upon the convention and being seized upon as a compromise candidate. Radical in his views, which commends him to certain groups in the West, and an anti-conscriptionist, which makes him unobjectionable to Quebec, his opportunity may come with refusal of Quebec to take Fielding and counter refusal of Ontario and the West to stand for Fisher.[14]

Carefully and cleverly King turned the last half of his speech into a plea for responsible government, a strong attack on the Unionist administration, and a eulogy to Sir Wilfrid Laurier. It proved to be an eloquent and moving tribute which brought the delegates to their feet at its conclusion. The Ottawa *Morning Journal* drew the correct conclusions when it reported:

> [King's] speech of Wednesday evening, when pointing dramatically to the picture of Sir Wilfrid which hung over the platform, he applied to him the moving lines of Tennyson on

[13] *1919 Report*, p. 135.
[14] *Ottawa Journal*, August 4, 1919, p. 2.

the Duke of Wellington, was a master stroke of strategy as well as a triumph in oratory, for it mobilized and consolidated the French-Canadian and the Laurier-Liberal vote. Up to that moment hostility to Unionism was existent but unorganized. Mr. King's eloquence pointed it to a figure around which its forces could rally.[15]

In the event, King's speech was unmatched by those of his three opponents and when voting on the leadership proceeded the next day, King had clearly established a claim as the man to beat.[16]

Pierre Elliott Trudeau's rise to the Liberal leadership was of quite a different nature. Although appointed as Minister of Justice in April 1967, Trudeau went relatively unnoticed until December of that year when, quite unexpectedly, he burst upon the national political scene with proposals for liberalized divorce laws and criminal code reforms. By early 1968, Trudeau gained further public attention when the nationally televised proceedings of the federal-provincial constitutional conference fortuitously provided an important forum through which the Justice Minister could express his pro-federalist constitutional views. The man who two months earlier had been a relative unknown in Canadian politics had suddenly emerged as a strong contender for his party's leadership, even though he had not indicated publicly that he wished to seek it.[17] Popular social reform proposals, constitutional

---

[15] *Morning Journal,* August 8, 1919, p. 1. F. A. McGregor confirmed the newspaper's version of the impact of King's speech: "It was common talk at the end of the convention and afterwards that Mackenzie King's fighting speech marked the turning of the tide in his favour." McGregor, *The Fall and Rise of Mackenzie King,* p. 338.

[16] King's age probably helped him win the leadership too. At forty-four, he was the youngest of the four candidates. When their party is in opposition, some delegates apparently favour younger as opposed to older candidates, fearing that the party would be out of power for some time and that nothing would be gained by having an older leader who would need to be replaced within a very few years. Such appears to have been the concern of some delegates in 1919 with the Liberals and, although to a lesser extent, in 1956 with the Conservatives. Interview with Senator A. W. Roebuck, Ottawa, May 30, 1969; Dawson, *William Lyon Mackenzie King: A Political Biography,* p. 306; and Dalton Camp, *Gentlemen, Players and Politicians* (Toronto: McClelland and Stewart Ltd., 1970), pp. 242-43.

[17] Helpful studies of Mr. Trudeau's meteoric rise to public attention are to be found in Blair Fraser, "The Sudden Rise of Pierre Elliott Trudeau," *Maclean's* magazine, April 1968, pp. 24 ff.; Elizabeth Iglauer, "Profiles:

views reassuring to many Canadians (more so because they were championed by a Quebecker), an adulatory press, combined with a personal image of remarkable contemporaneity, quickly drew Trudeau to the public's (and, ergo, to the delegates') attention. By the time he announced his candidacy for the leadership of the Liberal party (February 16), Trudeau appeared to many Canadians as the candidate most in keeping with the needs of the time and as the person best able to cope with the nation's most pressing problem: French-English relations and the future of Confederation.[18] Trudeau had succeeded in a remarkably short time in establishing a serious claim to the Liberal leadership. The Gallup poll released immediately prior to the April convention indicated that 32 per cent of the Canadian people felt Trudeau would make the best leader for the Liberal party — a percentage over twice that of the next favourite candidate, Paul Martin, who had led the poll up to that time for over three years.

Both Mackenzie King in 1919 and Trudeau in 1968 were regarded as highly contemporary men. Both were considered to be competent young reformers whose ideas and expertise were well suited to their times. Yet in King's case, virtually the entire thrust to capture the party leadership had to await the convention itself and it included, among other things, a highly effective convention speech. Not so with Trudeau. Constituency and regional meetings with party supporters and delegates during the two months preceding the convention helped to overcome in part one of Trudeau's major disabilities: that he was unknown to the Liberals of Canada. Furthermore, television contributed substantially to his meteoric rise to prominence for it carried him to a mass audience from

---

Prime Minister/Premier Ministre," *The New Yorker,* July 5, 1969, pp. 36 ff.; and Donald Peacock, *Journey to Power* (Toronto: Ryerson Press, 1968), chaps. 5-9.

[18] Prior to February 1968, Pierre Elliott Trudeau had never appeared on the Gallup poll list of likely or possible successors to Mr. Pearson. However, by early February, on a list of ten declared and undeclared candidates (and Trudeau had not at that point declared his candidacy), Trudeau placed second to Paul Martin, and well ahead of Hellyer, Sharp, Turner, Kierans and other prominent Liberals.

whom the response was, by and large, favourable. Television proved to be a medium for which Trudeau was particularly well suited. His television image, as Marshall McLuhan later described it, "ha[d] everything. . . . [It was] soothing, cool and include[d] all ages."[19] In his psychoanalytical study of Martin Luther, Erik H. Erikson has argued convincingly that leadership will not be denied those who "combine a universal enough new meaning with the mastery of a new technology."[20] Certainly Trudeau's rise to prominence would seem to confirm Erikson's judgment. Television was the technological device Trudeau used effectively over a short period of time to develop a positive public reaction to his ideas and his image. In its initial stages his appeal was clearly a mass appeal. It was left to the Liberals in convention to react to that appeal and to assess the party's prospects under a man whom many of them regarded (some with caution, others with scepticism) as an outsider.

John Bracken's selection as Progressive Conservative leader in 1942 was effected as a major step in overhauling the Conservative party. The party's fortunes had never been at a lower ebb, and to top it off its leader, Arthur Meighen, had, earlier that year, suffered personal defeat in the York South by-election.[21] Meighen was convinced, when he considered the various possible successors to his position, that no one could revive the party's fortunes better than John Bracken. Bracken had been the premier of Manitoba for twenty years, a position into which he had been co-opted from the presidency of the Manitoba Agricultural College. His leadership of the United Farmers of Manitoba, of the Progressives and of the Liberal Progressive governments had marked him as being a successful, efficient, but unspectacular leader. At the same time, he was looked upon as a reformer and a progressive. In fact, in mid 1942 so shrewd an observer of the

---

[19] Peacock, p. 135.

[20] *Young Man Luther: A Study in Psychoanalysis and History* (New York: W. W. Norton and Company, 1962), p. 225.

[21] On the Meighen–Bracken changeover, see Bell, "Conservative Party National Conventions," pp. 35-39; Graham, III, *Meighen*, 139-51; and Granatstein, pp. 136-50.

Canadian political scene as John W. Dafoe found it possible to believe that Bracken would run for the CCF at the time of the next federal election.[22] Bracken was looked upon as a friend of the farmer and was thought to be popular in the west. Moreover, he was known to have become increasingly dissatisfied with Mackenzie King's government, especially over its war policies.

Nothing materialized from an approach Meighen made to Bracken in 1941 to seek the Conservative leadership, but in 1942 Meighen made a second attempt to persuade the Manitoba premier to run for the party's leadership. Meighen, according to his biographer, summoned "all his argumentative powers to show that only the Manitoba Premier could attract sufficient support among anti-Mackenzie King Liberals to bring about the downfall of the Government, that he alone could mobilize the Conservative party to withstand the anticipated post-war surge of the C.C.F."[23] Additionally, Meighen felt that the Conservative party had to make inroads in the west if it were to survive.

Bracken, for his part, stipulated certain conditions that would have to be met before he would assume leadership of the party. The name would have to be altered to "Progressive Conservative" and the party would, in fact, have to become a truly progressive party by adopting policies based upon those suggested by the Port Hope Conference of reform-minded Conservatives earlier that year.[24] Significantly, support for Bracken came from important members of the party: the retiring leader, the leader of the Conservatives in the Commons, and the convention chairman, to name but three. But perhaps of even greater importance was the fact that many party supporters and convention delegates sensed the mood of change in Canada and they feared for the future of their party. The CCF appeared to be on the upswing and the direction of Canadian politics appeared to be changing. Unless acceptable progressive policies and leadership could be presented to the Canadian electorate in the immediate future, many

[22] Granatstein, p. 142.
[23] Graham, III, 139.
[24] Both conditions were met, although the name was not changed until after Bracken's election as leader.

Conservatives maintained, their party would no longer be a viable force in Canadian politics. John Bracken and his brand of "Progressive Conservatism" were to their liking. Accordingly, Bracken had little trouble winning the party's leadership.

When, with the retirement of George Drew in 1956, John Diefenbaker sought the Progressive Conservative leadership, he did so in the face of some powerful opposition from within his own party. The president of the party's national association, the retiring leader, the acting leader in the House of Commons, and all but two or three of the Conservative front-benchers in the House (that is, virtually all of the party's "old guard"), were known to be opposed to Diefenbaker. Additionally, the Quebec wing of the party was reportedly opposed to him almost to a man.[25] Diefenbaker, who had already been defeated in two convention attempts for the Conservative leadership, had many charges levelled against him by his opponents. It was alleged that he was too old (he was then sixty-one), that his health was too weak, and that he was too temperamental to ever develop into an effective leader. Furthermore, it was said that he would prove to be an electoral liability in Quebec, the one area in which the party had its greatest need to increase its representation. Because he attended caucus meetings infrequently and because he often chose to play a role quite independent of his parliamentary party, he was regarded as a poor team man. He was, unmistakably, a loner, and no party could last long with such a person at its head, Diefenbaker's critics argued.

Yet Diefenbaker was, at the same time, a man with a large popular following. By 1956, he had established an unrivalled reputation within the Conservative party. He was a devoted parliamentarian, the party's best parliamentary debater, and an orator much in demand in various parts of the country. He was well known to the Canadian public, both as a champion of civil liberties and as an outspoken, effective critic of the Liberal government.

---

[25] On Diefenbaker's selection, see Blair Fraser, "Why the Conservatives are Swinging to Diefenbaker," *Maclean's* magazine, November 24, 1956, pp. 30 ff., and Meisel, *The Canadian General Election of 1957*, pp. 25-33.

Shortly before the 1956 convention Blair Fraser noted that even Diefenbaker's "bitterest enemies concede[d] that if an election were held tomorrow, [he] would draw more votes to the Conservative party than any other leader in sight."[26] What he lacked in front-bench support, Diefenbaker more than made up (in numbers at least) from Conservative back-benchers. For some Conservative MPs support for Diefenbaker was looked upon as a matter of personal political survival: "My people are for John," one of them explained in 1956. "If I were to oppose him I'd probably lose the nomination and I'd certainly lose the election."[27] For others, only Diefenbaker's election as leader would provide them with the means to uproot and replace the "old guard" of the party — to displace those who for so long had occupied the most powerful positions within the party.[28] Diefenbaker may have been a loner, but he was a popular loner. He had attracted as personal supporters those who were not in positions of power or influence. Because he was a successful outsider he was clearly attractive to many other "outsiders" in the parliamentary party, the party in the country, and the general public. As a protector of civil liberties, as a champion of minority causes, as a fighter battling the power centres within his own party, as an orator making fiery, relentless attacks on the St. Laurent government, as one who defended (as he himself would say) "the little people," Diefenbaker proved that he was capable of appealing to a wide variety of people, many of whom, for a variety of reasons, felt socially or politically enfeebled. Diefenbaker's supporters argued that he, more than anyone else, could give substance and direction to any movement for intra-party and intra-societal change — that he could effect a peaceful revolution.

In assessing the theory of charismatic leadership, Robert Tucker has pointed out that

> the charismatic leader is one in whom, by virtue of unusual personal qualities, the promise or hope of salvation — deliverance from distress — appears to be embodied. He is a

[26] Fraser, "Why the Conservatives are Swinging to Diefenbaker," p. 30.
[27] *Ibid.*
[28] See Camp, pp. 232-55.

leader who convincingly offers himself to a group of people in distress as one peculiarly qualified to lead them out of their predicament. He is in essence a savior, or one who is so perceived by his followers. *Charismatic leadership is specifically salvationist or messianic in nature.*[29]

Diefenbaker's rise to power in the Conservative party may, quite properly, be understood as the rise to power of a charismatic leader. At the time (Diefenbaker was easily elected on the first ballot of the 1956 convention) references were made to the "Diefenbaker Revolution" within the Conservative party. But in little more than six months references were being made to the "Diefenbaker Revolution" in Canadian politics, for with the 1957 general election Diefenbaker began to make the same impression on much of the electorate that he had previously made on a number of the convention delegates and party supporters. Growing disenchantment on the part of the public with the Liberal government could not have been better timed to match Diefenbaker's political skills. One incident in Amherst, Nova Scotia, during the 1957 election campaign, and recounted by a then admirer of Diefenbaker, Dalton Camp, makes clear the sort of support Diefenbaker was able to attract to himself and to his party, as well as the nature of the man's appeal.

> Amherst is a town in which industrial activity and prosperity are of recent memory. It is now a little down at the heel, and the townspeople listen, fascinated, to Diefenbaker's comprehensive cataloguing of the area's problems — the chronic plight of the coal industry at Springhill, doomed to be shut down; the abandoned ferry service from Parrsboro

---

[29] Robert C. Tucker, "The Theory of Charismatic Leadership," *Daedalus* (Summer 1968), pp. 742-43. (Italics in original.) See also Max Weber, *The Theory of Social and Economic Organization* (Toronto: Collier-Macmillan Canada, Ltd.; 1964 edition of a work published initially in 1947), especially chap. III. In referring to charismatic authority as a "specifically revolutionary force," one of Weber's statements may aid in understanding Diefenbaker's career as leader and his ultimate fall from favour with so many Conservatives: "The only basis of legitimacy for [the position of power] is personal charisma, so long as it is proved; that is, as long as it receives recognition and is able to satisfy the followers or disciples. But this lasts only so long as the belief in its charismatic inspiration remains" (p. 362).

to Wolfville; the loss of local industry; the decline of agriculture; the out-migration of the young; the plight of the old, and the problems that are being created as the life is slowly squeezed from the Cumberland towns and once-prospering villages along the Fundy shore.

In the close, damp stillness of the packed hall, the only sound is Diefenbaker's vibrant, emotive voice, his the only face in the crowd — his eyes lit by the ceiling lights and by the inspiration of his calling. He invokes Suez and St. Laurent's scornful "superman" epithet, directed at the British; he excoriates "the six-buck boys" who cheated the pensioners of their just deserts. "I love Parliament," he says, abruptly, turning to the mysteries of the pipeline controversy and the secrets of parliamentary procedure.

All these concerns, vaguely felt by wounded spirits, become focused on this single man, whose face quivers from the suppressed torments of having known and suffered the rape of Parliament, the despoiling of the British connection, the humiliation of the old, and the long, steady, inexorable decline in the prospects of Cumberland County and the town of Amherst.

In Diefenbaker's passion is incorporated all the grievances of his audience; he absorbs their indignation and, at the end, after they have laughed with him, cheered him, felt their nerve-ends respond to his voice, they find that he has repossessed their hopes, and they believe in him as they have not believed in anyone in a long, long time, if even then.

I leave the hall, as the crowd's ovation begins, to find a taxi to drive me to Moncton. I sit in the back, remote and silent, discouraging conversation with my driver. It is a little like watching a nightly miracle, this recurrent chemistry between Diefenbaker and his audiences.[30]

What had begun as a movement for change with, initially at least, a small group of loyal followers clustering around the charismatic personality and accepting his authority, eventually culminated (in March, 1958), in the largest single electoral victory for any party in Canada's history. The conversion of the Progressive Con-

---

[30] Camp, pp. 333-34. Reprinted by permission of McClelland and Stewart Ltd., the Canadian Publishers.

servative party into the party of "Diefenbaker Conservatives" had been completed in sixteen months.[31]

The theory of leadership selection as an interaction of individual personality and of the socio-political requirements at particular points in time helps, to some extent at least, to explain the choice of such leaders as King, Trudeau, Bracken and Diefenbaker. Yet no one could rightly claim that the delegates' assessments of the various candidates' personalities, of the appropriateness of those personalities to societal requirements, and of the interaction of these two could be expected to explain completely why certain persons are chosen as leaders and others not. As will be noted in Chapter 8, other considerations, such as the ordering of individual delegate preferences, the formation of voting coalitions on the convention floor, as well as electoral and organizational tactics and strategies, must also be taken into account in trying to explain the outcome of a convention. Even these, in concert with the interactional theory, do not present the whole explanation for the choice of one person over another. For the truth is, as correctly pointed out by one of the foremost scholars in the study of leadership, "the final determiners of the rise to leadership remain somewhat of a mystery."[32]

[31] See Tucker, "The Theory of Charismatic Leadership," p. 739, for a discussion of a charismatic movement's growth. Tucker makes the important point that when a leader-personality is genuinely charismatic, that personality will manifest itself before the leader becomes politically powerful (pp. 740-41). Roger Graham finds little to support the theory of charismatic leadership in Canadian history in his "Charisma and Canadian Politics," in Moir (ed.), *Character and Circumstance*, pp. 22-36.
[32] Gibb, "Leadership," 265.

7

A Comment on the CCF and the NDP

Before proceeding to an analysis of candidate and delegate strategies during leadership contests (Chapter 8) a brief comment on leadership selection by the CCF and NDP is in order. The Co-operative Commonwealth Federation and the New Democratic Party are so unlike the two older Canadian parties they deserve separate attention. Examining the two social democratic parties together, one is reminded of the fact that during their forty-year history they have never been close to forming either a government or the official opposition at Ottawa. They have never received more than 18 per cent of the total popular vote at a general election. The parties' federal electoral successes have been confined exclusively to five provinces. Their House of Commons membership since 1935 has averaged 18 in a House the average size of which has been 260. So far, at least, the CCF and NDP have been something less than major electoral successes in Canadian national politics. However, equally important as a reason for considering the CCF and NDP separately from the Conservatives and Liberals is the fact that the parties have claimed

173

to have, as one might expect, a more orthodox socialist understanding of party leadership: according to the party's constitution, the leader is chosen regularly and frequently. He is to be held accountable for his term as leader by the members of his party meeting in convention, and he is expected to ensure that the party convention policy decisions are implemented once he and his colleagues have gained power.

The CCF came into being well after the introduction of national leadership conventions by the Liberals and Conservatives and apparently no consideration was given to the selection of its leader by any means other than by convention.[1] Even if such consideration had been given, the obvious, indeed the unquestioned, first leader of the party, J. S. Woodsworth, was very much a part of the 1932 Calgary meeting. The delegates present at that meeting seized the opportunity to elect Woodsworth as their first "President" — a rather curious term that was clearly intended to carry with it responsibility for the leadership of the party in the House of Commons.

Woodsworth's career in politics made him the natural choice for leader of the CCF in 1932. First elected in 1921 as one of two Independent Labour Party members, Woodsworth was re-elected to the House three more times before the Calgary meeting. During much of his first twelve years in the Commons Woodsworth had managed to gain, more or less consistently, the support of some six to ten United Farmers and Progressive party members: the loose coalition eventually known as "the Ginger Group." Woodsworth was clearly recognized by members of this group and by others as its leader. Indeed, formal recognition of Woodsworth's position as a leader in parliament did not have to await the formation of the Ginger Group. "By 1923," Walter Young states, "Woodsworth had established his right in the Commons to speak

---

[1] In his study of the CCF Dean McHenry writes: "The CCF adopted the convention plan in part because of its utility in a young movement not yet widely represented in provincial and national legislatures. The convention method of selecting was also in harmony with the emerging Canadian political practices of the preceding twenty-five years." Dean E. McHenry, *The Third Force in Canada: The Cooperative Commonwealth Federation 1932-1948* (Berkeley: University of California Press, 1950), pp. 32-33.

after Robert Forke (. . . leader of the Progressives) as the leader of a party, even though there were only two in his party, that is, Irvine and himself."[2] That Woodsworth's personal characteristics had much to do with his election to the presidency in 1932, there can be little doubt.[3] But that Woodsworth had established a claim on the leadership of the CCF through his experience in parliamentary politics and through his direction of a small dedicated group of supporters in the Commons, there can also be no doubt. Woodsworth had, in fact, "emerged" in the truest sense of that word as leader of the CCF. In his resignation letter some eight years later, Woodsworth recognized the fact of his emergence when he wrote: "Ever since the formation of the C.C.F. I have held two positions — first, that of House Leader and second, that of President. To the first position there was no formal appointment."[4] The leader of the movement had been evolved in a manner more traditional, more in keeping with pre-leadership convention Canadian politics, than that then being followed by the other Canadian parties. The CCF and NDP (never parties renowned for ignoring precedents in spite of what they might claim) were not to ignore this one in years to come.

Woodsworth's successor, M. J. Coldwell, had been actively involved in politics when, in 1940, he was chosen as parliamentary leader of the CCF; two years later he was elected president of the party in succession to Woodsworth. Coldwell had established substantial contacts within the party as its first national secretary (1934–1937) and its first national chairman (1938–1942). His earlier political career had included eleven years as a Regina alderman, the presidency of the Independent Labour Party in Saskatchewan from 1930-1932, and the leadership of the Farmer-

[2] Walter D. Young, *The Anatomy of a Party: The National CCF, 1932-61* (Toronto: University of Toronto Press, 1969), p. 29.
[3] See Young, pp. 156-62; Kenneth McNaught, *A Prophet in Politics: A Biography of J. S. Woodsworth* (Toronto: University of Toronto Press, 1959), pp. 30-57; and Grace MacInnis, *J. S. Woodsworth: A Man to Remember* (Toronto: Macmillan Company of Canada, 1953), pp. 261-97 and 319-30, for evidence suggestive of Woodsworth's charismatic qualities and the widespread devotion to him of his followers.
[4] PAC, *CCF Records*, M.G. 28, IV-I, Volume 8, Woodsworth letter of resignation, October 26, 1940.

Labour Party of Saskatchewan from 1932 to 1935. In addition, Coldwell had made important contacts across Canada in his capacity as president of the Canadian Teachers' Federation from 1928 to 1934. His election to parliament in 1935 followed by ten years an earlier defeat as a Progressive candidate, but by the time the party needed a new House leader in late 1940 Coldwell had begun his sixth year in parliament, had twice been elected to the Commons, and was extremely well known to active CCF supporters in various provinces. Two years later he was chosen without contest in convention to become the party's second president. Coldwell had clearly won for himself the right to the leadership of the party.

Coldwell's defeat in the 1958 election left the tiny remaining group of eight CCF MPs the task of choosing a House leader from their midst. The man they selected, by a margin of one vote with three candidates seeking the office, was Hazen Argue. Although undoubtedly not "a member of that inner circle which had been the core of the CCF since its inception,"[5] Argue had, if nothing else, been consistently elected to the Commons since 1945. He was also ambitious. This fact was made apparent in 1960 when, in the final national convention of the CCF, the party constitution was amended to overcome a difference between the caucus and the party council by creating a new position (that of "National Leader") especially for Argue. However, the CCF was, by that time, a spent force, and plans were well under way for a party new in name and organization to succeed it. Under the circumstances, leadership of the old party was of dubious value. For a variety of reasons Argue and his fellow MPs had managed to antagonize many of the extra-parliamentary notables by 1960. Almost to a man these notables favoured T. C. Douglas as the first leader of the New Party.[6] The first contest for the national

[5] Young, p. 235.
[6] For more on the differences between the parliamentary and the extra-parliamentary parties see Young, pp. 234-38. Argue's selection in 1960 came only as a consequence of some rather unusual intra-party manoeuvring. See *Report of the Sixteenth National Convention, Co-operative Commonwealth Federation,* August 9, 10, 11, 1960, Regina, p. 5, and *The Commonwealth* (Regina), August 17, 1960, pp. 1 and 6.

leadership of Canada's new socialist party was in the offing; it promised to be a contest between a small, belligerent, but quite powerless caucus, most of whose members supported their leader, and the extra-parliamentary party professionals in support of an electorally successful provincial premier. There was never any doubt who would win.

At the time he was chosen leader of the NDP in 1961 (by a vote of 1,391 to 380 over Argue on the first ballot), T. C. Douglas was fifty-six years of age. Douglas was then starting his eighteenth consecutive year as premier of Saskatchewan, having previously served nine years as a federal MP. He had been leader of the CCF in Saskatchewan for twenty years, and was a former national president of the CCF youth movement. As the leader of the only CCF party in Canada to have gained office, as an effective politician and a first-rate orator, Douglas's name and reputation were well known across Canada. For these reasons, the senior party officials clearly wanted Douglas to lead the New Party. The socialists were presented with their first opportunity to co-opt a successful provincial leader into federal politics, and they seized it.

With Douglas's retirement in 1971 as leader of the NDP, five candidates sought the party's leadership. Three (Ed Broadbent, Frank Howard and David Lewis) were members of parliament, whereas two (John Harney and James Laxer) had had no experience in either federal or provincial legislatures. From the early stages of the leadership campaign Lewis was plainly the man to beat, although four ballots were needed for him to win a majority of the delegates' votes (see Table 7-1). Without question, Lewis was one candidate whose political career had been headed in the direction of party leadership. He had served the party in different capacities during the leadership of Woodsworth, Coldwell, Argue and Douglas. There is no reason to question Young's assessment that in the CCF's formative years Lewis dominated the "socialist elite, as he did the whole party," that as CCF national secretary from 1938–1950 "he was the centre of party affairs," and that "his influence was not markedly diminished after he left the post of national secretary."[7] Within the party his skills were

[7] Young, pp. 163 and 166-67.

both managerial and political. From 1950–1961 he was elected to the CCF's vice-chairmanship, chairmanship and presidency, and he later served on the NDP executive as an elected vice-president. He sat continuously on the CCF's national executive from 1938 to 1961. Lewis ran for parliament eight times and was, on three of the last four occasions, successful. When in parliament he served as deputy leader of his party and was, by the time of the 1971 leadership convention, commonly regarded as "the NDP's most persistent critic of the Government."[8] Lewis's claim on the leadership of the NDP had been established.

In fact each of the five leaders of the CCF and NDP had established a legitimate title to the party leadership unmatched by any of his contemporary rivals. Each was experienced, available and by far the most suitable for the job. Each had, through years of service to the party in various capacities, worked his way to the top. No political dilettanti these: each was the heir apparent. The socialist party, the party most willing to experiment with leadership review and leadership accountability, the party claiming more openness and internal democracy than other parties, has been the one Canadian party since the introduction of leadership conventions to have selected as its leaders men who have followed the more traditional, the more hierarchical career pattern to the party's highest position. CCF and NDP leadership conventions have had the effect of altering only the way in which the men with extensive political experience are chosen as leaders, not the fact.

Why should this be so? The reasons lie almost exclusively with the relative size and importance of the party. Co-optation of extra-party notables could scarcely be effected by a small party holding out little chance of gaining power. Co-optations from outside a party will be minimal if the rewards are not commensurate with the risks involved, and minimal within the party from the provincial level of government to the federal if the party wins power only spasmodically and irregularly in the provinces. So far the one exception to selection of the party's leaders from within the ranks of the parliamentary group has been T. C. Douglas, a

---

[8] *Globe and Mail*, April 17, 1971, p. 7.

Table 7–1: NDP Convention, April 21-24, 1971, Ottawa, Ontario

Leadership Balloting: April 24

Candidates in order of rank on first ballot	First ballot	Second ballot	Third ballot	Fourth ballot	Parliamentary experience		Provincial experience	
					House or Senate	Cabinet	House	Cabinet
David Lewis	661	715	742	1046	6 yrs. 4 mo.	—	—	—
James Laxer	378	407	508	612	—	—	—	—
John Harney	299	347	431ª		—	—	—	—
Ed Broadbent	236	223ª			2 yrs. 10 mo.	—	—	—
Frank Howard	124ª				13 yrs. 11 mo.	—	3 yrs. 7½ mo.	—

ªEliminated as a result of this ballot.

fact hardly surprising given the party's success under him in Saskatchewan and the obvious desire of the national party, certainly no different from that of the Conservatives, the other long-term opposition party, to be led by someone with a record of electoral victories. The simple fact is, if the possibilities for co-optation are minimal, the party has little choice but to recruit from its own midst.[9]

Co-optation would also appear to be inconsistent with the party's socialist tradition and ethic. If the party were to employ co-optive practices quite consistently, then it would run the risk of appearing to be something other than what it claimed to be — of resorting to practices which any good socialist would renounce as undemocratic and elitist. Socialists seem to believe strongly in the individual proving himself a socialist by word and deed. The outsider, therefore, is viewed with suspicion until his "credentials" have been demonstrated. To establish any serious claim on the party leadership within the socialist context, then, means that an individual would have to have shown that he had worked assiduously for socialist interests in general and for the party in particular.

The CCF and NDP have prided themselves on being parties of regular leadership review. The NDP, for example, has insisted by constitutional provision that the "supreme governing body" shall be the party meeting in convention, that conventions, held regularly every second year, "have final authority in all matters of federal policy, program and constitution," and that they elect a leader who "act[s] as the leader of the Party in the Federal House of Commons."[10] In the event of a leadership vacancy between

---

[9] The NDP will have difficulty resisting the attraction of attempting to recruit as Lewis's successor one of the current NDP premiers who successfully leads his provincial party for the next few years. If that is the case, then the NDP will probably move increasingly in the direction of the Conservative party (in so far as co-optive practices are concerned) as it becomes better established and more electorally successful in provincial politics.

[10] *Constitution of the New Democratic Party* as amended, April 1971, articles V (2) and VII (2).

Table 7—2: CCF and NDP National Conventions

	Date	Place	Leadership Events of Note
CCF	August 1—3, 1932	Calgary	Woodsworth elected president, unanimously without contest
	July 19—23, 1933	Regina	
	July 17—19, 1934	Winnipeg	
	August 3—5, 1936	Toronto	
	July 28—29, 1938	Edmonton	
	October 28—29, 1940	Winnipeg	Woodsworth named honorary president[1]
	July 27—29, 1942	Toronto	Coldwell elected president unanimously without contest
	Nov. 29—Dec. 1, 1944	Montreal	
	August 7—9, 1946	Regina	
	August 19—21, 1948	Winnipeg	
	July 26—28, 1950	Vancouver	
	August 6—8, 1952	Toronto	
	July 28—30, 1954	Edmonton	
	August 1—3, 1956	Winnipeg	
	July 23—25, 1958	Montreal	
	August 9—11, 1960	Regina	Argue elected national leader unanimously without contest[2]
NDP	July 31—Aug. 4, 1961	Ottawa	Douglas elected leader on first ballot
	August 6—9, 1963	Regina	
	July 12—15, 1965	Toronto	
	July 3—6, 1967	Toronto	
	October 29—31, 1969	Winnipeg	
	April 21—24, 1971	Ottawa	Lewis elected leader on fourth ballot

[1] On November 6, 1940, caucus elected Coldwell acting house leader and on April 22, 1942, following Woodsworth's death, house leader.

[2] On April 23, 1958, following Coldwell's defeat, caucus elected Argue house leader. Coldwell remained president and national leader until the 1960 convention when he was elected honorary national leader.

regular conventions "the Council of the federal party may, after consultation with the parliamentary caucus, appoint an acting Leader to serve until such time as a Convention may be called."[11] But the party in convention, so the argument goes, regularly selects the leader who, in turn, and with his parliamentary colleagues, is expected to press for the implementation of the policies arrived at in convention. The convention's pre-eminent position means that the caucus "is not very important" as a policy-making body for it "has no choice but to follow" the policy directives of the convention.[12] The leader, specifically, accounts for his term of office every two years, and he may or may not be re-elected for a further two-year term by the party meeting in convention depending upon the mood of the party and the party's appraisal of his leadership up to that point.

Such is part of the official party line of many socialist parties. So far as the NDP is concerned, how well does it accord with the facts? To be sure policy is discussed, resolutions are debated and passed or defeated by the delegates at the party's biennial conventions. (For a list of CCF and NDP conventions, see Table 7-2, and for a breakdown of the delegate registration at the 1971 convention, see Table 7-3.) But, as the party has never been in power in Ottawa the supreme test has, of course, not had to be met. The experience of socialist parties elsewhere (Britain, for example,) would scarcely support the official party position on policy directives and the degree to which they are binding on the parliamentary party;[13] the same was certainly found to be the case with the CCF during its years in office in Saskatchewan.[14] Granting that a "vital role" was played by the CCF membership in the policy process at the national level ("if only by their mere presence and the leaders' consciousness of the democratic struc-

[11] *Constitution of the New Democratic Party*, article VII (3).
[12] Interview with Clifford A. Scotton, federal secretary, NDP, Ottawa, May 16, 1969.
[13] See McKenzie, *British Political Parties*, pp. 485-516.
[14] See Evelyn Eager, "The Paradox of Power in the Saskatchewan C.C.F., 1944-1961," in J. H. Aitchison (ed.), *The Political Process in Canada: Essays in Honour of R. MacGregor Dawson* (Toronto: University of Toronto Press, 1963), pp. 118-35.

Table 7–3: *1971 NDP Convention Delegate Registration** (Ottawa, April 21-24, 1971)*

Category	Potential	Actual	% of Total Provincial Registration	
			Potential	Actual
Provincial Delegates				
British Columbia	163	141	14.7	14.5
Alberta	56	39	5.1	4.0
Saskatchewan	295	237	26.8	24.3
Manitoba	99	98	9.0	10.1
Ontario	403	388	36.5	39.8
Quebec	42	40	3.8	4.1
New Brunswick	9	6	0.8	0.6
Nova Scotia	25	17	2.3	1.8
P.E.I.	1	1	0.1	0.1
Newfoundland	9	7	0.8	0.7
N.W.T.	1	—	0.1	—
Sub-Total	1103	974	100.0	100.0
Federal council	112	106		
Federal caucus	23	23		
Young New Democrats	135	94		
Affiliated local groups[a]	854	490		
Central labour bodies[b]	213	52		
Sub-total	1337	765		
TOTAL	2440	1739		

*Exclusive of Alternates
[a]*Constitution New Democratic Party* Article VI (4).
[b]*Constitution New Democratic Party* Article VI (5).
Source: Lists of potential and actual delegate registration provided by the NDP.

ture"), Young concludes that "it would be difficult to defend the proposition that CCF members actually made and shaped the party policy; this was the function of the party leaders."[15] There is no reason to believe that such a conclusion is less supportable in the case of the NDP as well. Memberships offer policy guidance; they are unable to control or direct in the fullest sense of those terms, no matter what their expectations and their determination.

It is equally difficult to accept the party line on leadership selection. Re-election of the leader at regular intervals for two-year terms is an act based on considerations markedly different from those involved in choosing a new leader of the party. Vacancies created through deaths and resignations present no serious problems and can be filled through the normal processes. But a challenge directed against the incumbent leader at the time he seeks re-election must be carefully planned and executed if it is to succeed, an enormously complex task given a convention selection system if the challenge is to be something more than token. In addition, the party runs the risk of suffering more from the wounds created by a leadership challenge than it gains from the fact of having a new leader. Within the Parliamentary Labour Party, a party with a much greater proclivity for disputes over leadership than the NDP, and a party with a relatively less cumbersome process of non-renewal of a leader's appointment when the party is in opposition, there have been only two occasions (both in the early 1960s over Gaitskell's leadership) on which the strength of the leader's support has been tested by electoral contest within the parliamentary group itself. Not so with the CCF and NDP. Not only have these parties been free of any open challenge with intent to remove their leaders, they have refused to accept the resignation of one leader who wished to retire and persuaded two others to remain as leaders until the time was more propitious for the selection of their successors. When Woodsworth submitted his resignation in 1940 (for policy and health reasons), the party in convention refused to accept it, changing instead his title from

---

[15] Young, pp. 155 and 228.

president to "Honorary President." Similarly, when Coldwell wished to resign in 1958, having just been personally defeated and having his group's parliamentary representation reduced from 25 to 8 in the election of that year (surely enough to test any leader's acceptability to his party), the party's council prevailed upon him to remain as national leader for a further two-year term. He did. Douglas first seriously considered retirement in 1968-69, but party officials successfully urged him to stay on as leader for a further two years for, according to Douglas himself, the timing of a leader's departure is "a matter of deciding if a new leader should be in the field two years before the election, 15 months before the election or 12 months. It's a matter of publicity and political strategy."[16] Indeed it is. Timing (uppermost in any politician's mind) is of major importance in leadership selection. Regular and frequent election of the leader means that the party has opted in favour of providing an institutional vehicle by which the incumbent may be challenged. But the allocation of fifteen minutes of time on the agenda of biennial conventions for the "Election of the Leader" indicates also that the exercise itself is seen by party officials themselves as more symbolic than real.

[16] *Globe and Mail,* May 6, 1969, p. 9.

8

The Politics of the Selection Process

Why Some Choose to Become Leadership Candidates

The mere presence of several candidates on the convention ballot does not itself guarantee a fiercely competitive race for the leadership. If a popular heir apparent is running, the competitive aspect of the contest will, in fact, be quite illusory, for the decision will almost certainly be settled by a sizable majority of the delegates on the first ballot. If "nuisance" candidates are running they can hope to gain nothing more than the publicity which they seek, for they stand no chance whatsoever of winning the leadership.[1] But there are others, much better

---

[1] "Native son" nominations (so common in American nominating conventions), intended as a gesture to reflect favourably upon the individual nominated as well as the province or region with which he is closely associated, are rare in Canadian leadership conventions. Perhaps the reason lies in the fact that the convention itself and the leadership voting system are not structured on a provincial basis. There is little encouragement in such a system for locally popular politicians to be nominated simply for the sake of promoting regionalism or provincialism. Allan MacEachen's

known to the public and to the members of their party than the nuisance candidates, who also allow their names to stand in nomination even though they too have little hope of winning the leadership. Why they should choose to do so, of course, is not always clear. Some, apparently, wish simply to protest against the convention as a possible "cut and dried affair."[2] But many of the others seem to fit into one of two roughly defined groups.

For younger and generally less well-known politicians who are highly motivated by a drive for career advancement, a leadership convention affords an excellent opportunity to gain both national attention and political promotion. Most such politicians would find it difficult to by-pass the opportunity of running in a leadership convention recognizing that, given the considerable exposure to the public and to their party during the convention and its campaign, they would likely stand to gain much more within their party than they would lose. Indeed, it might take little more than a particularly effective speech at the convention itself to give a substantial boost to such a politician's career, as M. A. MacPherson and J. J. Greene proved in 1938 and 1968 respectively.

MacPherson, a former Attorney General of Saskatchewan, was a virtual unknown to a number of Conservative delegates in 1938 and was a late candidate for the party's leadership as well. According to contemporary accounts, his surprisingly forceful nomination speech swayed many of the delegates, one of whom

---

candidature and support in 1968 more closely approximated that of a "native son" candidate than any in the history of Canadian conventions, yet it could scarcely be called successful. MacEachen openly sought the Maritime delegates' votes as a Maritimer himself, hoping to get a sufficient number of their votes to put him in a strong position on the first ballot. Most of his voting support came, in fact, from Maritime delegates, but as it was smaller than what he needed to continue in the balloting as a major force, and as much of it was committed to him for only the first ballot, MacEachen withdrew. See: *Telegram* (Toronto), April 4, 1968, p. 9, and Joseph Wearing, "The Liberal Choice," *Journal of Canadian Studies*, III (May 1968), 9-10.
[2] This was John Diefenbaker's reason for entering the 1942 Conservative leadership convention. See *Winnipeg Free Press*, December 8, 1942, p. 15.

later allowed that "the MacPherson whirlwind campaign almost
took the convention by storm. Although I'd never heard of Mac-
Pherson before, he attracted me right away, so I voted for him."[3]
MacPherson ran a respectable second on each of the two ballots
and earned a considerable reputation within the party as a result.
Greene's modest campaign for the Liberal leadership in 1968 had
made little impact on the delegates during the several weeks prior
to the convention. But this was partially corrected by his fighting,
highly partisan speech at the convention itself. The speech was
rated by many delegates as the best of the evening and without
a doubt gave more first ballot support to Greene than would
otherwise have been the case.

Given a moderately impressive convention and campaign showing, a politician of this type might properly expect a cabinet
position or a more prestigious cabinet portfolio than that which he
then held. His stature within the party would certainly be enhanced, and he might well receive enough favourable attention
to leave many of the party faithful convinced of his attractiveness
as a future leader of the party. The candidatures of R. J. Manion
(1927), M. A. MacPherson (1938), Davie Fulton (1956), J. J.
Greene (1968) and John Turner (1968) seem best explained in
this way.

For another group of candidates, however, their profound concern over the direction of their party's policies leads them to
allow their names to be placed in nomination for the leadership
of their party. Whereas to the members of the previous group
the convention proves to be a vehicle ideally suited for career
advancement, to this second type of candidate the convention
affords one further opportunity to attempt to direct his party toward certain policy goals. The two categories are by no means
mutually exclusive, for some candidates may well overlap the
two categories. But characteristically, the candidates in this second
group are older men of some prominence in their party who, although their association with their party has been a long-standing
one, have nonetheless frequently distinguished themselves by
publicly and harshly criticizing their own party. They enter the

[3] Bell, "Conservative Party National Conventions," p. 27.

race knowing full well that they have virtually no chance of winning the leadership, but because their desire to articulate certain policies is so strong, they seize the opportunity presented to them by a leadership convention to address their fellow party members. The sort of candidate who might be included in this category would be George Graham (1919), Robert Rogers (1927), H. H. Stevens (1942) and Eric Kierans (1968), but three better examples than Wallace McCutcheon (1967), C. G. Power (1948), and John Diefenbaker (1967) could scarcely be found.

Senator Wallace McCutcheon entertained no false illusions about his chances of being chosen Conservative leader in 1967.[4] He knew that he was a spokesman for a minority in the Conservative party. Yet McCutcheon became a candidate so that he might, both through his speeches across the country and through the forum of the convention itself, present to as wide an audience of Conservatives as possible his own views on the need to reduce government spending and to bring an end to what he called "the merciless rape of the Canadian taxpayer." "Like many of us," he argued in his campaign literature,

> I have watched with a growing sense of dismay, the gigantic auction market that has characterized Canadian politics over the past few years. I have looked on with incredulous disbelief as the various political parties — including, unfortunately, the Conservative Party — have all sought to outflank and outsmart each other by engaging in an orgy of promises and spending that has squandered the earnings and savings of millions of hard-working and thrifty Canadians.[5]

C. G. Power's candidacy in the 1948 Liberal leadership convention, when he ran against Louis St. Laurent and J. G. Gardiner, was of the same type. Power recorded in his autobiography:

> I never had anything like a glimmer of hope that I would be successful; but I was coming more and more to the conclusion that since I had in the past three or four years, in the House of Commons, in speeches, and in magazine articles,

---

[4] Johnston records that "No one expected [McCutcheon] to win, least of all himself" (Johnston, *The Party's Over*, p. 198).
[5] "The McCutcheon Express," a four-page pamphlet distributed to Conservative delegates attending the 1967 convention.

protested against the [Liberal] government's method of procedure and continued wartime controls, I could not at this time whitewash the past and give a blank cheque for the future. This was the time, when Liberals of all shades and degrees were assembled, to set forth my views, and if anyone wanted to vote for them, and for what I considered to be the true precepts of Liberalism, then I would give him an opportunity.[6]

John Diefenbaker's last-minute decision to allow his name to stand in the Conservative convention of 1967 was made in full knowledge of the fact that he could never gain the party's leadership in that contest.[7] Diefenbaker apparently persisted in entering the contest so that he might use the time allotted to him for his speech as a candidate to warn the party not to adopt the "two-nations" proposal contained in the policy committee's report. Coupled with the public warning was a behind-the-scenes threatened walkout by Diefenbaker and his supporters if the "two-nations" proposal was accepted. Such measures, Diefenbaker's confidants maintained, could at one and the same time be made possible and effective only so long as Diefenbaker was still in the running for his party's leadership. By agreement between Diefenbaker's advisers and convention officials, the policy committee report was tabled in the party's plenary session without discussion only moments before the leadership balloting was to begin, an action which led Diefenbaker to claim a policy victory even though he did not do well in the leadership balloting.[8]

---

[6] Power, *A Party Politician*, p. 396.
[7] James Johnston recalls the following conversation in Diefenbaker's hotel suite on the day of the leadership balloting:
> " 'You're going to be clobbered this afternoon, Chief,' I said, 'and [Senator] Dave Walker and I just want to remind you again.'
> " 'I know,' he replied, stretched out on his bed, perfectly relaxed. 'If that's what they want to do, it's all right by me, but there will be the greatest upset throughout this country' " (Johnston, p. 235).
[8] See Johnston, pp. 230-37.

Organizations, Strategies and Tactics

The candidate who seriously attempts to obtain his party's leadership in convention is naturally interested in effecting a victorious electoral coalition on the day of the leadership balloting.[9] That candidate's basic strategy, from which other strategies and tactics emanate, is clearly designed to obtain enough support to make his victory possible. Both the candidate's campaign and his organization are planned with this fundamental goal in mind. As a consequence, probably no one is more fully aware of the complexities of leadership selection by a party convention than the serious leadership candidate; for he learns (if he did not already know) that to construct an adequate organization, plan an acceptable campaign, and effect a winning coalition in a country with as varied a population and political interests as Canada's, is a truly major undertaking.

From the time of the Conservative convention of 1927, pre-convention campaigning and organizational efforts by candidates and their supporters have become increasingly characteristic of leadership conventions.[10] Not every serious candidate in the various leadership contests since then, of course, has campaigned actively for the office, but those who have chosen not to do so have usually enjoyed so undisputed a lead over their opponents that, for them, campaigning would have been a superfluous exer-

[9] Throughout this chapter, the term "coalition" will be used to refer to any grouping of individual delegates whose voting behaviour happens to coincide at a particular point in time in support of the same candidate. Such use of the term is naturally based on the assumption that there are individual voting behaviour preferences and individual preference rankings. It recognizes that such loosely knit groupings are both unstructured and highly ephemeral, and that their membership will change from one ballot to the next according to the ordering and intensity of voting preferences. "Coalition" should not be taken to mean (as one would interpret the term as it is applied to American nominating conventions) that it is simply a product of a bargaining type of situation, with various factional leaders in such powerful positions to be able to "deliver" blocs of votes *en masse*.

[10] Little in the way of organized campaigning on behalf of the various candidates took place during the pre-convention period of the 1919 Liberal convention, perhaps largely because no one knew with any certainty who the candidates would be until the convention itself met. See *Gazette* (Montreal), August 5, 1919, p. 1, and August 8, 1919, p. 1.

cise. Nonetheless, the basic point remains that there has been such a marked shift in the direction of increasingly vigorous campaigning on the part of all major contestants (reaching, as it did, its zenith in the 1967 Conservative and 1968 Liberal conventions) that it now appears that the candidate who preferred "not to seek the office, but to have the office seek him" is indeed a creature of the past.[11]

If they have the available financial and human resources, candidates typically establish (1) a campaign organization, (2) a headquarters' organization, and (3) a convention floor organization; they hope, naturally, that such organizational structures will aid them substantially in their drive for their party's leadership. But it is certainly as true in Canada as Nelson W. Polsby and Aaron B. Wildavsky found it to be in the United States: "there is an extra-ordinarily wide divergence among candidate organizations. They range from the comprehensive, integrated, and superbly effective to the fragmented, uncoordinated, and virtually non-existent."[12] The success of such organizational attempts depends, in no small way, on the political experience and the managerial abilities of those persuaded to serve in key staff positions. An examination of one candidate's organization serves to illustrate many of these points.

Davie Fulton was the first of the nine major contenders to declare officially that he was a candidate for the Conservative leadership in 1967. January 19, 1967, was the date Fulton chose to make his announcement. He clearly hoped for an early convention. It was a month, however, before the date of the conven-

---

[11] On earlier Conservative and Liberal candidates' campaigns for their party's leadership see Williams, *The Conservative Party of Canada, 1920-1949*, pp. 91-93; Herbert F. Quinn, "The Third National Convention of the Liberal Party," *CJEPS*, XVII (May 1951), 231; and Ward, "The Liberals in Convention," pp. 1-11. Quinn notes that in 1948 James Gardiner's "organization issued a large number of leaflets, engaged in intense lobbying among the delegates, and provided entertainment in the form of dinners and cocktail parties at which everyone was welcome" (p. 231). Gardiner's campaign may well have been the first of the very elaborate and expensive convention operations.

[12] Polsby and Wildavsky, *Presidential Elections: Strategies of American Electoral Politics*, 2nd ed. (New York: Charles Scribner's Sons, 1968), p. 89.

tion was set by the party's convention committee and it was not until September 5-9 that the convention itself was held. It is difficult to judge with any certainty, but Fulton's announcement may have been so prematurely timed that his campaign staled with the passing months and suffered accordingly. (In contrast, Stanfield and Roblin, the two top candidates in the convention voting, chose to wait until July 19 and August 3 respectively to declare their intentions to seek the leadership. Certainly both their organizations thrived on the freshness and excitement inherent in last-minute whirlwind campaigns.) V. O. Key, Jr., has noted the delicacy of the timing problem in American nominating conventions: "A tactical problem confronted by all aspirants is the timing of the announcement of their candidacies. One maxim is that a candidacy announced too soon may be blighted like an early-blooming flower; too late an announcement may give an advantage to other contenders."[13] There seems to be no reason to doubt the appropriateness of such a statement to Canadian leadership campaigns.

Having made his decision to become a leadership candidate, Fulton quickly set about constructing a campaign organization in both Toronto and Ottawa. He appointed an executive assistant (who served, in fact, as his campaign manager), a fund raiser, two staff assistants (one with special responsibility for Quebec), an executive secretary responsible for itinerary, travel arrangements and press liaison, a speech writer, a director of public relations (who was, additionally, charged with making the physical convention arrangements in Toronto), and a youth organizer. Local and regional supporters were contacted with a view to promoting the election by their constituency or appointment by their provincial organizations of delegates sympathetic to Fulton, provincial organizations were established, and a Fulton National Committee was struck. Twenty of that committee's members met in Ottawa in April to plan the strategy for Fulton's national campaign. By the time the delegates had gathered in Toronto for the convention, Fulton had travelled 76,000 miles and spent over $100,000 in his search for delegate support.

[13] Key, *Politics, Parties and Pressure Groups*, p. 401.

The majority of Fulton's campaign and headquarters staff were men under thirty years of age who, despite their youth, had a surprising amount of political experience and many valuable political contacts within the party. Fulton's staff proved to be more politically professional than Roblin's but undeniably weaker and less polished than Stanfield's. They were able to perform most of the essential tasks a serious candidate requires. Literature in the form of pamphlets, policy statements and press releases was produced during the pre-convention stage and, for the convention itself, signs, badges and other paraphernalia were prepared for distribution to the delegates. But Fulton's staff lacked administrative and organizational skills and his campaign suffered as a result. Proper delegation of responsibilities between the Ottawa and Toronto groups never materialized; correspondence with campaign workers and convention delegates was inadequately handled; and the campaign manager proved to be overly protective of the candidate, shielding him from much-needed criticism and advice, and restricting his lines of access to limited sources of information. Moreover, the Toronto and Ottawa offices never effectively meshed together as a cohesive campaign unit, and some essential tasks were completely overlooked. To their dismay, the Fulton organizers discovered as the balloting began on convention day that they had no floor manager, an oversight which was to prove costly in maintaining an effective communications network during the convention itself.[14]

Candidates and their organizers try desperately to avoid the sort of difficulties and problems that plague groups such as Fulton's, but few succeed completely. Those who do, however, undoubtedly deserve serious consideration from the delegates. For, if in addition to surviving an exhausting nationwide campaign of several

---

[14] Joseph Wearing has contributed a useful analysis of the 1967 Conservative convention, which sheds some light on the candidates and their organizations; see "A Convention for Professionals: The PCs in Toronto," *Journal of Canadian Studies,* II (November 1967), 3-16. The information on Fulton's campaign has been gathered from Wearing and Philip B. Lind, "Davie Fulton's Campaign for Leadership — 1967," (unpublished M.A. thesis, University of Rochester, 1968).

weeks duration, a candidate manages to bring together on short notice an experienced, politically knowledgeable staff, to assign responsibilities in such a way as to maximize expertise and minimize internal conflict, and to ensure considerable first ballot convention support for his candidacy, he has made a solid claim on his party's leadership.

Strategic and tactical moves, if properly conducted, may prove to be as valuable to a candidate's campaign as his organization, or they may even help to offset substantially the adverse effects of a weak organization. Examples of such moves by three winning leadership candidates (Diefenbaker, Stanfield and Trudeau) are worthwhile noting.

Among the charges levelled against John Diefenbaker in 1956 in his drive for the Conservative leadership was the allegation that he was so unacceptable to Quebec that the Conservative party would never be able to gain any significant electoral support from that province under his leadership. Left unanswered, such a charge could have severely damaged Diefenbaker's chances of becoming leader. It would not only have made Quebec support difficult to obtain; it would also have removed as likely supporters those non-Quebec delegates convinced of the need to have as a party leader one who could appeal to all sections of the country. To overcome the problem, Diefenbaker's strategists abandoned hope of winning large-scale Quebec support and concentrated instead on gaining as much publicity as possible in the English-language press across Canada for the speeches of Diefenbaker's few Quebec supporters and for the activities of a small committee of influential Quebec Conservatives pledged to support Diefenbaker. Their aim was to create the impression outside Quebec that Diefenbaker was acceptable to Quebec. By way of illustration, one speech delivered two weeks before the convention to a small audience in Toronto by the only Quebec MP supporting Diefenbaker was given wide coverage in many parts of Canada following its dispatch as a Canadian Press news item and was carried by the pro-Conservative Toronto *Telegram* on its front page under the heading "Quebec Swinging to Diefenbaker." According to John Meisel it was "most unlikely that [Diefenbaker's Quebec] committee, or the speeches made by some of its members, has the slightest effect on the Quebec delegation at the convention."[15] But as the stratagem was not designed to alter the Quebec situation as much as it was to boost Diefenbaker's campaign in other parts of the country, it was a success, for it helped to create a "climate of opinion favourable to Diefenbaker's election"[16] among non-Quebec delegates.

Following their bitterly divisive meeting in Ottawa in November 1966, Conservatives, with only the slightest provocation, were quick to label one another as being either of the Diefenbaker or the Camp factions of the party. To be unmistakably identified with one group, with no apparent support from the other, could well have proved costly to a candidate in 1967. In choosing Maurice Flemming as his campaign manager for the 1967 Conservative leadership contest, Robert Stanfield selected a well-known Diefenbaker loyalist who had recently defeated a "Camp" candidate for the presidency of the Nova Scotia Progressive Conservative Association. By making such an appointment, Stanfield shrewdly defused at least some of the potential criticism that could have been levelled at him as "Dalton Camp's Candidate." At the same time he broadened his appeal base in such a way as to make it easier for Maritime Diefenbaker loyalists in particular (to whom Flemming was especially well-known) to give their support to Stanfield.[17]

Fearing that if they stressed Trudeau's apparent lead over the other Liberal candidates they would unite his opponents behind a common "stop Trudeau" candidate before the balloting at the 1968 convention, the Trudeau advisers, in their discussions with delegates during the final few days before the election, deliberately played down the fact that Trudeau was the front-runner. Moreover, they claimed Trudeau's campaign workers were unmistakably non-professional and ill-organized, and quite unprepared to compete

[15] Meisel, *The Canadian General Election of 1957,* pp. 30-31.
[16] Meisel, p. 31.
[17] See the *Telegram*'s account of the 1967 Conservative convention, *Balloons and Ballots* (Toronto: Telegram Publishing Co., 1967), p. 108, and Coates, *The Night of the Knives,* pp. 102-106.

effectively with the party pro's who were assisting Martin, Winters and Hellyer. "As the Convention drew near," according to one account,

> the Trudeau people rather encouraged the idea that their organization was not strong. A man from Hellyer's head-quarters recalled having a Trudeau man bewail to him, "How can you do anything with the Church and the Establishment against you." These tactics were intended to contrast the Trudeau "amateurs" (as he himself called them) with Hellyer's "organization men." They also wanted to dilute the beat-the-leader feeling which is always natural at a convention and suggest that the leader was somehow an underdog.[18]

To counter the charge that Trudeau was so much an outsider to the Liberal party that his claim to becoming its leader lacked legitimacy, Trudeau's advisers understandably made the very most of two important events that occurred only four days before the balloting. Mitchell Sharp, Finance Minister, prominent Liberal, and candidate for the party's leadership, withdrew from the leadership race and announced that he was supporting Trudeau. The three federal cabinet ministers who had worked for Sharp's campaign joined him in making the switch. On the same day Joey Smallwood, the premier of Newfoundland and a man with valuable Liberal connections beyond his own province, announced that he too was supporting Trudeau for the Liberal leadership.[19] From that point on, Smallwood's and Sharp's frequent accompaniment of Trudeau in his meetings with the press, in his visits with groups of delegates, in his television appearances, and in his convention floor box, transferred a needed aura of acceptability to Trudeau's candidacy. Just as the presence of two privy councillors at the birth of a royal child in Britain has attested to the legitimacy of the child as a potential heir to the throne, so the presence of Sharp and Smallwood (two of Canada's best-known Liberals) attested to the legitimacy of Trudeau as a serious contender and

[18] Wearing, "The Liberal Choice," p. 12.
[19] On Sharp's and Smallwood's announcements see the *Globe and Mail* April 4, 1968, pp. 1 and 8.

potential heir to the Liberal leadership. The gesture was symbolic-
ally and politically important, for it helped to authenticate Trudeau's claim to his party's leadership.

Although it is customary for a retiring leader to remain publicly
neutral in the selection of his successor, on occasion (as with
Meighen's preference for Bracken and St. Laurent's for Pearson)
the leader's views are something of an open secret. Just before
the 1948 Liberal convention Mackenzie King feared that his
choice for a successor (Louis St. Laurent) might face rather stiff
competition from J. G. Gardiner, federal Minister of Agriculture.
King held Gardiner's candidacy in low regard and was distressed
at the prospect of Gardiner becoming leader of the Liberal party.
"It would be difficult for me if matters go too far, to refrain from
letting the party know for whom I stand," Mackenzie King recorded in his diary. "I wish I could hold back choosing as between colleagues but the interests of the country may demand a
final word. I am letting it be known through other sources just
how I feel about the importance of St. Laurent being chosen."[20]
But not satisfied with a deliberate "leak," Mackenzie King went
further. To assist in defeating Gardiner, King devised a strategy
whereby several prominent cabinet ministers would be nominated
for the leadership, decline the nomination from the convention
floor podium immediately before the leadership balloting, and
"in this way, the delegates will see that all the leading members
of the Cabinet without exception are for St. Laurent and none of
them for Gardiner."[21] Five federal cabinet ministers were duly
nominated, each of whom declined the nomination in a short
speech before the convention.[22] King's strategic manoeuvrings
proved to be unnecessary, however, for St. Laurent was widely
recognized within his own party as the heir apparent. He carried
into the 1948 convention more voting strength than any other

[20] J. W. Pickersgill and D. F. Forster, *The Mackenzie King Record, 1944-
1945* (Toronto: University of Toronto Press, 1970), II, 353-54.
[21] *Ibid.*, 358.
[22] *Ibid.*, 352-54, and National Liberal Federation of Canada, *Report of the
Proceedings of the National Liberal Convention, 1948* (Ottawa: 1948),
pp. 199-201.

candidate and won easily on the first ballot with 69 per cent of the vote.

Gardiner's candidature and, to a lesser extent, Power's, none-theless provided a vital service to the Liberal party in 1948; they made at least a token competition out of what would otherwise have been, for all intents and purposes, a coronation. St. Laurent was clearly marked as Mackenzie King's successor and the party was anxious to have him as its leader. But whereas an unop-posed candidate in a caucus selection system would be quite ac-ceptable under certain circumstances, the same could scarcely apply in a convention system. To generate intra-party enthusiasm and to attract public attention, conventions need some genuine competition, even if only for one ballot. It is difficult to conceive of a situation in which it would not be in the party's interests to ensure that some respectable competition to the obvious winner was provided.

Provincial Leaders and the "Delivery" of Votes

In American nominating conventions, bargaining among state party leaders is an essential part of the process of selecting a presidential candidate. Each leader, whether governor, congressman, important state party official, or elder stateman

represents a state party or faction within a state which is independently organized and not subject to control by out-siders. In the presence of disagreement and the absence of coercion, leaders must persuade one another, compromise, and form coalitions if they are to gain sufficient support to carry the day. Although the leaders may differ in their prefer-ences among possible candidates, they believe that participat-ing in the bargaining process will aid them in achieving their goals and inform them of the goals and tactics of others which in turn may help them in attaining their goals.[23]

[23] Polsby and Wildavsky, p. 80.

Naturally a candidate's success at an American convention depends to a very large extent on his ability to attract the support of the powerful leaders, for these are the men who are best able to mobilize and to direct delegate support. Such leaders are few in number, but they are exceedingly influential in determining the outcome of the convention. The evidence suggests that the same is not the case in Canada.

Acknowledged provincial party leaders and notables in Canada are not in control of blocs of delegate votes as are state leaders in the United States. Since the Canadian convention voting structure emphasizes the individuality of the delegate's role through the secret ballot, the power of provincial or regional leaders is reduced accordingly. Moreover, the national parties in Canada maintain a sufficiently independent existence of their own, quite unlike their American counterparts which are loose federations of state and local parties. Given such a difference, important American state party leaders understandably enjoy and exercise considerably more political power in national conventions than their Canadian counterparts.

No better example than the almost unbelievable one of William Fielding's candidature could be used to illustrate the inability of provincial party leaders to direct their delegates to support a particular candidate in sufficiently large numbers to form a winning coalition. Fielding was the only candidate in 1919 to be nominated by two provincial leaders; moreover, he had the known support of at least six of the eight Liberal provincial premiers in attendance at the convention.[24] Given such support, even a relatively insignificant matter such as the seating arrangement at the convention should have favoured Fielding, for the delegates were seated,

---

[24] It remains uncertain exactly how many of the Liberal premiers supported Fielding. The Liberals were in power in every province except Ontario, and the Ontario Liberal leader, Hartley Dewart, supported Graham. F. A. McGregor put the number of premiers supporting Fielding at six; R. MacGregor Dawson claimed it was seven; King's principal Ontario supporter and the man who moved his nomination (Sir Allen Aylesworth) as well as the *Ottawa Morning Journal* both suggested every one of the eight Liberal premiers supported Fielding. See McGregor, *The Fall and Rise of Mackenzie King*, 338-39; Dawson, *William Lyon Mackenzie King*, pp. 306-308; and the *Ottawa Morning Journal*, August 8, 1919, p. 1. Fielding's candidacy was further enhanced by Lady Laurier's claim (known to

unlike most subsequent conventions, by province and in the immediate presence of their respective provincial leaders. Yet Fielding lost to King on the third ballot by thirty-eight votes. One account of Fielding's defeat in 1919 makes it all too clear how one provincial premier who favoured Fielding (Sir Lomer Gouin of Quebec) fared at the hands of his provincial delegation. Sir Allen Aylesworth, who with Sydney Fisher placed Mackenzie King's name in nomination for the leadership, recorded the day following the balloting in 1919:

> I went down [to Ottawa] intending of course to do my utmost for Fisher — on the lines of Laurier and anti-Laurier. And that element continued in the struggle of course all through. But on those lines we should have won *easily*. So the Fielding and Graham crowd talked Socialism against King — and argued that Fisher was a rich man and an aristocrat — to beat *him*. We found that these lines of talk were getting lots of our Laurier Liberals in the West and in the Maritime Provinces to agree to forgive and forget — and so to vote Fielding or Graham. Accordingly we had to consolidate the Fisher men and the King men — or lose. And that course being decided on Fisher and I turned in and nominated King. That did the business — though it was a tight squeeze in so big a Convention where hundreds of delegates were complete strangers to all of us Easterners. But the Frenchmen did the grand thing. They met in caucus — and actually turned Gouin down *cold*. They told him in plain English — that is to say in plain French — that he could run his own Local Legislature, but that *they* would run themselves in Dominion matters — and they voted — practically solid — to stand by Fisher and me *because* we were English and had stood by Laurier and the French Canadian.[25]

---

convention delegates) that her husband had indicated shortly before his death that he wished Fielding to succeed him. Fielding's nomination paper, as well as those of the other candidates, was read to the convention only moments before the balloting began. It stated: "We hereby nominate the Hon. William Stevens Fielding, member of Parliament for Shelbourne and Queens, Nova Scotia, as candidate for the leadership of the Liberal party of Canada. (Signed) M. W. Martin, Prime Minister of Saskatchewan, [and] W. E. Foster, Prime Minister of New Brunswick." *1919 Report*, p. 167.
[25] Letter of Sir Allen Aylesworth to his brother George A. Aylesworth, August 8, 1919, as quoted in Dawson, *William Lyon Mackenzie King*, 308. (Italics in original)

Since 1919, claims by provincial leaders about their ability to deliver blocs of votes not only has been made infrequently in Canada, but on those rare occasions on which they have been made, the power of the leader has tended to be somewhat exaggerated. Joey Smallwood, more than any other recent premier, reportedly enjoyed enormous influence over his provincial party in both provincial and federal Liberal politics. Smallwood claimed, when he supported Trudeau in 1968, that he could deliver 95 per cent of the Newfoundland delegation's votes to Trudeau on the first ballot. Yet the evidence suggests that Smallwood's claim was unsupportable. The day before the convention balloting the *Telegram* reported that it had interviewed a good part of the eighty-four-delegate Newfoundland group and had found that thirty-three were supporting Winters.[26]

The very fact that the basic unit of delegate apportionment is the constituency and not the province markedly reduces the likelihood of the provincial association and its leader playing roles equivalent to those of American state organizations and their leaders. The combination of such an extremely weak system of intermediate leadership and a total absence of organized subgroups between the constituency and the Canadian convention

---

[26] *Telegram*, April 4, 1968, p. 9, and April 5, 1968, p. 1. Although one study seems to give more credence to Smallwood's claim by showing that 89 per cent of the Newfoundland delegation supported Trudeau, the percentage figure is, unfortunately, based on a small sample of only nine respondents from Newfoundland. See Lawrence LeDuc, "Party Decision-making: Some Empirical Observations on the Leadership Selection Process," *CJPS,* IV (March 1971), 112. LeDuc admits that his respondents showed a strong "true preference for Trudeau" quite apart from Smallwood's support of him. "How they might have behaved had Mr. Smallwood chosen to support another candidate is an intriguing but moot question," LeDuc states. "The survey evidence in the other provinces generally indicates that provincial leaders were not a significant force in delegate decision-making, and it is also clear that the convention structure does not produce the mechanisms which would be required to forge and control regional voting blocs" (p. 111). LeDuc's 305 respondents to a mail questionnaire represented 61 per cent of a sample population stratified by province and chosen randomly. According to the author, the sample conformed "quite closely to the original stratification" (p. 97).

itself, leads ultimately to the relatively greater independence of the Canadian national party leader from intermediate leaders when compared to his American counterpart. In noting these features, Professor Carl Baar correctly draws this distinction between Canadian and American party conventions:

> In Canada, the mass society convention develops out of the dispersion of apportioned delegates among a large number of categories, the use of secret ballot, and the development of rules which reduce the need for and efficacy of voting blocs and party factions — all of which arose out of the construction of a political institution which could establish a national base for a parliamentary party in a large and diverse federal polity. In the United States, the intermediate leadership arises out of the apportionment of delegates to states, open voting by state delegations, rules which facilitate and necessitate bargaining among sub-leaders to resolve conflict — all of which arose out of the construction of a political institution which could establish a national base for a confederated party with wide variations in appeal across geographical regions.[27]

What seems clear is that the combined costs of, first, attempting to direct his province's delegates within a highly atomistic voting structure to support a particular candidate and, second, risking large-scale identification with a potential electoral liability, prove too great for most provincial leaders to wish to assume.

Information: Its Availability and Reliability

For a delegate, the endorsement of a particular candidate by a party notable whose judgment he respects may simplify

---

[27] Carl Baar, "Party Organization, Convention Organization and Leadership Selection in Canada and the United States," paper delivered to the American Political Science Association, Los Angeles, September 11, 1970, p. 19.

his task by helping him decide whom to support. But the likelihood of the delegate relying exclusively, or even largely, on such limited information is slight. After all, the delegate is the object of considerable attention. The propaganda emanating from the candidates' offices, announcing that certain distinguished people have endorsed a particular candidate, is only one of a number of competing pieces of information available to him. He must establish to his own satisfaction its value in relation to all the other information he has at his disposal, and as he receives so much information this is not easily done. During the campaign and the convention itself the delegate gathers his information from a great variety of sources — formal and informal meetings with the candidates and their organizers, news reports and opinion polls carried by the media, contacts with other delegates and interested members of the public, party communications, the results of successive ballots and candidates' decisions on the balloting day — and none of these, either singly or in combination with the others, provides him with wholly dependable or complete information.

The problem of obtaining reliable information is, however, by no means exclusive to the delegates. The candidates, too, face many of the same sorts of difficulties. For one thing, the absence of preferential primaries, of provincial conventions for the selection of party delegates, and of roll-call votes during the convention balloting, denies to the Canadian candidates (as well as to the delegates) sources of information which prove to be of some value to their United States' counterparts. For another, their own elaborate communication networks operating during both the campaign and the conventions are not always able to provide the candidates with accurate and complete information on such important matters as delegates' voting intentions and various candidates' support bases. An organization's most reliable private estimate of its candidate's support may sometimes be quite unrealistic. For Paul Hellyer's organization in 1968,

> when the results of the first ballot were announced, there came a crisis in expectations. The 330 Hellyer votes were far less than any Hellyer supporter had been led to expect. The Hellyer organization's prediction [based on a computer analysis of information provided by Hellyer's staff] was that

Mr. Trudeau would be ahead of Mr. Hellyer by about 200 votes and that Mr. Hellyer would lead Messrs. Martin, Turner, and Winters also by about 200 votes. Although he did come second, more than 400 votes separated him from Mr. Trudeau and Mr. Winters, just 37 votes behind in third place, did better than expected.[28]

Moreover, candidates' organizations not only are involved in an active search for any information that will aid them in planning their strategies; they are also expected to serve as indispensable sources of information for the media, convention officers, party notables and convention delegates. Given the fact that the informational requirements and capacities of these various groups and individuals are not always alike, that perceptions and interpretations of identical pieces of information vary from one person to another,[29] and that candidates' organizations are expected to deal with literally thousands of politically motivated people, the dual responsibilities of those organizations as receivers *and* disseminators of the most accurate information possible are, understandably, formidable to execute.

Paradoxically, the very occasion on which delegates and candidates need their most reliable information happens also to be one of the least propitious times for accurate information flows: at the convention on the day of the leadership balloting. On that day rumours abound of deals, withdrawals, switches, endorsements, and promises. Names of candidates and other prominent politicians are linked in various ways and tossed about freely in hundreds of private conversations, each differing according to the interests and the objectives of the individuals involved. The excitement and the confusion on the convention floor combine to produce a situation in which such rumours are virtually impossible to deny satisfactorily.

If anything, the rules compound the difficulties. Floor microphones are banned. Candidates who have been eliminated or who have withdrawn voluntarily are not allowed to address the delegates from the podium stating their preferences or intentions.

[28] Wearing, "The Liberal Choice," p. 5.
[29] On this point, see Polsby and Wildavsky, pp. 76-78.

Although simple statements from the candidates indicating their withdrawal from the leadership race are read on the candidates' behalf by the convention chairmen, they are void of any direction to the candidates' supporters. At the same time, however, the candidates are free to state their views and intentions to newspaper reporters and on radio and television — and at the crucial moments they are invariably surrounded by a crush of reporters, cameras and microphones. The average radio listener or television viewer of a convention's proceedings, ironically, has more complete information provided to him than the average convention delegate. In 1967 and 1968 small groups of delegates gathered around the many television sets operating in the concourses and snack bars off the convention floors of Maple Leaf Gardens and the Ottawa Coliseum in an attempt to discover from the television reports and comments precisely what was taking place at the convention! Symbolic gestures (two candidates shaking hands publicly, or well-known supporters of one candidate replacing their badges, or stickers, or ribbons, or signs with those of another) assume added importance in such circumstances for they are often the safest and fastest way of transmitting information to the delegates.

Obviously such a situation is far from ideal. As a minimum, delegates should be given the same information as is provided the media by those candidates who, upon their elimination or withdrawal, choose to indicate their support for some other candidate still in the race. Short statements from the platform making their voting intentions known should be an option available to those candidates who wish to avail themselves of it. But should anything else be done?

Reforms aimed at improving the quality and accessibility of information could easily lead to new sorts of problems more objectionable than those to be corrected. No party would want to prohibit newsmen, reporters and television cameras from the convention, irksome and interfering as they may be, for the consequent loss of publicity with all that this would mean in reduced public interest and enthusiasm would be a greater price than any party would care to pay. At first glance, a proposal for reform to the effect that a twenty-four-hour adjournment should follow the first ballot "to encourage a higher degree of delegate rationality," appears attractive. It is based on the twin premises that convention delegates need more time than they are presently given to digest the first ballot results and to decide how they will then vote, and that the information available to the participants would be more accurate given a longer period of adjournment.[30] Yet such a modification could well alter the power structure within the convention in such a way as to play down the importance of the individual delegate. Any additional time available to candidates following the first vote would permit much more intensive and much more knowledgable drives for delegate support and for coalition formation by the candidates' organizers than is presently the case. The major thrust would almost assuredly be in the direction of striking acceptable bargains in two opposing directions: to ensure, on the one hand, the victory of the leading candidate and to attempt, on the other, to beat him. The process of bargaining, in other words, would be accentuated given the increased time to make use of first ballot information and the availability of less public opportunities in which to carry out negotiations. With such a change, it is fair to assume that a new set of relationships enhancing the power of the candidates, their organizers, and the intermediary intra-party leaders would begin to emerge which, in the long run, would likely tend to reduce the importance of the individual delegate and fundamentally alter the nature of Canadian conventions.

And for what purpose? Does the delegate, following the first

---

[30] D. V. Smiley has suggested that: "To encourage a higher degree of delegate rationality it is recommended that after the results of the first ballot the convention be adjourned until the next day. It is further suggested that on the first and subsequent ballots any candidate who fails to secure as many as one-third of the votes of the leading candidate be eliminated. These rules taken together would give delegates and candidates an opportunity to evaluate their positions after rigorous shakedowns of the contenders and in the light of more adequate information than was available at the recent conventions of how others are reacting." Smiley, "The National Party Leadership Convention in Canada," 395. Had such a proposal been operative in 1967 and 1968, six of the eleven Conservative candidates (Sawka, MacLean, Starr, Fleming, Hamilton and McCutcheon) and four of the nine Liberal candidates (Henderson, Kierans, MacEachen and Greene) would have been eliminated following the first ballot.

ballot, in fact need additional information and time? Surely not—unless, of course, one were to assume that the delegates had not given enough thought to the leadership question to know what they intended to do following the first ballot. But that is hardly an appropriate assumption. Delegates, after all, are politically aware and knowledgeable people who take their convention responsibilities seriously. Their political interests and activities prepare them for making decisions in rapidly moving, dynamic situations. This is an important point to note about delegates. For although they obviously have not contemplated appropriate actions for every particular combination of possibilities they might face following the first ballot, the individual delegates are nonetheless sufficiently well-informed and politically self-assured by the time the convention balloting begins to establish in their own minds and to their own satisfaction preference orderings of the various candidates. This is not to say that every delegate has necessarily placed in rank order all the candidates beyond his first two or three favourites. It means that if he were asked to do so, he could.[31]

---

[31] That delegates could easily formulate ordinal preferential listings of candidates was confirmed by interviews and conversations with convention delegates in 1967 and 1968. Robin Farquharson has noted in his excellent study of voting logic that once an individual delegate has expressed his preferences in a systematic fashion, such a preference scale remains constant "throughout the course of the voting. It may, of course, have been modified by earlier arguments or events, but it does not vary after voting has begun." Farquharson, *Theory of Voting* (New Haven: Yale University Press, 1969), p. 6. In a convention with a large number of candidates seeking the leadership, the likelihood naturally increases of some delegates temporarily abandoning their preference scale for the first ballot to support some candidate other than the one they genuinely would prefer as leader without much fear of losing their opportunity to vote for their true preference on a later ballot. This is what apparently happened in 1968. LeDuc found that 75 per cent of the Liberal delegates in 1968 voted for their true preference on the first ballot, but that the remaining delegates gave their first vote to other candidates for a variety of reasons: to return past political favours; to vote for a "favourite son"; to honour the man for his past services to the party; and so on (p. 100).

Coalition Formation

By taking into account the valuable information provided in the form of results of the successive ballots, and by assessing the situation at the time of each ballot in light of his predetermined preferences, the individual delegate is able to make reasonable judgments about how he will then vote. Take, as an illustration, an imaginary Conservative delegate who, in 1967, had ordered his preferences for leader of his party in the following way:

Candidates	Order of preference for candidates of one delegate
McCutcheon	1
Hees	2
Stanfield	3
Fulton	4
Fleming	5
Roblin	6
Hamilton	7
Diefenbaker	8
Starr	9

How might that delegate's subsequent actions be explained when, after the first ballot, he had this information available?

Candidate	First ballot vote	Delegate's preference
Stanfield	519	(3)
Roblin	347	(6)
Fulton	343	(4)
Hees	295	(2)
Diefenbaker	271	(8)
McCutcheon	137	(1)

Hamilton	136	(7)
Fleming	126	(5)
Starr	45	(9)

Given such information, the delegate might choose either (a) to continue to support McCutcheon, even though he realized McCutcheon's vote and ranking were so poor that he stood virtually no chance of winning, or (b) to shift his support to his second preference (Hees) if McCutcheon withdrew. In either case, the delegate would be voting *sincerely* for he would be choosing his highest-ranked preference.[32] If, however, the delegate sensed that both McCutcheon and Hees had little likelihood of winning, he might then decide, even though his first and second choices remained on the ballot for some time, that his subsequent votes would be better placed with Stanfield. Why? Not simply because Stanfield was his third choice, but because in voting for Stanfield he would then make it more difficult for those lower on his preference scale to win. Such is a *vulnerable* situation and clearly involves *strategic* voting.[33] The delegate's actions, whether they be sincere or strategic, will be determined largely by the intensity of his feelings in relation to his ranked preferences: the extent of his loyalty to McCutcheon, of his desire to see Hees, then Stanfield, win, and of his desire to see Roblin, then Fulton, *not* win.

Coalition formation in Canadian conventions, in other words, is an extremely complex process. It involves individual delegates in a dynamic situation, each acting according to his own scale of preferences and each casting either sincere or strategic votes on successive ballots. Unlike coalitions formed in American conven-

---

[32] "A voter votes sincerely . . . if he chooses the subset with the highest-ranked top. If the tops are equal, he chooses the subset with the highest-ranked second-to-top element, and so on" (Farquharson, p. 18).
[33] As Farquharson notes: "It is not always to a voter's advantage to act sincerely. In certain cases he will find that, had he chosen a different strategy, the outcome reached would have been different, and in his opinion preferable." A situation is vulnerable "if another situation (i) can be obtained from the first by substituting a strategy of at least one voter; (ii) is preferred to it by that voter, or those voters" (*ibid.*, p. 24).

tions, those of Canadian conventions are not primarily the products of bargaining by party notables. They amount to simple aggregates of individual delegates who are temporarily united through common voting support of particular candidates. They have ill-defined boundaries and an unorganized structure. They are, in point of fact, highly ephemeral entities.

With the elimination or withdrawal of a candidate, is there then any guarantee that that candidate's supporters will follow his lead *en masse* if he chooses to indicate his preference for someone else? The question might best be answered by comparing the movement of delegates supporting two candidates who withdrew from the same leadership race. When Mitchell Sharp withdrew from the Liberal leadership race in 1968 the day before the convention opened, he endorsed Pierre Elliott Trudeau. According to one study, 60 per cent of those delegates who would have preferred Sharp as leader voted for Trudeau on the first ballot and 80 per cent voted for him on the final ballot. Paul Martin, on the other hand, withdrew after the first ballot at the same convention but without indicating his preference for another candidate. Unlike Sharp's supporters, Martin's dispersed widely. Data from the same study of Liberal delegates suggest that of those who supported Martin on the first ballot, a few transferred their second ballot support to MacEachen or Greene, 17 per cent switched to Turner, 20 per cent to Hellyer, 23 per cent to Winters and 34 per cent to Trudeau. On the final ballot of those for whom Martin was first preference, 57 per cent voted for Trudeau, 34 per cent for Winters and 9 per cent for Turner.[34]

Perhaps the timing of Sharp's withdrawal had something to do with the substantial cohesiveness of his supporters during the balloting. With two or three days to persuade Sharp supporters of the wisdom of their candidate's move and of the desirability of supporting Trudeau, Sharp organizers were in a far better position to deliver a bloc of votes than the staffs of those candidates who withdrew between convention ballots. If so, this would seem to

[34] Figures on Sharp's and Martin's support are from LeDuc, p. 105, and computed from Appendix A, p. 117.

lend weight to the earlier criticism of the reform proposal for a twenty-four-hour adjournment. For if such a proposal were adopted, the Canadian convention could well move away from a relatively unorchestrated assembly to one more dependent upon bargaining and persuasion by group leaders, candidates and organizers.

In any event, it would be temptingly simple, but very wrong, to conclude from the Sharp–Martin comparison that a retiring candidate who publicly states his preference is able to deliver votes to whomever he wishes. After all, so much depends on the timing of the declaration, on the organizational abilities of the retiring candidate's closest workers, on the delegates' reasons for supporting or not supporting particular candidates, on the loyalty a candidate's delegates feel toward him, and on the weight they accord to his expressed views in relation to all the other considerations they must take into account, that a "declaration of support" may prove to be of little consequence. Moreover, and most importantly, as preference ratings are done by individuals, not by groups or leaders, the extent to which the preferences of individual supporters of a retiring candidate coincide becomes a significant determinant of the electoral cohesiveness of that group on subsequent ballots. (For more on coalition formation and the theory of conflict of interest, see Appendix G, p. 253.)

Factional Conflict and the Number of Candidates

As a final comment on the politics of the selection process it is worth noting that, as one would expect, the extent and intensity of factional conflict within a party at the time a new leader is chosen undoubtedly has a considerable bearing on the number of candidates running for its leadership. This, in turn, appears to bear some relationship both to the number of ballots needed to select a winner and to the size of the vote (that is, the size of the

Table 8—1: Number of Ballots and Number of Candidates per Convention, 1919-1968

Number of Ballots	Number of Candidates*		Winner's % of Vote on Winning Ballot	Party	Year
	On first ballot	On final ballot			
1	2	—	78%	Liberal	1958
1	3	—	69	Liberal	1948
1	3	—	67	Conservative	1948
1	3	—	60	Conservative	1956
2	5	3	62	Conservative	1942
2	5	4	53	Conservative	1938
2	6	6	50	Conservative	1927
3	4	2	52	Liberal	1919
4	8	3	51	Liberal	1968
5	9	2	54	Conservative	1967

*Excluding L. Henderson (1958 and 1968), John MacLean and Mary Walker-Sawka (1967).

winning coalition) of the successful candidate on the final ballot. (See Table 8-1.)

When factional conflict within a party has been most pronounced (as in the Liberal party in 1919 and 1968, and in the Conservative party in 1967), the number of candidates seeking the leadership has reflected the extent of the divisions within the party. But when there has been a readily apparent heir who was virtually assured of winning the leadership in convention, and who was, at the same time, acceptable to most of the important cliques within the party, the number of serious challengers entering the contest has been understandably small. Of the ten Liberal and Conservative leadership conventions since 1919 four clearly have been of this second variety. Each was easily won on the first ballot by a candidate who was widely recognized well in advance of the convention as the undisputed favourite. St. Laurent (1948),

Drew (1948), Diefenbaker (1956), and Pearson (1958) won handily, their first ballot vote having been 69, 67, 60, and 78 per cent respectively. The fact that each of these candidates faced only one or two opponents suggests not only a rather widespread recognition on the part of other politicians of the futility of running against a sure winner, but also a relatively low degree of factional conflict within the party at those particular points in time.

When there has been an apparent winner who, for a variety of reasons, has been unacceptable to a number of prominent members of the party (as was the case with the Conservatives in 1927, 1938 and 1942), cliques of various sizes and importance within the party have nominated their own candidates. Such factions have not always been clearly identifiable, but one might assume that they have tended to be formed according to the predictable Canadian divisions: by regions, by economic groupings, and by linguistic and religious factions. The fact that the conflict within their party at those times led four or five candidates to run for the leadership even though their chief opponents (Bennett in 1927, Manion in 1938 and Bracken in 1942) were odds-on favourites to win, produced an interesting, though somewhat paradoxical, result. The number of candidates on a ballot certainly helped to deny victory to the leading candidate' on the first ballot. But at the same time it also minimized the likelihood of ever defeating the favourite candidate, for it effectively ruled out a united-front opposition before the balloting commenced and made the formation of such an opposition virtually impossible once the voting had begun.

One is led to conclude, then, that as the number of candidates increases in Canadian conventions so does the number of ballots needed to choose a winner. Moreover, it is clear that the size of the winner's vote on the winning ballot bears an inverse relationship both to the number of candidates and to the number of ballots. In 1968, five candidates withdrew or had to be eliminated from the contest before the leader could be elected, and in both 1919 and 1967 the respective victors could not be declared until the number of candidates had been reduced to two for the final ballot. But do these features of leadership conventions really make much difference to the final outcome? Apparently not, for, based on past experience at any rate, the respective rankings of all the candidates

Table 8—2: *Candidate Rankings by Ballots, Liberal*
and Conservative Conventions * (1919-1968)*

Convention	Candidates	Ballots and Rankings				
		First	Second	Third	Fourth	Fifth
Liberal 1919	King	1	1	1		
	Fielding	2	2	2		
	Graham	3	3			
	McKenzie	3	4			
Conservative 1927	Bennett	1	1			
	Guthrie	2	2			
	Cahan	3	3			
	Manion	4	4			
	Rogers	5	5			
	Drayton	6				
Conservative 1938	Manion	1	1			
	MacPherson	2	2			
	Harris	3	3			
	Massey	4	4			
	Lawson	5				
Conservative 1942	Bracken	1	1			
	MacPherson	2	2			
	Diefenbaker	3	3			
	Green	4				
	Stevens	5				
Conservative 1967	Stanfield	1	1	1	1	1
	Roblin	2	2	2	2	2
	Fulton	3	3	3	3	
	Hees	4	4	4		
	Diefenbaker	5	5	5		
	McCutcheon	6	8			
	Hamilton	7	6	6	4	
	Fleming	8	7	7		
	Starr	9	9			
Liberal 1968	Trudeau	1	1	1	1	
	Hellyer	2	3	3		
	Winters	3	2	2	2	
	Turner	4	4	4	3	
	Martin	4				
	Greene	6	5	5		
	MacEachen	7	6			
	Kierans	8				

*For those six conventions that went beyond one ballot. Excluding John MacLean and
Mary Walker-Sawka (1967) and L. Henderson (1968).

in all the conventions have, with only two exceptions,[35] remained unchanged over all the ballots (see Table 8-2).

The one feature to emerge unmistakably from the oftentimes tortuous and time-consuming process of coalition formation is that from the beginning to the end of a convention's voting period nothing, except for the size of the different coalitions, has changed in terms of orderings.[36] The candidate favoured with the largest plurality on the first ballot has invariably been the choice of the clear majority on the last ballot. The leading candidate on the first ballot, even though he may have had as small a share as 23 per cent of the first ballot vote and as slight a lead over his next opponent as 7 percentage points (as was the case with Stanfield in 1967), clearly enjoyed a dominant position given the rules and procedures as well as the type of coalition formation processes that are followed in Canadian conventions. Perhaps this is merely a typical expression of an unstructured and relatively unmanipulated assembly composed of delegates from all parts of a heterogeneous country — delegates who not only have widely differing interests and concerns but who, by and large, are remarkably free from direction by factional leaders. Whatever the reason, the basic fact is hard to ignore: every leadership convention since 1919 could have been adjourned following the first ballot and not one final outcome would have been different.

[35] Those two exceptions occurred in 1967 when, on the second ballot, McCutcheon dropped from sixth to eighth place and Hamilton and Fleming moved up one place, and in 1968 when Winters and Hellyer switched ranks on the second ballot from their first ballot positions.

[36] The same features, by the way, hold true in the NDP. Douglas very handily beat his only opponent (Argue) on the first ballot in 1961, with 79 per cent of the vote. Ten years later it took the favoured candidate, Lewis, four ballots to beat his four opponents. The rank ordering remained unchanged over those four ballots:

	Ballots and rankings			
	First	Second	Third	Fourth
Lewis	1	1	1	1
Laxer	2	2	2	2
Harney	3	3	3	
Broadbent	4	4		
Howard	5			

The fact that Lewis's final ballot vote of 63 per cent was somewhat higher than one would expect from a five-candidate convention going four ballots, may well be an indication of the extent to which the party was split at the time between the Waffle (Laxer candidacy) and non-Waffle factions.

9

Leadership Conventions and the Canadian Political System

Late in December 1911, Mr. Herbert B. Ames, Conservative member of parliament for Montreal–St. Antoine (and later Sir Herbert Ames, financial director of the League of Nations' secretariat), delivered a paper to the annual meeting of the American Political Science Association. Ames chose as his topic "The Organization of Political Parties in Canada." He was a person well qualified to speak on such a matter, for in practical terms he knew a good deal about Canadian politics. He had served as an alderman in the city of Montreal for eight years, as an MP for seven years, and had just recently been re-elected for the third consecutive time to the House of Commons. His electoral survival for some period of time as a Conservative in Quebec spoke well of his political abilities.

In one passage of his speech, Ames chose to illustrate his points about the role of an opposition party in the Canadian parliament:

> Let us imagine that there has recently been a general election. A strongly entrenched government is in power. A vigilant and fairly numerous opposition occupies the seats to the left of the speaker. Although, in the ordinary course of events, a period of four or five years would elapse before

217

there would again be an appeal to the electorate, the opposition commences at once to prepare for that event. No sooner have the formalities attendant upon the opening of Parliament terminated than the first party caucus is called. It is a strictly private gathering to which none but members are admitted, and attendance thereat is regarded as a tacit admission that the member is willing to abide by the will of a majority of his colleagues. *By majority vote, a leader is chosen. He becomes the mouthpiece of his party in the House of Commons and its "Chief" before the country at large.* The only other recognized officers of an opposition are the chief whip and his associates, whose duties are mainly to secure the maximum party attendance at important votes in the House.

From the opening day of the first session of a new parliament, the idea of originating proposals that "will take with the country" is never lost sight of by a vigilant opposition.

Resolutions are brought forward in the House, at first tentatively, then with a view of securing support. These are discussed in caucus, argued before the Commons, and, if pushed to a vote by the opposition with the approval of the leader, become planks in the party platform. *In former days a party convention, comprising delegates from the general electorate, was considered necessary to ratify a platform and endorse a leader. This procedure, however, no longer is in common use. The members of the party having seats in the House are held to be sufficiently acquainted with the feeling of the country to give expression to the views held by the party at large; hence conventions have fallen into disuse, and the leader and his House-following are taken to adequately represent the party as a whole.*[1]

Presumably the "former days" of party conventions to which Ames was referring were those of the 1850s, 1860s and 1893. What is abundantly clear from his remarks is that Ames (and no doubt many others in Canadian politics shared his views on this matter) not only considered the parliamentary party to be the supreme branch of the party; it was, for all intents and purposes, the only branch. To them, party conventions belonged to Canadian history.

[1] Herbert B. Ames, "The Organization of Political Parties in Canada," *Proceedings of the American Political Science Association*, 1911, VI (February 1912), 184-85. (Italics added)

Yet within less than eight years of the time that Ames read his paper, the Liberal party convened a large national gathering to discuss organization, to establish policy and to elect a leader. Insofar as the selection of leaders is concerned, that convention set the precedent which was followed eventually not just by the Liberals, but by the other parties as well. And ironically, conventions became popular for the very reason Ames thought they would no longer be needed: on representational grounds. Writing as he did in 1911, Ames might well have thought that the national parties (then at the very zenith of the Canadian two-party system) had developed sufficiently to ensure adequate representation for Canada's burgeoning and heterogeneous population. But Ames was in no position to foresee the effect on the traditional parties of an external war, with its highly divisive internal social consequences; of a new regionally defined economic and political power base in Western Canada; and of the increasingly diversified ethnic population. The parliamentary parties were soon believed to be unequal to the challenge of coping with the representational problems created by those developments. An acceptable alternative to the parliamentary groups' dominance of Canadian politics had to be found.[2]

When conventions were first introduced, therefore, it was easy

[2] Even *after* the first leadership convention, the impact of the 1919 convention on Canadian politics was ignored. Writing ten years after Ames's speech, George M. Wrong quite incredibly paid no attention to the 1919 convention, apparently assuming that political conventions were American, not Canadian, institutions: "National leadership is also becoming more difficult in Canada. There are no nation-wide newspapers. It is hard to move British Columbia by cries effective in Nova Scotia. But difficulties of leadership are softened in Canada by the mode of choosing them. It is the members of parliament, knowing their men, who choose the leaders, and not conventions of a thousand people with bands and songs and organized shouts for favourite sons. But in Canada because the leader is chosen by the few, it is long before he is known to, and trusted by, the many." Wrong, "Democracy in Canada," *CHR*, II (December 1921), 330-31. However, it was not beyond W. B. Munro, in his Marfleet Lectures of 1929, to sense the change: "The parliamentary caucus, so far as the choice of party leadership is concerned, has given way to the national party convention on the American model. Sir Wilfrid Laurier and Sir Robert Borden were chosen by the method of parliamentary caucus; but the present prime minister of Canada was chosen leader of the Liberal

to make the case that the new system of choosing party leaders was both more "representative" and more "democratic" than any previous system in Canadian history. The same rationale has remained a part of political conventions ever since. But in Britain, where the parliamentary parties have managed to retain the exclusive right to choose their own leaders, precisely the same reasons have been accepted to justify the authority of the parliamentary wing of the party in this matter.

The typical member of parliament in Britain carefully defends his parliamentary party's monopoly in choosing its leaders. His position would be much more difficult to maintain, however, were it not for the willing support given him by important extra-parliamentary party officials. The general secretary of the Labour party (an influential official elected by the party in conference and someone who might be expected to favour an enlarged role for the extra-parliamentary party in leadership selection) typifies the attitude of extra-parliamentary officials when he rejects any suggestion of change in the British system. "The party conference," he claims,

> could never properly assess potential leaders; whereas the MP (by virtue of his position and his expertise), can. The party meeting in conference is an inappropriate body to attempt to judge the calibre of the potential leaders, for it emphasizes oratorical ability, not political and administrative judgment. The MP, on the other hand, is a professional politician. As such, he is expected to become fully acquainted with the various potential leaders' characteristics in preparation for the time when he is called upon to play a part in choosing a new leader.[3]

---

party, which was then in Opposition, by a convention of delegates representing Canadian Liberalism on a nation-wide scale. Mr. Bennett, leader of the present Conservative Opposition, was chosen by the same process. There is every indication that the precedent will be followed." Munro, *American Influences on Canadian Government* (Toronto: The Macmillan Company of Canada, 1929), p. 64.

[3] Interview with Mr. Harry (now Sir Harry) Nicholas, general secretary of the Labour party, Transport House, London, July 14, 1970.

When asked to list in order of importance the various qualities needed by a politician to be a successful leader, the deputy chairman of the Conservative party (Sir Michael Fraser) gave the following as the single most important in his opinion: "The potential leader must have proved himself in parliament and in his ministerial office as a man of sufficient

The argument is accepted in Britain, but it does not seem to be in Canada, that because the MP is chosen by an electorate of tens of thousands of people in a *democratic* election, and because he is expected to serve in a variety of ways as the *representative* of those people, one of his tasks in "getting on with his job" is to choose, in company with his fellow parliamentarians, his party's leader.

Surely, with respect to both Britain and Canada the point is this: if a satisfactory leadership selection mechanism were one which was completely open and completely democratic, with complete representation and participation then, in truth, it would also be completely chaotic and unworkable. The responsibility for choosing leaders must, therefore, be delegated. The pressing question to be answered in judging the appropriateness of a particular form of delegation has to do with the suitability and equitableness of that system to a particular country's political system. This means, for example, that the standard by which Canadian conventions ought to be measured should be one that assesses the extent to which conventions provide acceptable solutions to the matter of political leadership, given the variety of problems and particular needs within the Canadian political culture. Compared to others, how adequate is that particular form of delegation of responsibility for leadership selection? Does the delegation of responsibility and authority accord well with the values of the culture and with the needs of the political system? On balance, the Canadian convention system seems to measure up well in these respects.

This is not to say, however, that the switch from the pre-1919 intra-parliamentary party selection processes to leadership conventions has been accomplished without costs to the political system. For one thing, to have leaders chosen by the party conventions apparently means that at least one of the traditional features of the

calibre to handle the job of leader. To do this he must have come up through the hierarchy of the party proving himself to the parliamentary party as he advances each step." Sir Michael made the point that in his opinion it looked as if Canada and Britain now followed exactly opposite principles in leadership selection: in Britain the parliamentary party imposes its choice of leader on the whole party, whereas in Canada the whole party imposes its choice of leader on the parliamentary party. Interview with Sir Michael Fraser, London, July 15, 1970.

Canadian constitution has been altered. Except under truly extra-ordinary circumstances, it would now seem that during the two or three month period immediately prior to a leadership convention of one of the major parties, a *de facto* limitation has been imposed on (a) the prime minister's right to advise dissolution of parliament and to call an election, and (b) the opposition's power to force an election through acceptance of a want of confidence motion against the government in the House of Commons. The reasoning for the change is simple: a party about to hold a leadership convention would be in a strong position to argue the "unfairness" both to that party and to the electorate if an election were called and held immediately prior to its selection of a new leader.

The defeat of the Pearson government in February 1968, on the third reading of an income tax bill, is a good case in point. The defeat came during the early stages of the Liberal leadership campaign (the convention being held in April of that year) and led the prime minister to charge that the "vote was contrived by the Opposition" to force the government into an election before its leadership changeover had been effected.[4] The leader of the opposition (Mr. Stanfield) replied quite correctly to the prime minister's charges by insisting on the distinction between the request for dissolution of parliament following immediately upon the defeat of the government and the issuance of election writs some time after that dissolution. These writs could then have provided for an election after the Liberal leadership convention.[5] However, his argument was lost in the excitement of the moment. The prime minister's claim apparently helped to generate at least some public support for the government, and within a matter of days, the minority government survived a subsequent test of confidence in the House of Commons. It would seem that in this respect, at least, conventions may have lessened the degree of flexibility that previously obtained in one area of the Canadian parliamentary system: the operative constitution has been made relatively more rigid during the period immediately prior to the selection of the new leader of one of the major parties.

[4] *Globe and Mail*, February 21, 1968, p. 8.
[5] *Ibid.*, February 22, 1968, p. 8.

In another rather curious respect the Canadian constitution appears to have remained somewhat more faithful to the traditional British example than has the British itself — and oddly enough, *because* of leadership conventions. On some occasions in the past when he exercised the prerogative power of the Crown in naming his first minister, the Governor General not only selected the prime minister but, in doing so, he in effect also named the new party leader. During the twentieth century the opportunities for the Crown to exercise this sort of discretionary power have been removed as the parties have consistently preferred to name their own leaders free of consultation with the Sovereign's representative. Nonetheless the prerogative power of the Crown has not disappeared; it has remained a part of the constitution which, quite conceivably, could be brought into use if the occasion warranted it.

If, for example, a prime minister suddenly died, a new one would have to be chosen as quickly as possible. Yet the party would be unable to meet in convention for some time (likely not for several months given the time necessary to organize a modern convention), in which case the party's parliamentarians would have to choose a temporary leader.[6] Within the parliamentary party, soundings would have to be taken and votes would have to be held to determine who ought to be asked to serve as prime minister.

If, however, there were no one unmistakably favoured candidate; or if there were a serious deadlock within the party over the

---

[6] Conventions take longer to organize than politicians (and the public) generally realize. To his horror, Lester Pearson discovered that when he announced his resignation as Liberal leader in December 1967 and asked the party to call a convention to name his successor, it would take considerably more time than he had hoped. "I also thought," Pearson later reflected on his decision to retire,

> it would be easier than it turned out to be because we could have a convention quickly. When I talked to Keith Davey about this and I said "Now I want this convention at the earliest possible date naturally," he said he would have it at the earliest possible date. But after I had announced my resignation he had had a few days then to make more public inquiries, and he said: "We can't have this convention until April." And I said, "You're crazy!"

Transcript of the CBC television show "The Tenth Decade," Program 8, pp. 4-5. The convention was held in April 1968.

succession; or if no clearly acceptable procedure could be agreed upon to choose a temporary leader; then the Governor General, in consultation with the senior members of the party, might well have to make the choice himself from among the leading contenders. In other words, this would be a clear-cut situation inviting the use of the royal prerogative. It would be the result of a unique combination of events: the parliamentary party's failure to come up with the name of a temporary leader, and the party's inability to meet in its accustomed way to choose its leader. It would subsequently be up to the party in convention to decide whether or not to accept the Governor General's choice, but that would come some time later. It is difficult to imagine a parallel situation in Britain in which the Sovereign might be expected to exercise her discretionary power, for both the Conservative and Labour parties have now opted for formal parliamentary party election procedures for the selection of their leaders which take remarkably little time to execute. As the British parliamentary party can be assembled on short notice, and as its decision can be made and its choice presented to the Sovereign all in a matter of a few days at the very most, the potential for the use of the royal prerogative in Britain appears to be even more limited than in Canada.

The struggle within the Conservative party during the 1960s over John Diefenbaker's leadership brought the whole matter of the relationship between the parliamentary and extra-parliamentary wings of Canadian parties to a head. By resolving that issue as they did, the Conservatives made it clear that the extra-parliamentary party was to rule supreme on matters of leadership: specifically on the selection and the replacement of leaders. Ironically, the issue had to be resolved within the very party that one might well have expected to have been more deferential toward its leader than any other; but when "democracy" becomes the rationale for a popular battle, deference stands little chance of survival.

The issue of the relationship of those two groups within Canadian parties to one another is more serious than might at first appear. For, over time, the continued dominance of the parliamentary party by the party in convention may well alter substantially both the understanding of politics in Canada and the nature of the

Canadian political system. Certainly the parliamentary group could be placed in the position of having to accept as its leader someone other than the person a majority of the caucus would wish to have lead them. But there is nothing new in this, especially within the Conservative party. In 1920, Sir Thomas White was asked to form a government even though a majority of the caucus had indicated in their ballots to Borden that their first preference was Meighen; and in 1896, the Governor General persisted in his refusal to accept Bowell's resignation as prime minister even though a cabinet revolt had taken place and a majority of the party favoured bringing in Tupper as leader. The real danger resulting from the preeminent position of the extra-parliamentary party lies in a different direction.

A party leader chosen in Britain, or Australia, or New Zealand, or India, or some other country using a parliamentary system modelled on Westminster, has as his power base and as the group to which he is politically indebted the parliamentary party. He does not have available to him as a weapon or as a threat, to be used against his cabinet or parliamentary colleagues, the fact that he was chosen by thousands of delegates assembled in convention and that it is to them that he must hold himself responsible. His power base and his responsibilities are defined according to parliamentary parameters. Having replaced those parameters with others, Canadians now run the risk of fostering a plebiscitary mentality with respect to Canadian politics which, so far at least, has remained alien to their country's political tradition. It is all too easy for a powerful prime minister to place himself above his cabinet colleagues; but when he has been chosen in convention, and when it is that body which has established its right to remove him from party office, it may well prove to be easier still. From the time of its first introduction to English-speaking politics in the seventeenth century through to the present, the meaning of the word "convention" has been perfectly clear. It has carried with it connotations of political philosophies more in keeping with plebiscitary than parliamentary politics: the sovereignty and natural rights of the people; the social compact of the political unit; the nature and direction of political responsibility between the individual leader and the assembly; and the authority of the convention as something derived from the rank and file.

If Canadian national parties were less dominated on the matter of leadership selection by the party in convention, if their existence were more dependent upon arrangements made by various provincial and local factions and competing intra-party organizations, perhaps the parties' parliamentary caucuses would be better able to withstand the pressures of their extra-parliamentary wings, for they might then find themselves in a relatively stronger position within the party as a whole. But, unlike American "national" party conventions, those of Canadian parties are not groupings of local political baronies assembling once every four years to choose a presidential candidate and then dispersing. They are not one-shot affairs. As they have developed since the mid 1960s, the Liberal and Conservative national federations have emerged as close approximations of continuing bodies. Through amendments to their constitutions they have now assumed considerable powers to determine not only who their leader should be but whether the leadership of the party should be reassessed in convention at particular points in time or under certain conditions. The point is not that challenges to a party's leadership are inappropriate. Rather, it is that challenges conducted by way of an extra-parliamentary forum may well, in the long run, weaken the fibre of Canadian parliamentary institutions by advancing the plebiscitary cause.

Both Canada and the United States are federal countries. Both Canadian and American parties have adopted a leadership selection mechanism one of the characteristics of which has been to facilitate the entry into national leadership positions of politicians with non-federal, non-legislative backgrounds. In the United States, for nearly one hundred years this enabled state governors to emerge as strong contenders for the presidential nomination. At the same time, state-based politicians became exceedingly powerful in the presidential nominating process. But events of the past decade suggest that at least in part this has changed. Senators and vice-presidents have now replaced governors as the most likely pool from which presidential nominees are drawn, even though state-based politicians have retained their considerable influence in the selection process. Rules, procedures and the voting system in United States' conventions have served to sustain and to enhance the power of the state-based politicians, certainly when compared with Canadian conventions. In Canada, the general absence of instructions to constituency or provincial organizations, combined with the secret individual vote at conventions, appears to have effectively removed the likelihood of Canadian equivalents of American state delegations or powerful state-based politicians controlling blocs of votes.

Indeed, one of the striking contrasts of conventions in the two countries is that the American voting procedures visibly reinforce American federalism, whereas those of Canadian conventions could scarcely do less to suggest that Canada is a federal country. If an outsider were introduced to Canadian politics for the first time through attendance at a national leadership convention he could easily gain the impression that Canada had a unitary, not a federal, system of government. Perhaps the difference could be accounted for by the fact that in the United States a political expression of federalism seems justified in a body such as a political convention because the constitutional expression of federalism has waned in importance, whereas in Canada the parts are so much more constitutionally viable that the unity of the nation deserves to be procedurally stressed at national conventions.[7]

Similar developments in leadership selection in both Canada and the United States (principally, the representational inadequacies of the congressional and parliamentary parties leading to the adoption of the convention selection system in both countries) have not met with similar results. For one thing, what an American party wants, as James Bryce astutely perceived in the late nine-

---

[7] To one American observer at a Canadian convention, the failure to accentuate the provincial units makes for less interesting conventions in Canada than in the United States: "Canadian convention delegates vote by secret ballot and the result of each ballot is announced *in toto* only, not by provincial delegation. This detracts from the show. I longed to hear: 'Quaint Quebec yields to sunny Saskatchewan.'" G. Gerald Harrop, "Canadian Conventions: 'Un Homme Qui . . . '," *The Reporter,* XVI (January 24, 1957), 31.

teenth century, "is not a good President but a good candidate. The party managers have therefore to look out for the person likely to gain most support, and at the same time excite least opposition."[8] Bryce may have taken his cue from Walter Bagehot who, twenty years before Bryce's book first appeared and in contrasting American parties with those of a parliamentary system, noted that though a party in a parliamentary system

> might not select the very best leader, they have the strongest motives to select a very good leader. The maintenance of their rule depends on it. Under a presidential constitution the preliminary caucuses [conventions] which choose the president need not care as to the ultimate fitness of the man they choose. They are solely concerned with his attractiveness as a candidate; they need not regard his efficiency as a ruler. If they elect a man of weak judgement, he will reign his stated term; even though he show the best judgement, at the end of that term there will be by constitutional destiny another election. But under a ministerial government there is no such fixed destiny. The government is a removable government; its tenure depends upon its conduct. If a party in power were so foolish as to choose a weak man for its head, it would cease to be in power. Its judgement is its life.[9]

A party in a parliamentary system, in other words, requires something more than a good candidate as its leader. The vicissitudes of parliamentary politics demand it. One of the major consequences of leadership selection in a parliamentary system is the almost certain likelihood of a party having to live with its choice of leader for a number of years whether the party gains power under his leadership or not. This is in marked contrast to the American presidential system which, with its national nominating conventions three or four months before a fixed election date, and with no institutionalized role for a defeated presidential candidate following the November election, stresses little more than

[8] Bryce, *The American Commonwealth*, 2 vols. (New York: G. P. Putnam's Sons, 1959; originally published in 1888), I, 239-40.
[9] Bagehot, *The English Constitution* (Garden City: Doubleday and Company, Inc., n.d.; originally published in 1867), pp. 115-16.

short-term effects on the losing party. What Canadian parties must realize, then, is that they have combined a leadership selection mechanism originally designed for short-run political activities with a governmental system based on the principle of occupancy of parliamentary positions of leadership on either side of the House of Commons over a period of several years.

The acceptance and widespread use of co-optive practices has been one of the distinguishing features of twentieth-century Canadian leadership selection. If, in this respect, one were to choose a successful party leader whose views on political leadership would likely have influenced the Canadian leadership norm more than those of any other party leader, it would almost assuredly be Mackenzie King. That King was a highly successful party leader, in electoral terms at least, there can be little doubt. The party he led in seven general elections succeeded in gaining or retaining power in all but one of them. Frank Underhill, one of King's most severe critics for many years, eventually came around to the view that King had succeeded because he had proven to be "the representative Canadian, the typical Canadian, the essential Canadian, the Canadian as he exists in the mind of God."[10] The lesson that King had learned well was how to master the art of compromisory politics. King's central position in Canadian politics for nearly thirty years meant that he had a considerable influence directly over the other men's political careers and indirectly on the standards that would be regarded as acceptable for the recruitment and selection of party leaders.

How did such a man conceive of leadership in the context of Canadian parliamentary politics? Perhaps the most apparent answer lay in the fact that, in playing the role of political broker so successfully, King also developed the skill of substituting for parliamentary representation a "much more direct but also much more indefinable relationship between himself and the Canadian people."[11] He was neither fond of parliament, nor did he care to develop special skills as a parliamentarian. Yet, paradoxically,

[10] "W. L. Mackenzie King," in *In Search of Canadian Liberalism*, p. 127.
[11] *Ibid.*, p. 134.

he served as prime minister longer than any other person in the history of the Commonwealth. King's failure to have followed a parliamentary career route to the leadership of his party as well as his distinct lack of interest in the parliamentary process itself brought no measurable harm either to himself or to his party.

Moreover, King subscribed to the peculiar notion that the civil service constituted, in his own words, "the stepping stone to the ministry."[12] Before King finally settled on St. Laurent as his successor, at one point, slightly more than a year away from his retirement, he was convinced that Lester Pearson, the Under Secretary of State for External Affairs, and a man with no experience in either parliamentary or party politics, would be the best man to succeed him as prime minister. Had he been asked to choose between Harold Lasswell's three political personality types — agitators, theorists and administrators — King undoubtedly would have favoured the last group.[13] Administrative politicians might lack political experience, but to King their conciliatory background suited them well for brokerage-style politics. They might not be dynamic, but they would at least be safe. And this was an important consideration, for to King a successful political leader was one who moved slowly and cautiously. "Mackenzie King genuinely believed and frequently said," J. W. Pickersgill has recorded, "that the real secret of political leadership was more in what was prevented than in what was accomplished."[14] Thus, in terms of the recruitment and selection of party leaders, King's legacy cannot be ignored, for it no doubt helped to prepare the way for acceptance of the idea that co-optive practices and extra-parliamentary career routes could be quite respectable components of Canadian party politics. Its meaning was unmistakably clear. Party leadership would not necessarily be denied to those who had followed the more traditional parliamentary career routes, but

---

[12] As quoted in Eugene Forsey, "Parliament Is Endangered by Mr. King's Principles," *Saturday Night*, October 9, 1948, pp. 10-11.
[13] See Harold D. Lasswell, *Psychopathology and Politics* (New York: The Viking Press, 1960; originally published in 1930).
[14] J. W. Pickersgill, *The Mackenzie King Record, 1939-1944* (Toronto: University of Toronto Press, 1960), I, 10.

it would be made more difficult to attain, given the acceptability, indeed the encouragement, of co-optive practices. Relatively new faces on the political scene would be hard for the seasoned political veterans to match.

In this respect, the leadership selection pattern has not gone full circle in Canada as it has in the United States. Experience in national politics has once again emerged as an important qualification for serious contenders for the American presidency, but similar experience remains relatively less important in Canada. The explanation may well rest in the differences that exist between political career opportunities in the two countries. The American vice-presidency and membership in the Senate are offices that permit the individual office-holders to gain publicity on their own and to develop into truly national figures. There are no roughly equivalent positions in the Canadian parliamentary system. A cabinet post would seem to offer the best hope for a federal politician in Canada to gain national stature; but even then a minister with many years in the cabinet faces the likelihood of being by-passed in favour of an apparently attractive co-opted notable whose meteoric rise to prominence may have little or nothing to do with his performance as a minister of the Crown. The weight of party discipline, the principle of cabinet solidarity, the extreme unlikelihood of an individual MP warranting sustained national attention, as well as the short tenure of Canadian MPs, combine to minimize the chances of all but the most ambitious and out-spoken of Canadian parliamentary politicians developing into nationally pre-eminent figures by way of parliamentary careers.

By replacing the leadership selection model based initially on British parliamentary practice (but modified to meet Canadian political conditions) with a leadership convention model originally designed for a governmental system with separate rather than fused legislative and executive offices, major alterations have taken place in Canadian politics. It might be argued that in effecting such a change Canada has ended up with the worse, rather than the better, of two possible worlds. The hierarchical career structure which emphasized political experience and placed some importance on service in parliament (thereby strengthening parliament itself) no longer obtains. As there are no compensating institutional bodies at the national level equivalent to the vice-presidency and the American Senate which would enable aspiring leaders in the governing party to operate free of collective responsibility and rigid party discipline in articulating their own views on policy, an unavoidable contradiction comes into play between the candidate's need to appeal for delegate support and the need to support the government. In 1968, for several weeks before the Liberal leadership convention, the seven federal cabinet ministers seeking the party leadership canvassed party delegate support from one end of the country to the other. This naturally meant they were able to devote less time to their governmental duties and departmental responsibilities. This, in turn, contributed to the government's defeat in the House of Commons in February of that year. Government policies and the principle of cabinet solidarity took severe beatings whenever the candidates were frank enough to express their personal policy views. Without such frankness the delegates would have been treated unfairly, for they would have been unable to determine the policy positions of the various candidates; but with it, the solidarity of the government was open to serious question. Such a dilemma seems inherent in combining the parliamentary system with leadership conventions. In all, the leadership recruitment and selection pattern which once obtained in Canadian politics appears to have been altered in the direction of American presidential politics. This could certainly add support to the arguments of those who fear for the future of parliamentary institutions in Canada.

Yet such a judgment may well be too harsh. Canadian leadership recruitment and selection practices have achieved a remarkably flexible quality — a quality which almost certainly would not obtain if the parties were to insist on rigorous political apprenticeships for their leaders. Moreover, the additional manoeuvrability granted parties through lateral entry of individuals into positions of leadership, while it quite clearly has the unfortunate effect of discounting the value of politics as a career, can, at the same time, be defended on the best of all possible Canadian grounds: it is in keeping with the requirements of a political system highly attuned to its federated structure. Of the problems facing Canadian political leaders throughout much of the twentieth century, few have been of greater magnitude than that of finding acceptable ways of maintaining a viable Canadian federalism. "The essential task of the national leader," Frank Underhill correctly concluded, "remains what it has always been, to discover the terms on which as many as possible of the significant interest-groups of our country can be induced to work together in a common policy."[15] Could it be that in a federated system as diverse as Canada's, the considerable extent to which politics is leader-oriented simply reflects the society's basic need for a strong federal symbol?[16]

To cope with a whole set of unique problems, Canadian political institutions have developed a character of their own. Naturally, the appropriateness of the standards and practices of British parliamentary politics to non-British problems has diminished accordingly. The Canadian political culture, with its distinctive party system, its federal structure, and its ethnic and linguistic mix, encouraged experimentation with many institutions that more accurately reflected the variety of Canadian society and politics than parliament itself. The adoption and development of the convention system as the vehicle for leadership selection should be

[15] Underhill, p. 133.

[16] Such a symbol may help to counteract the tendencies toward regionalism and localism that are so much a part of a federal union. One example of the way in which the Canadian prime minister plays a more conspicuous symbolic role than his British counterpart is to be found in the contrasting part that each takes in the opening of his respective parliament. In Britain, during the opening of parliament the attention focuses unmistakably on the Sovereign. The prime minister, by custom, proceeds no further than any of the other members of the Commons to hear the Queen's speech: to the Bar of the House of Lords, located just inside the entrance to the upper house. He is much less visibly associated with the speech than is the Canadian prime minister at the opening of parliament in Canada. In Ottawa, the prime minister accompanies the Governor General to and from the Senate chamber and sits to the right of the vice-regal representative during the reading of the speech from the throne. His presence is more obvious and it makes more apparent the fact that the speech is *his* government's speech than is true in Britain. In this sense, the prime minister is recognized as *pas comme les autres*, for he is not with the group of commoners assembled at the entrance of the Senate chamber to hear the speech.

understood in that context. By simply taking into account the variety of functions they perform, it is obvious that conventions are extremely useful as consensus-finding vehicles. They serve, certainly, as pure balloting devices whereby one or two thousand party activists may express their preferences on the matter of their party's leadership. But they also act as avenues for the articulation of policy views, as means for the aggregation and identification of intra-party conflicts of interest, and as an acceptable way to determine the common ground on which those differences may be minimized or even eliminated. All of this comprises something no serious Canadian party can afford to be without.

As the parties have been charged with the responsibility of playing a conciliatory role in Canadian politics, they have needed the freedom to adjust to the demands of the moment and to attract leaders who would serve them well in that task regardless of the extent or nature of their political background. For a variety of reasons (perhaps not the least of which is that they too have evidenced a capacity to deal in federal-provincial matters) provincial premiers have been favoured by the Conservatives. Because the Liberals have tended to be the governing party, and because they have made maximum use of the greater opportunity available to them to co-opt potential leaders directly into the cabinet from the extra-political world, they have successfully managed to establish an apostolic relationship between their leaders and those who succeed them which is really quite remarkable. From King through to Trudeau, each of the successors has been brought not only into the cabinet but indeed into federal politics itself by his immediate predecessor. In that sense, there has been a natural "evolution" of leadership in the Liberal party in Canada not unlike that of the Conservative party in Britain. But, regardless of the particular customs and preferences of the major Canadian parties, the fact remains that both have settled for a leadership convention system as a reasonable and equitable way to choose a party leader in a heterogeneous society.

For it is not that the caucus system, or the convention system, or some other system is inherently better. It is, instead, that the convention system seems to accord well with the Canadian experience, with Canadian values, and with the Canadian political culture. It has provided a forum whereby rational discussion of policies and party organization may take place. In turn, these are activities which involve people with some expertise, some experience, and some interest in the political process. Views of various competing interests within the body politic may be freely expressed in a convention setting, a fact which encourages members of the party both to fulfill their obligations to the community as a whole and to sustain their concern for political matters. Moreover, the forum within which the views are expressed and the leaders chosen is recognized and accepted as the *legitimate* forum within which such tasks should be performed in Canada. These are significant accomplishments the ultimate effect of which cannot be minimized. That conventions provide an opportunity to unite and to enthuse party supporters for campaigning purposes, as well as to generate widespread and positive public interest in their particular party, its policies and its leader, is an extra bonus for which the party organizers and professional politicians are only too thankful.

A convention delegate, for his part, knows that the support a leader most wants is from a united party. His desire to identify positively with the new leader, even though the nominee may not be the delegate's first choice as leader, serves to remind the delegate that the interests of his party are paramount and, indeed, are accepted on an *a priori* basis as being paramount. Delegate status seems to carry with it an implicit understanding that so long as policy positions are not seriously jeopardized and so long as the party remains electorally credible, the delegates will abide by their party's decision.

In the United States the "national" party is too much a sum of its parts for the same to be true. Depending upon the nature and strength of their objections, significant elements within an American party may refuse to endorse and support their party's presidential nominee. They may even go so far as to organize a splinter party and present their own candidate at the time of the presidential election, although admittedly such an extreme course of action is rare. But in Canada, it is rarer still. The Action

Canada movement, initially organized in 1971 by Paul Hellyer, may be seen as a belated rejection of the 1968 Liberal convention's leadership decision; if so, it is not only a much delayed, but a historically unique reaction to a Canadian party's leadership decision.

Naturally, not all intra-party differences disappear following the choice of a new leader — some even tend to surface with embarrassing regularity. But, by and large, a new leader can expect a substantial closing of the ranks after his selection. For the fact of the matter is, the national party is a sufficiently strong entity in its own right to survive the periodic intra-party conflict over its leadership. In this respect, the last, symbolic act of the convention is helpful. For through it the delegates, the various factions and the contestants renew their identification with their party and indicate (at least publicly) their acceptance of their new leader. The final request before the adjournment of the convention (something also characteristic of the best tradition of American nominating conventions) takes the form of one or more of the losers in the leadership contest urging that the election of the new leader be made unanimous.

What better example of that fact than 1967? Having been replaced as leader of his party by that convention following one of the most deeply divisive party battles in the history of Canadian politics, John Diefenbaker made his way to the platform when the results of the final ballot were announced bringing to an end the 1967 Progressive Conservative Centennial Convention. He wished to address the delegates. When he spoke he did not urge the withdrawal of his supporters from the party, as well he could have; nor did he display bitterness at the results of the balloting by the members of the party he had led for eleven years. "My fellow Conservatives," he began, to the cheers of his audience:

> I join with all of you in welcoming the new leader of this party, the Honourable Robert Stanfield. For him I ask above everything else, loyalty from the rank and file of this party. . . . Always remember those who have on their shoulders the mantle of leadership. They are subjected, and expect to be

subjected, to persistent attack. . . . Do not, as the fires of controversy burn around your leader, add gasoline to those fires. My course has come to an end. Out of my heart I thank you for having given me the opportunity to serve in my day and generation.

Nemine contradicente, and all are together once again.

Appendices

APPENDIX A

Procedure for the Selection of the Leader of the Conservative and Unionist Party (Great Britain)

1. There shall be a ballot of the Party in the House of Commons.
2. The Chairman of the 1922 Committee will be responsible for the conduct of the ballot and will settle all matters in relation thereto.

Nominations and Preparation of the Ballot

3. Candidates will be proposed and seconded in writing. The Chairman of the 1922 Committee and a body of scrutineers designated by him will be available to receive nominations. Each candidate will indicate on the nomination paper that he is prepared to

---

Source: Conservative and Unionist Central Office, Press Release #9221, February 25, 1965.

accept nomination, and no candidate will accept more than one nomination. The names of the proposer and seconder will not be published and will remain confidential to the scrutineers. Nominations will close twenty-four hours before the first and second ballots. Valid nominations will be published.

4. The scrutineers will prepare a ballot paper listing the names of the candidates and give a copy to each voter at a meeting called by the Chairman of the 1922 Committee for the purpose of balloting and consisting of all Members of the House of Commons in receipt of the Conservative and National Liberal Whips.

First Ballot

5. For the first ballot each voter will indicate one choice from the candidates listed, and hand the ballot paper to the scrutineers who will count the votes.

6. If as a result of this ballot one candidate *both* (i) receives an overall majority *and* (ii) receives 15 per cent more of the votes cast than any other candidate, he will be elected.

7. The scrutineers will announce the number of votes received by each candidate, and if no candidate satisfies these conditions a second ballot will be held.

Second Ballot

8. The second ballot will be held not less than two days and not more than four days after the first ballot, excluding Saturdays and Sundays. Nominations made for the first ballot will be void and new nominations, under the same procedure as for the first ballot, will be submitted for the original candidates if required and for any other candidate.

9. The voting procedure for the second ballot will be the same as for the first, save that paragraph 6 above shall not apply. If as a result of this second ballot one candidate receives an overall majority he will be elected.

Third Ballot

10. If no candidate receives an overall majority, the three candidates receiving the highest number of votes at the second ballot will be placed on a ballot paper for a third and final ballot.

11. For the final ballot each voter must indicate two preferences amongst the three candidates by placing the figure '1' opposite

the name of his preferred candidate and the figure '2' opposite the name of his second choice.

12. The scrutineers will proceed to add the number of first preference votes received by each candidate, eliminate the candidate with the lowest number of first preference votes and redistribute the votes of those giving him as their first preference amongst the two remaining candidates in accordance with their second preference. The result of this final count will be an overall majority for one candidate, and he will be elected.

Party Meeting

13. The candidate thus elected by the Commons Party will be presented for election as Party Leader to the Party Meeting constituted as at present.

APPENDIX B

Election Rules and Procedures for the Selection of the Leader of the Progressive Conservative Party, September 9, 1967

1. *Nominations*:
   (a) All nominations shall be made in writing on the form to be provided by the Convention Committee.
   (b) All nominations must be proposed by a minimum of twenty-five and not more than fifty accredited delegates who shall execute the nomination form.
   (c) All nominations shall require the acceptance in writing of the person nominated in the terms of the nomination form.
   (d) Nominations shall close at 10.00 a.m., E.D.S.T. on Friday, September 8, 1967.

Source: Schedule 4 of the *Report of Executive Committee of the Executive Officers of the Progressive Conservative Association of Canada being the Convention Committee of the Progressive Conservative Centennial Convention to the Convention* (Presented to the Toronto Convention, September 7, 1967).

(e) All nominations must be delivered in person or by prepaid registered mail so as to be received by Convention Headquarters at the Royal York Hotel or Suite 1530 at 101 Richmond St. West, Toronto, prior to the close of nomination.

(f) At the close of nominations, the Chief Elections Officer will announce the names of all properly nominated candidates and will notify each candidate of all other candidates properly nominated.

(g) Any candidate wishing to withdraw at any time after the close of nominations may do so by advising the Chief Elections Officer in writing of his withdrawal. The Chief Elections Officer will immediately notify one of the Co-Chairmen of the Convention who shall be authorized to inform the Convention of such withdrawal.

2. *Nomination Speeches*:

(a) The names of all nominated candidates may be put in nomination by a proposer and seconder of the candidate's choice on the afternoon of Friday, September 8, 1967.

(b) The proposer and the seconder are required to be accredited delegates or alternates to the Convention.

(c) The length of the speeches of the proposer and seconder shall be set by the Convention Committee and announced to the Candidates before 6.00 p.m. (EDST) Thursday, September 7th, 1967.

(d) The order of all speakers shall be determined by lot, with the draw supervised by the Chief Elections Officer.

(e) Demonstrations in support of any candidate shall be permitted for a period not exceeding five minutes after each candidate's name is put in nomination by the proposer.

(f) The Co-Chairman may deduct speaking time from the seconder for protracted demonstrations which exceed the five minute limit.

(g) All speakers shall be notified by the Co-Chairman one minute before their speaking time elapses. After the full time has elapsed, the Co-Chairman shall immediately terminate further remarks by the speaker.

(h) Each nominated candidate shall be entitled to address the Convention on the evening of Friday, September 8th; the length of the speeches of the candidates shall be set by the Convention Committee and announced to the candidates before 6.00 p.m. (EDST) Thursday, September 7th, 1967.

(i) The order of the candidate's speeches shall be determined by lot with the draw under the supervision of the Chief Elections Officer.

(j) No demonstrations shall be allowed in support of any candidate after a candidate's speech other than for normal applause.

3. *Scrutineers and Agents*:

(a) Each candidate shall be entitled to appoint in writing an official agent and two scrutineers to represent them in reviewing all nominations and elections' procedures.

(b) All such appointments shall be made on a prescribed form to be provided by the Convention Committee.

4. *Voting Methods and Procedures*:

(a) Registration and accreditation of delegates shall cease at 11.00 a.m. (EDST) on Saturday, September 9th, 1967.

(b) At the close of accreditation, the Credentials Chairman shall deliver to the Chief Elections Officer a list of all accredited voting delegates, such list to be in numerical order, according to the number of the credentials certificate.

(c) The Chief Elections Officer shall allocate delegates to specific polling stations on the basis of the numerical order supplied by the Credentials Chairman and shall announce the allocation.

(d) Voting shall be carried out by means of the Shoup Voting Machine supplied by the Canadian Voting Machine Company of Canada.

(e) At 1.00 p.m. (EDST) Saturday, September 9th, 1967, the voting shall commence and voting delegates shall be given thirty minutes to join a voting queue. Voting shall continue until all delegates in the queue have voted.

(f) Each delegate other than an alternate delegate shall be entitled to one vote on each ballot.

(g) The Chief Elections Officer shall immediately tally the results from each voting machine and prepare a total result of all votes cast.

(h) The total result may be shown electronically and shall be announced officially by a Co-Chairman.

(i) The candidate receiving the lowest number of votes on each ballot shall be dropped from the list of eligible candidates.

(j) In the event of a tie vote between two candidates receiving the lowest number of votes, the voting will be done again.

(k) A period of fifteen minutes shall be allowed after the announcement of the results of each vote for the purpose of allowing withdrawal by any candidate in the manner hereinbefore referred to.

(l) Voting shall then recommence and continue until a candidate is elected as leader.

(m) Immediately that the first ballot commences, the amphitheatre at the Maple Leaf Gardens shall be deemed to be the polling area for election purposes.

(n) The Sergeant-at-arms on the Convention staff shall be authorized to take all such steps as are necessary to maintain order while the voting is in process.

(o) Immediately the first ballot commences no delegate shall be entitled to be heard from the floor, but any complaint or grievance relating to any alleged voting irregularity or any other matter pertaining to the election shall be made to the Chief Elections Officer. The decision of such complaint or grievance shall be made by the Chief Elections Officer after consultation with the Co-Chairman. Such decision shall be final and binding. No appeal lies from the decison of the Chief Elections Officer.

5. *Election of Candidate as Leader:*

(a) The candidate first receiving a majority of the votes cast on one ballot shall be elected as leader of the Party.

APPENDIX C

A Note on Campaign Expenses

Convention campaign costs for individual candidates need not be exorbitant. Neither should serious potential leaders be handicapped because of their inability to raise substantial sums of money. Consideration ought to be given by the Liberals and Conservatives in future to a plan not unlike that approved by the NDP for their 1971 convention whereby (a) a maximum would be placed on candidate campaign costs and (b) each candidate would receive a small grant from the party's treasury. There is obviously a risk that such a plan if adopted would encourage token candidates. But that eventuality might well be minimized by a party regulation that no reimbursing grant would be forthcoming from the party to any candidate receiving less than one per cent of the total first ballot vote. In 1967 such a requirement would have meant that a Conservative candidate needed twenty-two votes, and in 1968 a Liberal candidate would have needed twenty-four votes to qualify for financial assistance from his party. Such a regulation in 1967 would have entitled Michael Starr to Conservative party support, but not John MacLean or Mary Walker-Sawka. In 1968 the cut-off line for Liberal party support would have been drawn between Eric Kierans and Lloyd Henderson. In 1971, the NDP regulations took the following form:

Rules for the Conduct of Campaign for the Federal Leadership of the New Democratic Party 1971, Approved by the Federal Council (Sept. 20, 1970)

1. (a) A candidate, for the purposes of these regulations and participating in benefits outlined herein, is any member of the Party in good standing who, in writing, files with the Secretary of the Party a written declaration of his candidacy signed by 50 members of the Party in good standing, including members from at least three ridings and two provinces.

    (b) A candidate shall not be eligible for any benefits provided herein unless he files for nomination in accordance with Rule 1 and is nominated, pursuant to Rule 8, or unless the Federal Executive decides otherwise.

2. Provincial sections of the Party, constituency or affiliated organizations are requested to provide equal opportunity, as far as possible, to all candidates to speak to and meet members of the Party.

3. (a) The Party shall arrange one Cross-Canada joint tour for all candidates who have declared their intention to be candidates. The Party shall arrange for the use of halls, at suitable places, for public meetings to be addressed by the candidates. At such meetings, an appeal for contributions shall be made to pay some of the Party costs of the tour.

Source: New Democratic Party Headquarters, Ottawa.

(b) The Party shall, after the convention, recompense candidates by reimbursing them for monies expended by them on account of the campaign, but not exceeding for any one candidate the sum of $1,000: the aggregate amount for this purpose shall not exceed $7,000 and should this total provide less than $1,000 per candidate, the $7,000 total amount shall be pro-rated equally among the eligible candidates.

4. Each candidate shall notify the Secretary of the name of a member of the Party in good standing who will be the candidate's official representative for consultation and liaison purposes. The official representative shall be entitled to notice of, and to attend, with voice but no vote, meetings of the 1971 Federal Convention Committee.

5. Each candidate shall appoint an official agent for purposes of accounting for all campaign expenses and contributions of goods and services and for certifying to the accuracy of the statement referred to in Rule 6.

6. Each candidate shall file with his nomination paper an itemized statement, signed by the candidate and his official agent, showing the total amount of the value of goods and services expended (NB: From the date of the adoption of these rules by the NDP Federal Council) and estimated to be still expended on the campaign, by the candidate or by others on his behalf, to the best knowledge of the signators of the statement; and the names of donors of money, goods or services. Contributions of less than $50 may be grouped under the heading 'Miscellaneous Contributions'. Copies of these statements shall be distributed to all delegates.

7. The total expenditures by any candidate shall not exceed 3¢ multiplied by the total number of NDP members in Canada (as of this date 350,000).
   It is understood that expenditures during the period of the actual convention are to be part of the global limitation outlined above.

8. *Candidates:*

   Must be members in good standing of the Party.

   Must obtain nomination forms from the Federal Secretary.

   Must submit nomination forms indicating acceptance and signed by not less than 50 persons qualified and approved by the appropriate authority as delegates.

   Must submit nomination forms by noon on April 22, 1971.

Must name a speaker to nominate them before noon
of April 22, 1971.

(Note: A preliminary list of delegates to be prepared and made available to all candidates by April 6, 1971).

9. *Candidates' Speeches:* On April 23, 1971.
Order of speaking determined by lot.

10. *Balloting:*

By seating blocks (not geographically) of perhaps
100 delegates.

Counting of ballots in the convention hall.

Announcement of balloting results by blocks and
consolidated figure by chairman of balloting committee.

Any candidate with less than 50 votes on a ballot
and the candidate with the lowest vote on each
ballot to be dropped after each vote.

If two candidates are tied for the least number of
votes on any ballot yet neither has less than 50
votes, both shall be included on the next subsequent ballot.

The winning candidate shall receive more than 50%
of the ballots of delegates present and casting
valid ballots.

Candidates may, by written notification to the Secretary, withdraw before any ballot but must do so
before the announcement of the taking of the
subsequent ballot. (Time between ballots to be
determined).

During balloting only delegates should remain in the
voting area.

11. *Delegate Totals:*

For the purpose of convention representation, the
provisions of the NDP federal constitution, Article
VI, shall apply.

12. *Convention Demonstrations:*

Non-delegate demonstrations be banned within the convention
area. Delegate demonstrations on behalf of candidates should be
such as not to interfere unduly with convention progress.

Clifford A. Scotton,
Federal Secretary.

September, 1970.

APPENDIX D

Call for a National Convention of the Liberal Party of Canada Ottawa, April 4-6, 1968

Pursuant to a request made by the Leader of the Liberal Party of Canada, the Rt. Hon. L. B. Pearson, on December 14, 1967, and in conformity with a decision of the Executive Committee of the Liberal Federation of Canada, at a meeting held in Ottawa on December 17, 1967, a National Convention of the Liberal Party of Canada is hereby called, to take place at OTTAWA, Capital City of Canada, on April 4th, 5th and 6th, 1968.

The purposes of the Convention shall be:

1. To elect a Leader of the Liberal Party of Canada.
2. To consider aspects of Liberal policy of particular importance at this time.
3. To consider party organization.
4. To elect Officers of the Liberal Federation of Canada.

Following the plans adopted at the four prior National Liberal Leadership Conventions, all held in Canada's first century, (1893-1919-1948-1958), and having regard to subsequent developments, including a decision of the Executive Committee (April 30th, 1966) to the effect that the terms "constituency" and "federal electoral district" as used herein 'shall mean constituencies and federal elecoral districts as redistributed and applicable to the next general election, the representation at this, the fifth National Liberal Leadership Convention, shall be as follows:

REPRESENTATION

1. All the Liberal Members of the Privy Council, of the Senate (including retired members of the Senate) and of the House of Commons, and where any constituency is not represented in the House of Commons by an adherent of the Liberal party, the Liberal candidate defeated in the last election and if a new Liberal candidate has been nominated in a redistributed constituency, such new candidate.

2. The Leaders of the Liberal party in the ten provinces of Canada.

Source: *National Liberal Convention, Ottawa, 1968* (Handbook presented to all Liberal delegates). The Call is in error in stating that the 1893 convention was a leadership convention.

3. All the members of the Executive Committee of the Liberal Federation of Canada, the Women's Liberal Federation of Canada, the Young Liberal Federation of Canada and the Canadian University Liberal Federation.

4. Four members of the Executive Committee of each Association, Federation or party Organization listed in Clause No. 2 of the constitution.

5. In addition to the president, two other officers of each of the ten provincial organizations of Liberal Women and of the ten provincial organizations of Young Liberals.

6. Two representatives of each of the University Liberal Clubs in Canada and of the five regional organizations of the Canadian University Liberal Federation.

7. The co-chairmen of the standing committees of the Federation and the appointed members of each of the standing committees of the Federation.

8. Six delegates from each federal electoral district at least one of whom shall be a Liberal Woman and one a Young Liberal, and three alternates, all of whom shall be elected at a constituency meeting, to be called for that purpose.

9. The Liberal members of each provincial assembly and the Liberal candidates defeated at the last provincial assembly election in each province or new candidates nominated, acting jointly, shall have the right to select from among themselves a number of delegates equal to one-fourth of the total membership of each provincial assembly.

REGULATIONS

To assist the Convention Organization Committee in the preparation of the Convention, the following regulations shall apply:

1. The Call of the Convention shall be sent to each Provincial Liberal Leader, to each Provincial Liberal Association or Federation, to each Provincial Liberal Association or Federation President, to each Liberal Senator, to each Liberal Member of the House of Commons, and where a constituency is not represented by an adherent of the Liberal party, to the defeated Liberal candidate in such constituency; and if a Liberal candidate has been nominated in a redistributed constituency to such new candidate, to the Presidents of Provincial Women's and Young Liberals' organizations, and to the President of each University Liberal Club.

2. In each federal electoral district a meeting shall be called not later than 35 days (February 29, 1968), prior to the opening of the Convention, for the election by a majority of the votes of those

present at the meeting, of the number of delegates and alternates to which the constituency is entitled. To ensure a representative attendance at each such meeting, sufficient advance notice shall be given by advertisement or otherwise, and the date, hour, place and purpose of meeting shall be mentioned in such notice.

3. Each Provincial Liberal Association or Federation shall, in conjunction with each federal member or candidate, as the case may be, and the Constituency Liberal Association, arrange the date, place and hour of this meeting.

4. In each constituency, the sitting Liberal member or the defeated Liberal candidate or, if a new Liberal candidate has been nominated, such new candidate, as the case may be, shall co-operate with the President of the constituency Association in all matters relating to the calling and holding of the meeting for the election of the said delegates and alternates.

5. At each of the said constituency meetings, each elected delegate and alternate shall be furnished with a certificate of his election as such and each of the said certificates shall be signed:

    (i) by the chairman of the meeting electing delegates;

    (ii) by the secretary of the meeting;

    (iii) by the delegate or alternate himself.

6. When any delegate elected under paragraph 8 of the representation rules is unable to attend the Convention, he must be replaced by an alternate already elected for his constituency, and a new alternate may then be appointed. Request for cancellation of delegates' credential, promotion of alternate to delegate status and appointment of new alternate must be made on the prescribed form signed by the same persons who signed the original certificates or by the President and the Secretary of the Provincial Association or Federation mentioned in Clause 2 of the constitution.

All substitutions of alternates for delegates shall cease 24 hours after time of opening of the Convention or at the same time registration closes, whichever is earlier.

7. Similar certificates shall be issued by the Association or Federation included in Clause No. 2 of the Constitution, to the last defeated Liberal candidate in each constituency not now represented in the House of Commons by an adherent of the Liberal party; similar certificates are also to be issued by the local organization to the newly nominated candidates in a redistributed constituency.

8. Similar certificates shall also be issued over the signature of the president and secretary of their respective associations to delegate selected under paragraphs 4-5-6-7 of the representation rules.

9. Forms of certificates shall be prepared under the direction of the Convention Organization Committee at Ottawa, and the persons

to whom they are mailed will be held responsible for their proper distribution and return.

10. Each of such certificates duly filled in and signed as aforesaid, shall be mailed to the General Secretary of the Convention Organization Committee at Ottawa, not later than 30 days (March 5, 1968), prior to the opening of the Convention. Upon receipt of the said certificates, the said General Secretary shall issue and mail credentials to the delegates entitled thereto. Only one single, non-transferable credential shall be issued to one person to qualify as a delegate.

11. Credentials for all other persons entitled to attend the said Convention shall be issued as required by the said General Secretary.

Dated at Ottawa, the 1st day of January, 1968.

"L. B. Pearson"
Leader of the
Liberal Party

"J. L. Nichol"
President, Liberal
Federation of
Canada

APPENDIX E

Rules to Govern Choice and Seating of Delegates at Progressive Conservative National Convention, 1956

1. Delegates or alternate delegates wherever practicable shall be elected at Meetings of the Progressive Conservative Association in each riding, called for such purpose.
2. Delegates or alternate delegates representing each riding shall be permanently resident in such riding or *closely* identified with the organization and work of the Progressive Conservative Party in such riding, and in the latter circumstance, must be permanently resident in the Province in which the riding is situated.
3. In any case where no Progressive Conservative Association or similar organization exists in any riding, steps shall be taken to call a meeting of party supporters to elect delegates and alternate delegates. If, in any case, the Provincial Executive certifies to the

Source: Progressive Conservative Party Headquarters, Ottawa.

Convention Executive Committee that such a course is not feasible, the Convention Executive Committee may authorize the Provincial Executive to name the delegates and alternate delegates to represent such riding, provided however:

(a) Wherever possible, such delegates and alternate delegates shall be resident of such riding; or closely identified with the organization and work of the Progressive Conservative Party in such riding;

(b) In any event, such delegates and alternate delegates shall be permanent residents of the Province in which the riding is situated;

(c) That a full list of delegates so chosen, together with all relevant documents is submitted to the Credentials Committee at the Convention, which Committee shall have full power, when it considers any abuse has occurred, to refuse for that reason to approve the credentials of any person so chosen.

4. Delegates-at-large and Youth delegates-at-large must be permanently resident in the Province which they are selected to represent.

5. University delegates-at-large must be enrolled at the University which they are selected to represent.

6. An alternate delegate will not be seated at the Convention if the delegate for whom he is entitled to substitute is registered at the Convention.

APPENDIX F

Progressive Conservative Delegates-at-Large, 1967 Convention

11. (iv) *Delegates-at-Large:*

(a) *General:* The following delegates-at-large from each province and the territories:

Yukon — Three; N.W.T. — Three; British Columbia — Thirty; Alberta — Twenty-five; Saskatchewan — Twenty-

Source: *Report of Executive Committee of the Executive Officers of the Progressive Conservative Association of Canada Being the Convention Committee of the Progressive Conservative Centennial Convention to the Convention* (Presented to the Toronto Convention, September 7, 1967).

five; Manitoba — Twenty-five; Ontario — Ninety; Quebec
— Ninety; New Brunswick — Twenty; Nova Scotia —
Twenty; Prince Edward Island — Ten; Newfoundland —
Fifteen.

The general delegates-at-large are to be appointed in each
province by the provincial president for the province, the
provincial vice-president for the province and the two
federal directors for the province.

(b) *Women:* Nine delegates-at-large from Ontario and Quebec to be appointed by the Women's Provincial Association. Three delegates-at-large from each of the other provinces and each of the territories to be appointed by the
Women's Provincial Association or Territorial Association.

(c) *Y.P.C.:* Nine delegates-at-large from Ontario and Quebec, three of whom must be women to be appointed by the
Y.P.C. Provincial Associations in conjunction with the
federal Y.P.C. Association. Three delegates-at-large from
each of the other provinces and each of the territories one
of whom must be a woman to be appointed jointly by each
Y.P.C. Provincial Association and the federal Y.P.C. Association.

APPENDIX G

A Note on Coalition Formation and the Theory of Conflict of Interest

Why are certain coalitions more likely to form than
others?[1] Understandably, there is no simple explanation that might
be given in response to that question. Indeed, before a satisfactory
answer could be expected, adequate data would have to be collected
on a great many variables, including the roles, perceptions, interests
and goals of convention delegates and leadership candidates. A theoretical framework would be needed within which such data could

[1] Once again the term "coalition" is to be understood as meaning a loosely
knit grouping of individuals voting for the same candidate on a particular
ballot, not a product of bargains struck by factional leaders controlling
blocs of votes.

be analysed and the results explained. It would not be unfair to say that social scientists in Canada have really only begun the enormous job of gathering and interpreting the necessary data.[2] Recognizing all this, it is nonetheless of some interest to speculate on the process of coalition formation by examining a theory of politics based on conflict of interest.

According to the theory of conflict of interest[3] certain coalitions have a greater likelihood of forming than others. Those potential coalitions with less incompatibility of goals among their members are more likely to form and to remain more durable than other potential coalitions with greater conflict of interest among their members. Just as it is true that the various parties in a multi-party system have differing goals, but that "a given party has goals that are more similar to those of some of the parties than of others,"[4] so is it also true that the various candidates and delegates in a leadership contest differ from one another, but that given candidates and delegates share more in common with one another than with others. Robert Axelrod has illustrated the theory of conflict of interest in the following way:

> Suppose that the [candidates and their respective delegate supporters] are labeled A, B, C, D, E, F, and G in order of their positions from left to right on the policy dimension. In an ordinal policy dimension, the dispersion of the coalition consisting of . . . A, B, and C cannot be compared to the dispersion of the coalition consisting of B, C, and D. However, the coalition consisting of . . . A, B, and C is certain to be less dispersed than the coalition consisting of A, B, and D. For this reason, a coalition consisting of adjacent [members], or a *connected coalition* as it can be called, tends to have relatively low dispersion and thus low conflict of interest for its size.
>
> Of course, the property of a coalition's being connected does not take into account its total spread or dispersion. The coalition ABC has less dispersion than the coalition ABCD. Therefore ABC has less conflict of interest than ABCD, even though both coalitions are connected. Thus the size as well as the connectedness of a coalition affects its conflict of interest.[5]

[2] Two published studies of particular relevance to this subject are Lele, Perlin and Thorburn, "Leadership Conventions in Canada," and LeDuc, "Party Decision-Making."

[3] See Robert Axelrod, *Conflict of Interest: A Theory of Divergent Goals with Applications to Politics* (Chicago: Markham Publishing Co., 1970), especially chap. 8.

[4] *Ibid.*, p. 166.

[5] *Ibid.*, pp. 169-70. (Italics in original)

Naturally the coalition has to be a *winning* coalition to get the candidate chosen as leader. But the winning coalition does not have to be large in numbers, for the smaller the coalition the lower its conflict of interest. In a Canadian convention, 50 per cent plus one of the delegates' votes would be the ideal size, for it would be "minimal in the sense that it can lose no member . . . without ceasing to be connected and winning."[6] Accordingly, the coalition predicted by the theory might best be defined (in Axelrod's terminology) as a *minimum connected winning coalition.*

Could it be that in 1967 and 1968 the sorts of coalitions predicted by the conflict of interest theory materialized? Perhaps. The data (neither as refined nor as complete as one might hope) are at least suggestive, if nothing more, of some support for the conflict of interest theory.

Ignoring distances between the candidates and assuming that the following arbitrarily defined "Left-Right" political spectra appropriately place the 1967 Conservative and 1968 Liberal leadership candidates, the theory of conflict of interest appears to help in furthering our understanding of the sorts of coalitions formed during the convention balloting in 1967 and 1968.

Such spectra are, at best, very crude and approximate guesses at the relative location of the candidates. They are based simply on an intuitive approximation of a composite nature, and have attempted to take into account the candidates' views on a variety of subjects, but not in any systematic way: taxation, the role of the government in the economy, social welfare, French-English relations, and such matters. The spectra are designed to be of use in the development of the line of reasoning in the text and are not expected to locate *exactly* (either in absolute or relative terms) the various candidates. Certainly there will be differences of opinions over the location of particular candidates. One illustration of that fact will do. Some may choose to place Fleming further to the Right on the Conservative spectrum. Yet it should be remembered that for some time before the 1967 convention many Diefenbaker loyalists (particularly prairie MPs) were more attracted by the possibility of having Fleming as their leader than by any of the other candidates except Diefenbaker. For them, Fleming's position on the spectrum was not far removed

---

[6] *Ibid.*, p. 170. Earlier work by William Riker and others argued that political coalitions will be of minimal rather than of maximal size. According to Riker, minimum winning coalitions, subjectively defined by the participants because of the absence of perfect information, are preferred to coalitions that are larger than necessary to win, for they ensure the best distribution of the spoils to the individual coalition members. See Riker, *The Theory of Political Coalitions* (New Haven: Yale University Press, 1962), chaps. 2 and 4.

from Diefenbaker's and to a considerable degree they were responsible for getting Fleming to agree to run.[7]

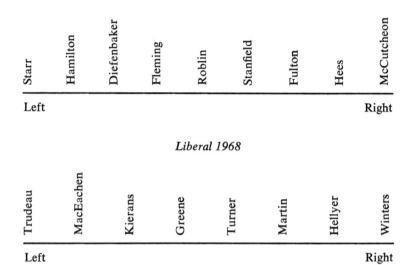

Conservative 1967

Starr — Hamilton — Diefenbaker — Fleming — Roblin — Stanfield — Fulton — Hees — McCutcheon

Left   Right

Liberal 1968

Trudeau — MacEachen — Kierans — Greene — Turner — Martin — Hellyer — Winters

Left   Right

The evidence suggests that there was a marked tendency on the part of those delegates and candidates who switched their support to move to a position of supporting one of the major, relatively compatible candidates. Naturally there were exceptions (as when nearly one-half of MacEachen's supporters on the first ballot switched to Winters on the second ballot), but they tended to be rare and clearly reflected the disparate first ballot support bases of some candidates.[8] A few appropriate examples might be given.

An analysis of the totals for each of the twenty voting machines at the Conservative convention of 1967 suggests that, in general terms and in varying degrees, over the course of the convention's five

---

[7] Delegate placement of the Liberal candidates by LeDuc's questionnaire respondents very closely approximates the Liberal spectrum designed for this Appendix. See LeDuc, "The Leadership Selection Process in Canadian Political Parties: A Case Study" (unpublished Ph.D. dissertation, University of Michigan, 1970), p. 72.

[8] MacEachen figures computed from LeDuc, "Party Decision-Making," Appendix A, p. 117. As noted previously in chapter 8, much of MacEachen's support was apparently in the nature of first ballot "native son" support which then, quite logically, moved to its true preferences following the first ballot.

Table G-1: A Comparison of Fourth and Fifth Ballot Results by Candidate and by Voting Machine, Progressive Conservative Convention, 1967

(12 of 20 machines)

Voting Machine Number	1	2	3	5	6	9	10	11	12	13	15	16	Totals
Fourth ballot: number voting	115	114	105	58	111	107	95	110	119	113	116	123	1286
Fulton	13	17	6	5	8	41	7	17	27	13	17	22	193
Hamilton	20	8	3	2	3	9	16	2	11	8	11	9	102
Roblin	35	32	20	10	24	22	34	39	37	38	58	46	395
Stanfield	47	57	76	41	76	35	38	52	44	54	30	46	596
Fifth ballot: number voting	116	112	106	57	108	105	96	108	115	111	111	120	1265
Roblin	60	40	25	13	23	30	48	42	48	46	73	57	505
Stanfield	56	72	81	44	85	75	48	66	67	65	38	63	760

Source: Official voting totals by ballot and by voting machine provided to the author by a campaign manager of one of the candidates.

ballots the Starr–Hamilton–Diefenbaker–Fleming supporters tended to move ultimately to a position of voting for Roblin, whereas the McCutcheon–Hees–Fulton supporters tended to vote for Stanfield when their favourite candidates were no longer in the race.[9] Of those candidates who were eliminated or who withdrew from the contest, three indicated that they personally supported Stanfield: McCutcheon, Hees and Fulton. No such endorsements were made on Roblin's behalf, although key workers for some of the retiring candidates closer on the political spectrum to Roblin than to Stanfield (for example, top Diefenbaker aides Gordon Churchill, James Johnston and Joel Aldred) showed their support publicly for Roblin once their candidate withdrew. Comparing the results of the last two ballots of the Conservative convention, the transferability of support from Hamilton to Roblin and from Fulton to Stanfield was apparently a dominant feature at a majority of the voting machines[10] (see Table G-1).

At the Liberal convention of 1968 the voting coalitions were not formed in a centripetal fashion as were those of the 1967 Conservative convention. With the first ballot results at the Liberal convention it was obvious that the leading candidates were not only some distance apart, but at the opposite ends of the political spectrum. Nonetheless, it was around them that the major coalitions began to form. The principle of connected voting coalitions (formed, of course, on each of the successive ballots) appears to have obtained, just as it had at the Conservative convention. When Kierans withdrew following the first ballot of the Liberal convention, virtually all of his supporters gave their second-ballot votes to the two closest major candidates: 57 per cent to Trudeau and 36 per cent to Turner, with the remaining 7 per cent switching to Greene. Of those delegates who originally

---

[9] Official voting totals by ballots and by separate voting machines for each of the ballots, as well as a complete list of delegates by voting machines (indicating those voting on the respective ballots) have been provided to the author by a campaign manager of one of the candidates. Much of the information in this section is taken from those data and lists. A useful analysis of the same data was written by Scott Young and David Slocombe, "Party Brass Elected Stanfield," *Globe and Mail*, September 20, 1967, pp. 1 and 2.

[10] Most of the remaining machine totals suggested a different type of transferability: Fulton's Quebec supporters apparently preferred Roblin on the fifth ballot to Stanfield. Hees's Quebec supporters had reacted in much the same way once their candidate retired from the race after the third ballot. As a general rule, it seems fair to conclude that Roblin was much more acceptable to Quebec delegates than Stanfield. For Table G. 1 the assumption is made that the Roblin and Stanfield supporters on the fourth ballot voted the same way on the fifth ballot.

supported Hellyer but who abandoned him at some point during the convention, or who were forced to choose another candidate once he withdrew after the third ballot, over twice as many (63 per cent) chose to vote for Winters compared to anyone else. Of the Liberal candidates who decided, upon their elimination or withdrawal from the contest, to indicate their particular preference for leader, Mac-Eachen and Greene both selected Trudeau, but Hellyer favoured Winters. Martin and Kierans, on the other hand, preferred to retire from the race following the first ballot without making their choices public.[11] Turner's inability to establish a sufficiently acceptable claim to the leadership on the first ballot (he tied for fourth place) proved costly to him, for it meant that any potential he may have had as a satisfactory compromise candidate was lost as more and more delegates switched support away from the centre of the spectrum and towards its extremes.

[11] The figures used in this section are computed from LeDuc, "Party Decision-Making," Appendix A, p. 117.

Selected
Bibliography

Abbreviations:

APSR   American Political Science Review
CHR   Canadian Historical Review
CJEPS   Canadian Journal of Economics and Political Science
CJPS   Canadian Journal of Political Science
JCS   Journal of Canadian Studies
JP   Journal of Politics

I. *Political Leadership (General)*

BURNS, James MacGregor. "A Note on the Study of Political Leadership." *Roosevelt: The Lion and the Fox.* New York: Harcourt, Brace and World, Inc., 1956.

DION, Leon. "The Concept of Political Leadership: An Analysis." *CJPS,* I (March 1968), 2-17.

EDINGER, Lewis J., ed. *Political Leadership in Industrialized Societies.* New York: John Wiley and Sons, 1967.

————. "Political Science and Political Leadership; Reflections on the Study of Leadership." *JP,* XXVI (May and August, 1964), 423-439 and 648-676.

ERIKSON, Erik H. *Young Man Luther: A Study in Psychoanalysis and History.* New York: W. W. Norton and Company, 1962.

261

GIBB, Cecil A. "Leadership." *The Handbook of Social Psychology.* Vol. IV, 2nd ed. Edited by Gardner Lindzey and Elliot Aronson. Don Mills: Addison-Wesley Publishing Co., 1969.

GOULDNER, Alvin W. *Studies in Leadership.* New York: Harper and Brothers, 1950.

JAMESON, J. Franklin. "The Early Political Uses of the Word Convention." *Proceedings of the American Antiquarian Society,* XII (1899), 183-196.

LASSWELL, Harold D. *Psychopathology and Politics.* New York: The Viking Press, 1960.

MARVICK, Dwaine, ed. *Political Decision-Makers: Recruitment and Performance.* Glencoe, Illinois: Free Press of Glencoe, 1961.

MICHELS, Robert. *Political Parties.* New York: Dover Publications, Inc., 1959.

"Philosophers and Kings: Studies in Leadership." *Daedalus* (Summer 1968), pp. 683-1082.

PREWITT, Kenneth. "Political Socialization and Leadership Selection." *Annals of the American Academy of Political and Social Science,* 361 (September 1965), 109-110.

———, and Eulau, Heinz. "Social Bias in Leadership Selection, Political Recruitment and Electoral Context." *JP,* XXXIII (May 1971), 293-315.

SELIGMAN, Lester G. "The Study of Political Leadership." *Political Behavior: A Reader in Theory and Research.* Edited by Heinz Eulau, Samuel J. Eldersveld and Morris Janowitz. Glencoe: Free Press, 1956.

TUCKER, Robert C. "The Theory of Charismatic Leadership." *Daedalus* (Summer 1968), pp. 731-756.

WEBER, Max. *The Theory of Social and Economic Organization.* Toronto: Collier-Macmillan Canada, Ltd., 1964.

II. *Selection of Party Leaders: Great Britain*

BERKELEY, Humphry. *Crossing the Floor.* London: George Allen and Unwin, 1972.

BUTLER, D. E., and King, Anthony. *The British General Election of 1966.* Toronto: Macmillan Company of Canada, 1966.

BUTLER, Lord. *The Art of the Possible.* London: Hamish Hamilton, 1971.

CHURCHILL, Randolph S. *The Fight for the Tory Leadership.* London: William Heinemann Ltd., 1964.

GUTTSMAN, W. L. "Changes in British Labour Leadership." *Political Decision-Makers: Recruitment and Performance.* Edited by Dwaine Marvick. Glencoe, Illinois: Free Press of Glencoe, 1961.

HUTCHINSON, George. *Edward Heath: A Personal and Political Biography*. London: Longman Group Limited, 1970.

KING, Anthony, ed. *British Politics: People, Parties and Parliament*. Lexington, Massachusetts: D. C. Heath and Co., 1966.

LOEWENBERG, Gerhard. "The British Constitution and the Structure of the Labour Party." *APSR*, LII (September 1958), 771-790.

MACLEOD, Iain. "Lord Home Emerges." *The Spectator* (January 1964), pp. 65-67.

MCKENZIE, R. T. *British Political Parties: The Distribution of Power Within the Conservative and Labour Parties*. 2nd ed. London: Heinemann Educational Books Ltd., 1963.

PUNNETT, R. M. "The Parliamentary and Personal Backgrounds of British Prime Ministers, 1812 to 1963." *Quarterly Review*, 302 (July 1964), 254-266.

SHAW, Malcolm. "An American Looks at the Party Conferences." *Parliamentary Affairs*, XV (Spring 1962), 203-212.

III. *Selection of Party Leaders: United States*

CHASE, James S. "Genesis of the First National Political Convention: A Case Study in the Development of an American Institution." *Social Science Quarterly*, L (June 1969), 92-105.

———. "Jacksonian Democracy and the Rise of the Nominating Convention." *Mid-America*, XLV (October 1963), 229-249.

DAVID, Paul T.; Goldman, Ralph M.; and Bain, Richard C. *The Politics of National Party Conventions*. Washington, D.C.: The Brookings Institution, 1960.

Democratic Party's Commission on Party Structure and Delegate Selection. *Mandate for Reform*. Washington: Democratic National Committee, 1970.

GAMSON, William A. "A Theory of Coalition Formation." *American Sociological Review*, XXVI (June 1961), 373-382.

———. "An Experimental Test of a Theory of Coalition Formation." *American Sociological Review*, XXVI (August 1961), 565-573.

———. "Coalition Formation at Presidential Nominating Conventions." *American Journal of Sociology*, LXVIII (September 1962), 157-171.

JANOSIK, Edward. "The American National Nominating Convention." *Parliamentary Affairs*, XVII (Summer 1964), 321-339.

KEY, V. O., Jr. *Politics, Parties and Pressure Groups*. 5th ed. New York: Thomas Y. Crowell, 1964.

MEADOWS, Paul, and Braucher, Charles L. "Social Composition of the 1948 National Conventions." *Sociology and Social Research, 1951-1952*, XXXVI (Sept-Oct. 1951), 31-35.

MORISON, Samuel E. "The First National Nominating Convention, 1808." *American Historical Review,* XVII (July 1912), 744-763.

MURDOCK, John S. "The First National Nominating Convention." *American Historical Review,* I (July 1896), 680-683.

PLAISTED, Thais M. "Origins of National Nominating Committees and Platforms." *Social Studies,* XXX (May 1939), 199-206.

POLSBY, Nelson W., and Wildavsky, Aaron B. *Presidential Elections: Strategies of American Electoral Politics.* 2nd ed. New York: Charles Scribner's Sons, 1968.

POMPER, Gerald. *Nominating the President: The Politics of Convention Choice.* Evanston, Illinois: Northwestern University Press, 1966.

SOULE, John W., and Clarke, James W. "Amateurs and Professionals: A Study of Delegates to the Democratic National Convention." *APSR,* LXIV (September 1970), 888-898.

IV. *Leadership Selection and Party Conventions in Canada (General)*

BAAR, Carl. "Party Organization, Convention Organization and Leadership Selection in Canada and the United States." Paper delivered to the American Political Science Association, Los Angeles, September 11, 1970.

DAWSON, R. MacGregor, ed. *Constitutional Issues in Canada, 1900-1931.* London: Oxford University Press, 1933.

———. *The Government of Canada.* 5th ed. Revised by Norman Ward. Toronto: University of Toronto Press, 1970.

FORD, Arthur R. *As the World Wags On.* Toronto: The Ryerson Press, 1950.

GRAHAM, Roger. "Charisma and Canadian Politics." *Character and Circumstance: Essays in Honour of Donald Grant Creighton.* Edited by John S. Moir. Toronto: Macmillan Company of Canada, 1970.

HAMELIN, M., ed. *Les Idées Politiques des Premiers Ministres du Canada.* Ottawa: Les Editions de L'Université d'Ottawa, 1969.

HARRILL, Ernest Eugene. "The Structure of Organization and Power in Canadian Political Parties." Unpublished Ph.D. dissertation, University of North Carolina, 1956.

HARROP, G. Gerald. "Canadian Conventions: Un Homme Qui . . . ." *The Reporter,* XVI (January 24, 1957), 29-31.

HOCKIN, Thomas A., ed. *Apex of Power: The Prime Minister and Political Leadership in Canada.* Toronto: Prentice-Hall of Canada, 1971.

HOUGHAM, George M. "Minor Parties in Canadian National Politics: 1867-1940." Unpublished Ph.D. dissertation, University of Pennsylvania, 1954.

JONES, Elwood H. "Ephemeral Compromise: The Great Reform Convention Revisited." *JCS*, III (February 1968), 21-28.

KNOWLES, Stanley. *The New Party*. Toronto: McClelland and Stewart, 1961.

LEDERLE, John W. "National Party Conventions: Canada Shows the Way." *Southwestern Social Science Quarterly*, XXV (September 1944), 118-133.

————. "The National Organization of the Liberal and Conservative Parties in Canada." Unpublished Ph.D. dissertation, University of Michigan, 1942.

LELE, J.; Perlin, G.; and Thorburn, H. "Leadership Conventions in Canada: The Form and Substance of Participatory Politics." *Social Space: Canadian Perspectives*. Edited by D. I. Davies and Kathleen Herman. Toronto: New Press, 1971.

MACQUARRIE, H. *The Conservative Party*. Toronto: McClelland and Stewart, 1965.

MALLORY, J. R. "The Royal Prerogative in Canada: The Selection of Successors to Mr. Duplessis and Mr. Sauvé." *CJEPS*, XXVI (May 1960), 314-319.

————. *The Structure of Canadian Government*. Toronto: Macmillan Company of Canada, 1971.

McHENRY, Dean E. *The Third Force in Canada: The Cooperative Commonwealth Federation 1932-1948*. Berkeley: University of California Press, 1950.

McWHINNEY, Edward. "Prerogative Powers of the Head of State." *Canadian Bar Review*, XXXV (January 1957), 92-96. (Comments followed the publication of this article by J. R. Mallory, Eugene Forsey and Edward McWhinney in *Canadian Bar Review*, XXXV (February 1957), 242-244, and XXXV (March 1957), 368-371.)

MEISEL, John. *The Canadian General Election of 1957*. Toronto: University of Toronto Press, 1962.

MULLER, Steven. "The Canadian Prime Ministers, 1867-1948: An Essay on Democratic Leadership." Unpublished Ph.D. dissertation, Cornell University, 1958.

PICKERSGILL, J. W. *The Liberal Party*. Toronto: McClelland and Stewart, 1962.

PUNNETT, R. M. "Selection of Party Leaders: A Canadian Example." *Journal of Commonwealth Political Studies*, VIII (March 1970), 54-69.

REGENSTREIF, Peter. "Note on the 'Alternation' of French and English Leaders in the Liberal Party of Canada." *CJPS*, II (March 1969), 118-122.

SANDWELL, B. K. "The Convention System in Politics." *Queen's Quarterly*, LV (Autumn 1948-49), 343-349.

SMILEY, D. V. "The National Party Leadership Convention in Canada: A Preliminary Analysis." *CJPS*, I (December 1968), 373-397.

THORBURN, H. G. "An Approach to the Study of Federal Political Parties in Canada." Paper presented to the First Colloque sponsored by the Canadian Political Science Association and La Société Canadienne de Science Politique, Ottawa, November 10, 1968.

WINHAM, Gilbert R., and Cunningham, Robert B. "Party Leader Images in the 1968 Federal Election." *CJPS*, III (March 1970), 37-55.

YOUNG, Walter D. *The Anatomy of a Party: The National CCF 1932-61*. Toronto: University of Toronto Press, 1969.

V. *Leadership Selection in Canada: Biographical Studies*

BEAL, John R. *The Pearson Phenomenon*. Toronto: Longmans, 1964.

BORDEN, Henry. *Robert Laird Borden: His Memoirs*. 2 vols. Toronto: Macmillan Company of Canada, 1938.

BUCKINGHAM, William, and Ross, Hon. George W. *The Hon. Alexander Mackenzie: His Life and Times*. Toronto: Rose Publishing Company, 1892.

CREIGHTON, Donald. *John A. Macdonald*. 2 vols. Toronto: Macmillan Company of Canada, 1952 and 1955.

DAWSON, R. MacGregor. *William Lyon Mackenzie King: A Political Biography, 1874-1923*. Toronto: University of Toronto Press, 1958.

FERNS, H. S., and Ostry, B. *The Age of Mackenzie King: The Rise of the Leader*. London: William Heinemann Ltd., 1955.

GRAHAM, Roger. *Arthur Meighen*. 3 vols. Toronto: Clarke, Irwin and Company Limited, 1960, 1963 and 1965.

HARKIN, W. A., ed. *Political Reminiscences of the Rt. Hon. Sir Charles Tupper*. London: Constable and Co., 1914.

HOPKINS, J. Castell. *Life and Work of the Rt. Hon. Sir John Thompson*. Toronto: United Publishing Houses, 1895.

HUTCHISON, Bruce. *The Incredible Canadian: A Portrait of Mackenzie King*. London: Longmans, Green and Co., 1953.

JOHNSON, J. K., ed. *The Letters of Sir John A. Macdonald, 1836-1857.* Ottawa: Public Archives of Canada, 1968.

LONGLEY, J. W. *Sir Charles Tupper.* Toronto: Makers of Canada [Morang], Ltd., 1916.

MACINNIS, Grace. *J. S. Woodsworth: A Man to Remember.* Toronto: Macmillan Company of Canada, 1953.

MCGREGOR, F. A. *The Fall and Rise of Mackenzie King: 1911-1919.* Toronto: Macmillan Company of Canada, 1962.

MCNAUGHT, Kenneth. *A Prophet in Politics: A Biography of J. S. Woodsworth.* Toronto: University of Toronto Press, 1959.

NEATBY, H. Blair. "Laurier and a Liberal Quebec: A Study in Political Management." Unpublished Ph.D. dissertation, University of Toronto, 1956.

———. *William Lyon Mackenzie King, 1924-1932: The Lonely Heights.* Toronto: University of Toronto Press, 1963.

NICHOLSON, Patrick. *Vision and Indecision.* Don Mills: Longmans, 1968.

PEACOCK, Donald. *Journey to Power.* Toronto: The Ryerson Press, 1968.

PICKERSGILL, J. W. *The Mackenzie King Record, 1939-1944.* Vol. I. Toronto: University of Toronto Press, 1960.

PICKERSGILL, J. W., and Forster, D. F. *The Mackenzie King Record, 1944-1945, 1945-1946, 1947-1948.* Vols. 2-4. Toronto: University of Toronto Press, 1968 and 1970.

POPE, Joseph. *Memoirs of the Right Honourable Sir John Alexander Macdonald.* 2 vols. Ottawa: J. Durie and Son, 1894.

———. *Correspondence of Sir John Macdonald.* Toronto: Oxford University Press, n.d.

SAUNDERS, E. M. *The Life and Letters of Rt. Hon. Sir Charles Tupper.* London: Cassell and Company, 1916.

SCHULL, Joseph. *Laurier: The First Canadian.* Toronto: Macmillan Company of Canada, 1965.

SKELTON, O. D. *Life and Letters of Sir Wilfrid Laurier.* 2 vols. Toronto: Oxford University Press, 1921.

THOMSON, Dale C. *Alexander Mackenzie: Clear Grit.* Toronto: Macmillan Company of Canada, 1960.

———. *Louis St. Laurent: Canadian.* Toronto: Macmillan Company of Canada, 1967.

VAN DUSEN, Thomas. *The Chief.* New York: McGraw-Hill, 1968.

WATKINS, Ernest. *R. B. Bennett.* London: Secker and Warburg, 1963.

WILLISON, Sir John S. *Sir Wilfrid Laurier and the Liberal Party: A Political History.* 2 vols. Toronto: George N. Morang and Company Limited, 1903.

VI. *Leadership Selection in the Conservative Party*

Balloons and Ballots. Toronto: Telegram Publishing Co., 1967.

BELL, Ruth M. "Conservative Party National Conventions, 1927-1956." Unpublished M.A. thesis, Carleton University, 1965.

CAMP, Dalton. *Gentlemen, Players and Politicians.* Toronto: McClelland and Stewart, 1970.

CLARK, Lovell C. "The Conservative Party in the 1890's." *Report of the Canadian Historical Association* (1961), 58-74.

————. "Macdonald's Conservative Successors, 1891-1896." *Character and Circumstance: Essays in Honour of Donald Grant Creighton.* Edited by John S. Moir. Toronto: Macmillan Company of Canada, 1970, 143-160.

COATES, Robert C. *The Night of the Knives.* Fredericton: Brunswick Press, 1969.

FRASER, Blair. "Why the Conservatives are Swinging to Diefenbaker." *Maclean's* magazine, November 24, 1956, pp. 30ff.

GRANATSTEIN, J. L. "How the Tories of Old Switched Leaders." *Globe and Mail,* October 27, 1966.

————. *The Politics of Survival: The Conservative Party of Canada, 1939-1945.* Toronto: University of Toronto Press, 1967.

JOHNSTON, James. *The Party's Over.* Don Mills: Longmans Canada Limited, 1971.

LIND, Philip B. "Davie Fulton's Campaign for Leadership — 1967." Unpublished M.A. thesis, University of Rochester, 1968.

MacNICOL, John R. *National Liberal-Conservative Convention Held at Winnipeg, Manitoba, October 10 to 12, 1927.* Toronto: Southam Press, 1930.

PUNNETT, R. W. "Leadership Selection in Opposition: The Progressive Conservative Party in Canada." *Australian Journal of Politics and History,* XVII (August 1971), 188-201.

SAYWELL, John T., ed. *The Canadian Journal of Lady Aberdeen, 1893-1898.* Toronto: The Champlain Society, 1960.

————. "The Crown and the Politicians: The Canadian Succession Question: 1891-1896." *CHR,* XXXVII (December 1956), 309-337.

SCOTT, Morley S. "Foster on the Thompson-Bowell Succession." *CHR,* XLVIII (September 1967), 273-276.

VINEBERG, Michael. "The Progressive Conservative Leadership Convention of 1967." Unpublished M.A. thesis, McGill University, 1968.

WALLACE, W. Stewart. *The Memoirs of the Rt. Hon. Sir George Foster.* Toronto: Macmillan Company of Canada, 1933.

WEARING, Joseph. "A Convention for Professionals: The PCs in Toronto." *JCS,* II (November 1967), 3-16.

WILLIAMS, John R. *The Conservative Party in Canada: 1920-1949.* Durham, N. C.: Duke University Press, 1956.

————. "The Selection of Arthur Meighen as Conservative Party Leader in 1941." *CJEPS,* XVII (May 1951), 234-237.

YOUNG, Scott, and Slocombe, David. "Party Brass Elected Stanfield." *Globe and Mail,* September 20, 1967.

VII. *Leadership Selection in the Liberal Party*

BANKS, Margaret A. "The Change in Liberal Party Leadership, 1887." *CHR,* XXXVIII (June 1957), 109-128.

BROWN, George W. "The Grit Party and the Great Reform Convention of 1859." *CHR,* XVI (September 1935), 245-265.

FRASER, Blair. "The Sudden Rise of Pierre Elliott Trudeau." *Maclean's* magazine, April 1968, pp. 24ff.

HARDY, H. Reginald. *Mackenzie King of Canada.* London: Oxford University Press, 1949.

IGLAUER, Elizabeth. "Profiles: Prime Minister/Premier Ministre." *The New Yorker,* July 5, 1969, pp. 36ff.

JONES, Elwood H. "Ephemeral Compromise: The Great Reform Convention Revisited." *JCS,* III (February 1968), 21-28.

LAROCQUE, Paul T. "Leadership Selection in the Liberal Party." Unpublished B.A. thesis, Carleton University, 1968.

LEDERLE, John W. "The Liberal Convention of 1893." *CJEPS,* XVI (February 1950), 42-52.

————. "The Liberal Convention of 1919 and the Selection of Mackenzie King." *Dalhousie Review,* XXVII (April 1947), 85-92.

LEDUC, Lawrence. "Party Decision-Making: Some Empirical Observations on the Leadership Selection Process." *CJPS,* IV (March 1971), 97-118.

————. "The Leadership Selection Process in Canadian Political Parties: A Case Study." Unpublished Ph.D. dissertation, University of Michigan, 1970.

"The Liberal Leadership." *The Round Table,* IX (June 1919), 593-594.

The National Liberal Convention, Ottawa, August 5, 6, 7, 1919: The Story of the Convention and the Report of its Proceedings. Ottawa: n.p., n.d.

Official Report of the Liberal Convention Held in Response to the Call of Hon. Wilfrid Laurier, Leader of the Liberal Party of the Dominion of Canada. Toronto: Budget Printing and Publishing Co., 1893.

POWER, C. G. *A Party Politician: The Memoirs of Chubby Power.* Edited by Norman Ward. Toronto: Macmillan Company of Canada, 1966.

QUINN, Herbert F. "The Third National Convention of the Liberal Party." *CJEPS,* XVII (May 1951), 228-233.

Report of the Proceedings of the National Liberal Convention, 1948. Ottawa: National Liberal Federation of Canada, n.d.

Report of the Proceedings of the National Liberal Convention, 1958. Ottawa: National Liberal Federation of Canada, n.d.

SANTOS, C. R. "Some Collective Characteristics of the Delegates to the 1968 Liberal Party Leadership Convention." *CJPS,* III (June 1970), 299-308.

UNDERHILL, Frank H. *In Search of Canadian Liberalism.* Toronto: Macmillan Company of Canada, 1961.

WARD, Norman. "The Liberals in Convention: Revised and Unrepentant." *Queen's Quarterly,* LXV (Spring 1958), 1-11.

WEARING, Joseph. "The Liberal Choice." *JCS,* III (May 1968), 3-20.

Index